CW00684213

A History of
CRAWLEY

High Street, Crawley

A History of CRAWLEY

Peter Gwynne

Phillimore

1990

Published by
PHILLIMORE & CO. LTD.
Shopwyke Hall, Chichester, Sussex

ISBN 0 85033 718 6

Printed and bound in Great Britain by
STAPLES PRINTERS ROCHESTER LIMITED
Love Lane, Rochester, Kent.

Contents

List of Illustrations

Acknowledgements

The author is grateful to the following for giving their permission to reproduce illustrations: British Library, 8, 14 and 37; the Vicar of St Margaret's, Ifield, 17, 33 and 51; Crawley New Town Corporation, 68 and 69.

The author gratefully acknowledges the help and assistance given to him over the years by local people who share his interest in the history of Crawley. The first and most enthusiastic of these were the late Mrs. Hepzibah Carmen and Miss Daisy Warren, whose collections of their own and their families' past are a mine from which we can dig for many years yet.

Introduction

The use of the word 'Crawley' to define an area may seem in itself to be adequate, but this is not so. When this book was first considered, it was intended that by the end of the narrative the reader would be reading about the area which now comprises the Borough of Crawley. Even so, it is clear that the boundaries of the urban area which is described as Crawley have spread outside the official council local government boundaries, and some local residents vote for neighbouring councils rather than Crawley Borough Council. In the 1970s, the area of Gatwick Airport, which hitherto had been included in Surrey, was added

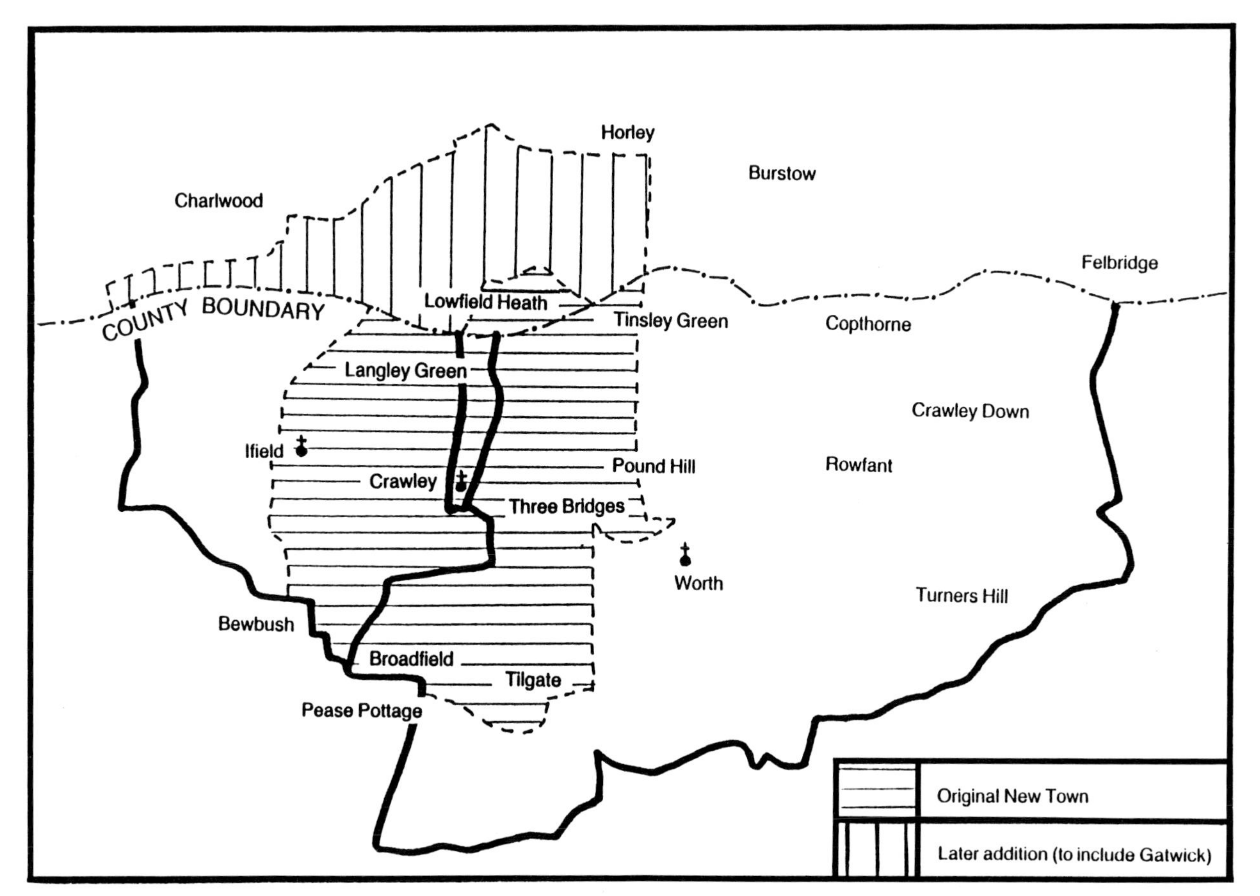

1. Crawley, showing the area discussed in this book. The three parishes, shown with a bold outline and bordering the original county boundary, are from left to right Ifield, Crawley and Worth. The shaded areas show the New Town as designated in the 1940s and the borough boundary as it expanded in the 1970s to take in Gatwick Airport.

to the town. The only definition that is likely to be sensible to the reader is to say that this book will eventually focus upon that area which most people would describe as Crawley.

When Crawley New Town was designated in 1946, it took in (i) the old parish of Crawley, (ii) much of the parish of Ifield which, in fact, included over half of the village of Crawley, and (iii) the western part of the parish of Worth, which included the village of Three Bridges. In the 19th century, the parish of Worth had itself been reduced in size by the creation of several new parishes, consequent on the building of more churches in the area. Since old documents do not always indicate which part of a parish is being referred to, the author has decided to begin this history by concentrating in the history of the early years on the three ancient parishes of Worth, Crawley and Ifield. As the chapters pass there will be an inevitable drawing in of the scope of the book to concentrate, eventually, on the present urban unit.

The map of the area (Ill. 1) shows the three parishes, with the neighbouring ones, and superimposed is the area of the Borough of Crawley as it is in 1990. The New Town area was slightly smaller than that of the present borough; in particular the large area, formerly in Surrey, which mainly comprises Gatwick Airport was a much later addition. Local residents will recognise the places named in the text, but those unfamiliar with the area may find it useful from time to time to consult this map. It must always be borne in mind that the present settlement pattern is not necessarily that of the past. The focus of the area has changed from time to time, but the High Street of Crawley is perhaps the 'centre' of the district with which this history will be concerned.

Chapter 1

Crawley's Site and Situation

Though the beginnings of Crawley New Town are well documented, the origins of the first settlement at Crawley can only be conjectured. There is obviously no single factor which can answer the question 'How did Crawley begin?' A knowledge of local geography, study of the general history of Sussex and the evidence of place-names will give conjecture greater credibility. Let us start by looking at the site.

Human activity takes place in a physical setting. The study of very early history is sometimes said to be all geography. Rather a sweeping statement perhaps, but the men who were the first to settle in and colonise an area were very much at the mercy of their surroundings and the weather. The types of soil, the water supply, the vegetation — these give a partial explanation of the first settlers' means of livelihood. From early times man has learned to modify soil, drainage and vegetation; however, climate he has had to take as it is. The following physical description of the area indicates how settlement could have been distributed, what routeways were available, and what minerals and food resources were there for exploitation. The Crawley area had its possibilities, and the settlers made use of them.

Geological structure and soil

In north Sussex there are two main geological divisions which have determined our local landscape. First of all there are sandstone layers, collectively known as the Hastings Beds, which dip northwards. On top of these are the softer layers, mostly clay, known as the Weald Clay. To the south the clays have been eroded, leaving the sandstones exposed as higher ground (*see* Ill. 2). The ridge at the boundary of the sandstone and clay is clearly seen to the south of Crawley, for example Pease Pottage Hill, and it also curves around the east of Crawley, as at Pound Hill.

This rather simple diagram is complicated in three main ways: (i) among the Hastings Beds there are some layers of clay; (ii) Among the Weald Clay Beds there are some thin layers of limestone and sandstone — where these occur the clay has not been eroded so much, leaving outposts of higher ground in the clay vale; (iii) there is a geological fault which has left an area of clay in the south of Crawley, the vale occupied by Tilgate. As a final modification, there are localised deposits of gravel from older river systems, some large as at Norwood Hill, and some small, for example, Rowley's Farm. These provided well-drained sites for settlers wishing to avoid damp, often flooded, soil (*see* Ill. 3).

The area, therefore, has a mixture of heavy and lighter soils, depending on the nature of the underlying geological strata. In general terms, the clay makes a heavy dark brown soil, but when roadworks or building foundations dig into the clay below the topsoil, the clay itself can be seen to vary greatly in colour from black to white, from bright yellow to dark red. The white clay was often used in the past to make clay pipes, as some Crawley residents have found when digging over their new garden plots. The sandstone makes a lighter but poorer soil. Again, building works show that its colour can also vary widely. To most people, there is little visible difference between the topsoil above the clay or the sandstone. Most Crawley gardeners complain about the clay soil, even when the geological map shows that they are not on the clay!

The Weald Clay itself has been useful to local inhabitants in the past as a raw material

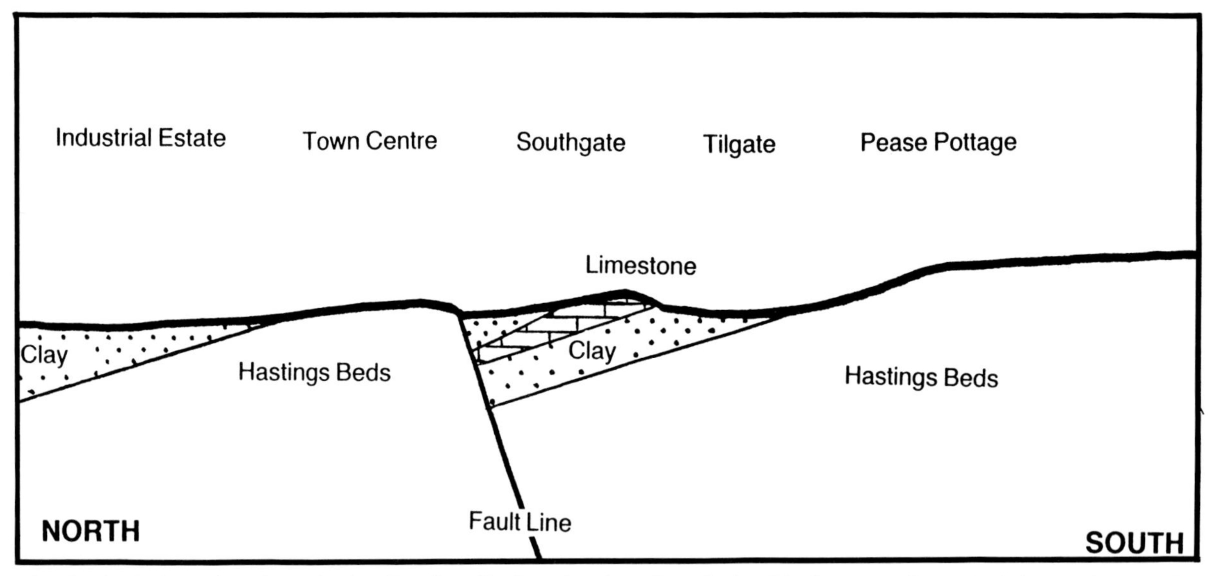

2. Geological section through the Crawley district, showing the relationship between the underlying geology and the settlements which developed on the ridges locally.

3. The basic geology of Crawley (simplified). This map shows the local boundary between the flat Weald Clay area and the higher ground of the Hastings Beds, mostly composed of sandstone. Between Crawley and Tilgate there is a small ridge of limestone in the Weald Clay, on which was an early Iron Age settlement.

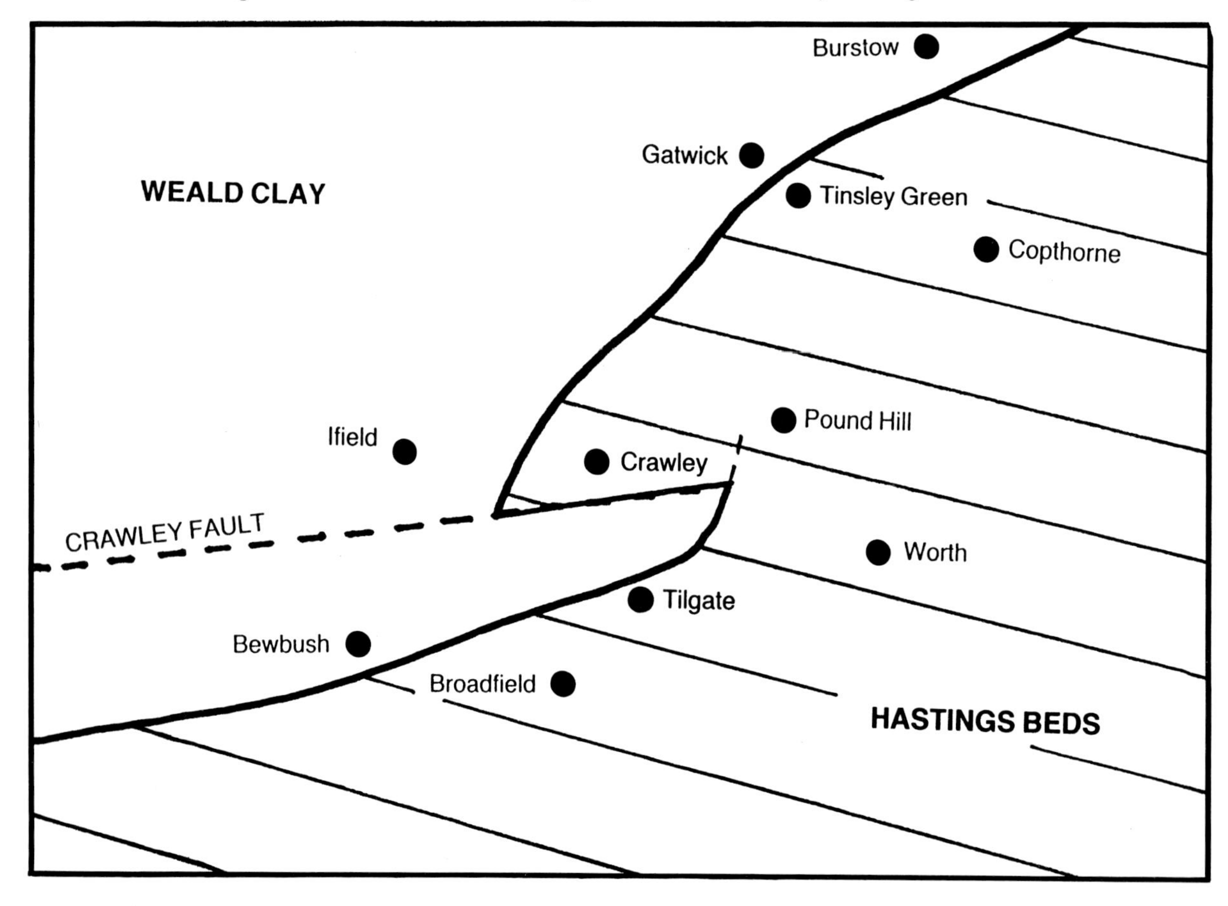

for pottery, brick-and tile-making, or simply daubed on a wooden lattice to form a wall (wattle and daub). In Sussex there have been hundreds of such small works. An advert in the 1896 Crawley Parish Guide states: 'R.Cook and Sons, Builders, Contractors, etc. Proprietors of the New Town Brick, Tile, Pipe and Pottery Works, Crawley'. The development around Springfield Road and West Street was at that time known as New Town. When the firm of James Longley moved to Crawley from Turners Hill in 1882, it purchased Malthouse Farm, which included a small brickworks. The lawns surrounding 'The Beeches' have many shallow indentations which show where the earth was removed to make the bricks of which the house was built. But for most Crawley residents, however, the clay is simply a difficult soil to work, and before modern drainage it must have been even more water-logged in wet weather.

In the Weald Clay there occur from time to time thin layers of limestone and sandstone. Locally there is a ridge in the clay which forms the site of Gossops Green and Southgate West, and can be traced as far east as Three Bridges station. One wooded field which existed by Grattons Drive in Pound Hill was called Chalky Pits. Until recently, when a housing estate was built on it, there were still many depressions which showed where the limestone had been extracted in the past. Another field in Northgate was called Kilnmead, a reminder that limestone had to be burned to make lime for the farmers to dress their fields and for the iron masters to help in iron smelting.

The flat or rippled sandstone which occurs in the clay is varied, but one common type is known as Horsham Stone or Horsham Slab. This was once widely used as a paving stone and for roof coverings. Some of the older buildings, with oak rafters, still show its use, for example the roofs of the Ancient Priors, the chancel of Crawley church, and the older part of the *George*. At times shale is found in the clay, and its existence has led oil companies to drill for traces of usable oil in the shale deposits. Some was found in a boring near Three Bridges station a few years ago, but not in sufficient quantities, at the time, to be commercially viable.

The local sandstone of the Hastings Beds is generally fine-grained and pale in colour. Around Crawley it is mostly Upper Tunbridge Wells stone, which at Three Bridges is about 250 ft. (80 m.) thick. One particular local stone, which contains some limestone, is known as Tilgate Stone. The sandstone which was used to build Crawley church probably came from a quarry in West Hoathly.

The soil around Crawley which has formed on the sandstone does not give rise to particularly good farmland, though modern methods can improve it. The approximate edge of the sandstone boundary is the forest ridge which forms the southern and eastern boundaries of the town. The main reason why the forest is still in existence is that it proved uneconomic to cultivate. Trees have been the most important crop, and rich landowners have learned that light woodland is excellent hunting country for deer and game-birds.

One last point about the clay and the sandstone is that both contain types of iron-ore. Usually it occurs in economic quantities in narrow clay belts — either within the Hastings Beds sandstone or just below the Horsham stone in the Weald Clay. There is a somewhat isolated area by The Hawth, in central Crawley, and a small area lies to the north of Ifield church, but the main area is along the line of the present A264 road to Horsham, and the adjacent railway line. Many depressions still mark where the ore has been extracted, and The Hawth in particular has scores of them, as generations of small children at play have well known.

Drainage and water supply

As would be expected, the drainage pattern of the area is broadly one of many small streams originating on the high land to the south and flowing northwards across the clay vale. Most are tributaries of the River Mole which flows across Gatwick, through Horley, and so towards Dorking. The two largest streams in the area, flowing through Three Bridges and Ifield, are both called by the local residents River Mole, though the stream by Three Bridges should more accurately be called Gatwick Stream. Reference to 19th-century maps shows that the whole of the present Crawley area was, at one time, drained by a large system of small streams. Clay is impermeable and the water stays for a long time on or near the surface before it drains away. The clay tends to have a heavy, water-logged soil in winter and, before the advent of modern farming methods, would have presented difficulties for farmers.

The best farms on the clay are those with some gravel deposits which give better drainage. Although we think of a large flat expanse of clay between Crawley and Horley, where it is over 1,000 ft. (320 m.) thick, travellers who walk or cycle across it are conscious of these localised drier areas of higher ground. It is likely that the first settlers in the area would have concentrated on the less boggy soils and depended on animals rather than grain. Indeed, in view of the wet nature of the soil, they would have raised cattle, pigs and horses rather than sheep.

During the 19th century many old streams were slowly filled in and, as new building took place, the remaining streams were channelled and kept open. Since the coming of the New Town, with its comprehensive main drainage, much of the original pattern of streams is no longer visible except in shallow ditches or by noting the lines of trees. Occasionally, after heavy rain, the present drainage system cannot cope with all the surface water, which temporarily resumes its former routes along forgotten stream beds, as local householders discover to their cost.

The 1836 tithe maps also show many ponds. It is usual to picture, in the mind's eye, a farm with its duck pond: Woolborough Farm, for example, had one. What is not realised is the extent to which most homes had some sort of pond nearby. The word may, of course, be a euphemism, and one cannot now imagine the state of such 'ponds' in an age before hygiene was understood and piped water supplies and waste disposal were generally available. The ponds did, however, represent an essential part of human needs — a regular water supply.

On the higher ground to the south there are many springs, but it is rare to find them on the clay unless there is a local layer of sandstone or limestone within it. The first Romano-British settlement at Southgate West probably got its water supply this way since there was a layer of Horsham Stone below the surface. Otherwise, people in the area relied on small streams, reasonably pure since they rose on the sandstone, forest area to the south.

In 1897 all the local water supply still came from garden wells or pumps, in many cases close to the cesspool, and a great many of these water sources had been condemned as health hazards. At that time some land in Goffs Park Road was purchased by a local syndicate of businessmen and a three-inch bore was undertaken. At 950 ft. (305 m.) water was finally reached and piped to an on-site reservoir, from where it was available for the whole of Crawley and Three Bridges villages. The Crawley and District Water Company was finally disbanded in 1926 when the Rural District Councils became responsible for water supply. Since then water has always had to be brought into the area from outside.

Until 1897, therefore, each householder had to obtain water in the best way that he could. At the rear of The Tree House and in other local houses there are still pumps in existence to remind us of the problems which for centuries faced local inhabitants.

Vegetation

It is difficult to talk about 'natural' vegetation since man has radically altered the original vegetation cover. When settlement first took place in this area, the country was predominantly forest, especially oak and beech. Modern forests do not necessarily reflect this; most of them have been cleared in the past, used and coppiced. Trees planted by man outnumber those naturally established. The oak forests on the heavier clay soils developed after the last Ice Age and were a rich natural resource for the inhabitants, as fuel, building material and raw material — charcoal and bark.

Crawley's last link with the old oak forests vanished in the early 1970s. In the grounds of Craigans, previously known as Tudor Oak and before that Lyons Farm, was an oak which was probably at least 400 years old. It was known to all the Ifield residents as the Ifield Oak, or the Tudor Oak and, though partially hollowed, was still alive and standing. When Craigans, itself a listed building in good condition and over 500 years old, was demolished to become the site of another housing estate, attempts were made to save the tree. Neither the developers nor the local authority would agree to do so and it was destroyed. It is ironic that the developers at first called the site 'Tudor Oak Estate'. The name, it seems, was more important than the tree itself.

What sort of vegetation would one find in the oak forest area? Briefly, it can be described as follows: (i) large trees: oak, birch, wild cherry, aspen, alder, poplar, wych elm; (ii) small trees: holly, crab-apple, rowan, yew; (iii) shrubs: hazel, hawthorn, blackthorn; (iv) climbing plants: ivy, honeysuckle. Some of our oldest farm-names derive from these. Examples are Ewhurst (yew), Hazelwick (hazel), Crabbett (crab-apple), and Naldretts (alder).

On the lighter, sandstone areas, beechwoods were most common, though one would also encounter some oak in the sandstone forests, such as Worth, Tilgate and St Leonard's forests. There was a general tendency towards heathlands, scrub or semi-wooded areas too, with bracken and gorse. Otherwise, the same type of smaller trees and shrubs would also occur, as in the oak forests.

Weather

There is not much which needs to be said about the local weather. Crawley has a typical south-east English climate, whatever that may be! The average annual rainfall is between 30 in. and 32 in. (75 cm. and 82 cm.) and the temperatures seldom fall below 0°C. or rise above 23°C. Variations are not so much concerned with rainfall and temperature as with the incidence of fog or groundfrost. The lower lying areas (mostly the clay) experience more of each than do the higher areas. To the east of Worth parish, the higher ground is noticeably cooler. Turners Hill often gets snow cover which Crawley itself has escaped. Similarly, anyone who drives into Crawley from the south will often experience a marked change in the weather at Pease Pottage, where bright sunshine can give way to dense fog.

As residents of Crawley know, this is a damp area and not ideal for those with chest complaints. Though the clay attracts much winter fog it is clear that Gatwick Airport, further north on the clay, has more fog and showers than the comparatively high ground at Crawley. It is possible to stand at the top of one of the high buildings in Crawley and see fog and rain over Gatwick which Crawley has escaped. Early settlers would have been aware of this and the higher land to the south would have been more attractive than the flatter, but damper, land to the north.

It is difficult to decide whether the present climate is markedly different to that which existed 5,000, or even 500, years ago. The most one can say is that it is probably drier and cooler today than in the past.

Conclusions

To conclude, the physical geography of the Crawley area can provide us with some hints as to why and how people first came to the district. The first point to note is that until quite late in the colonisation of Sussex a large forest existed in the Weald, known to the Saxons as 'Andredswald', between the North and South Downs. In the ninth century, when a writer described it as a 'Mickle-wood' (or great wood), it was about one hundred and twenty miles long from west to east and thirty miles wide from north to south. Large-scale clearances had to await the Norman occupation of England.

Secondly, the forest was a barrier, though never an impassable one, between the Sussex coastal settlements and those along the Thames Valley. Man settled in the Weald slowly. The hard work involved in clearing forest by hand was not attractive as long as better quality land was still available on its borders.

Thirdly, communications through the forest would have been slow and dangerous. It was truthfully said that travellers through the forest should travel with caution and a cudgel! Once on the clay, movement of heavy loads would only really be easy on the occasions when the ground was baked hard in summer or frosted in winter. Until the last hundred years or so Sussex roads were a source of wonder or amusement to the whole country; few people willingly travelled far and rarely would do so for pleasure. The local streams were too small to make water transport practicable.

Fourthly, what would attract a person into the forest? Obviously food and animal life: in particular deer, wild boar and birds. Fruit and nuts were available, too. Later, wood itself was a valuable commodity both for building and for fuel. Some domestic animals could be kept. Wild animals were not always useful; it is recorded that in 1209 the bishop of Winchester, who had a farm at Mardon in Hampshire near the Sussex border, lost two foals, which were eaten by wolves.

Finally, what would induce a person to settle in this area? The soil is not particularly well-suited to farming with primitive implements; there is not much good quality water available; the area is a long journey from other areas which are known to be early sites where man congregated. It is damp on the clay. True, the existence of iron-ore reasonably near the surface attracted men skilled in metal-working. The Romans recorded that the British produced iron, which made the south of England attractive enough to be included within the limits of the Empire, but iron-workers rarely stayed in one place for any length of time. Perhaps all this accounts for the lack of evidence of long-term intensive settlement before the Normans. Obviously there was some, the place-names prove it, but this occupation would have consisted of isolated, defended farmsteads rather than gregarious village communities.

The sort of people who choose a remote, isolated area in which to live are likely to be those who do not feel a need for company or those who are escaping or forced to move from another area. The early settlers in the north of Sussex are likely to have been taciturn, suspicious of strangers, and difficult to control.

Chapter 2

The First Evidence

Many books have been written about the general prehistory of the south of England. Over the last 500,000 years the area has been affected by four main Ice Ages, during which times the sea level and the temperature varied widely. The last Ice Age ended about 25,000 years ago, and there is evidence in Sussex to show how from that time Man, *homo sapiens*, entered and slowly settled in our region.

The approximate dates which are given to the prehistoric divisions in Sussex are as follows:

I	Stone Age	(i)	Palaeolithic (Early Stone Age) Any time before *c.* 10,000 B.C.
		(ii)	Mesolithic (Middle Stone Age) From *c.* 9,000 B.C.
		(iii)	Neolithic (New Stone Age) From *c.* 4,000 B.C.
II	Bronze Age		From *c.* 2,000 B.C.
III	Iron Age		From *c.* 500 B.C.

We will look at each of these in turn and see what we can find out about prehistoric man in the Crawley area.

The Stone Age

The first men to tread our locality would have been the various Palaeolithic hunters. The oldest traces in Sussex of such early people have been dated to about 350,000 years ago, but not in the north. In the Weald itself, the oldest flints found distributed over a wide area are from the Mesolithic period. The high ground to the south of Broadfield seems to have been a popular place for the Mesolithic hunters of about 5,000 B.C. and later. Many flints have been found here, probably in association with a phenomenon known as an 'animal funnel'. Deer and other large wildlife moving across the Weald tend to stay on the ridges and to cross the clay at its narrowest point. Bewbush Vale is one such point upon which animals still converge. It is, and was, a good place to hunt. Many flints (or microliths) have been found locally on the ridge extending from Pease Pottage to Horsham. These show common characteristics in the way that they are shaped, and are described as having the 'Horsham Point'. They all originated in St Leonard's Forest. In fact, the whole area from Tilgate to Horsham is one where over a long period of time, perhaps for over 2,000 years, a particular Mesolithic settlement group existed, now called the 'Horsham Culture'.

This seems to be the only area of Britain where a particular identifiable group is known, and is an example of how the Weald formed an 'island' in which early settlement developed its own recognisable style. For several thousand years early man lived overlooking our area, slowly developing his ability to provide for himself. It is ironic that construction work on archaeological sites often reveals unexpected evidence which suggests the work should be halted. Excavations for the M23, for example, yielded flints left by Mesolithic hunters.

Neolithic flints have also been found and it seems certain that the use of flint continued during the Bronze and Iron Ages. Merely looking at a flint is rarely sufficient to date it: one must also establish where it was found and what else was found with it. If Crawley were part of a hunting area, it would be reasonable to expect to find flints over a wide area, not just in one place. This is basically the case around Crawley. That they are not found over an even wider region can be explained by the facts that subsequent farming and settlement have destroyed or covered up the flints, or they are just not recognised when seen. It tends to be the neglected areas — like continuously wooded or recently developed lands — where flints are found which are likely to have been undisturbed since they were last used. It would be even more interesting to find a large group of flints in a small area, indicating a longer-lasting settlement.

Flints come from chalk and had to be brought to Crawley from the Downs. Although the North Downs are nearer to us, most discoveries of flint mines have been made on the South Downs. There are at least two local sites where collections of flints and chippings from worked flints have been found. One is along Parish Lane, leading eastwards from Pease Pottage, where many hundreds of worked flints have been picked up and can still be found in the fields, especially after ploughing. The second, smaller, site was at Southgate West, by Hogs Hill Farm. Both places are on high ground, where prehistoric settlements are usually found. Parish Lane is the more interesting, and even now it would be rewarding to carry out an investigation of the area. It is lightly wooded heathland which during colder climates had even less vegetation cover, and is an obvious site for a camp.

To sum up, Stone Age man passed through three stages over a period of 7,000 years: first, man the hunter; second, man the pastoralist, using clearings in the forest to breed and feed animals — at first only seasonally but eventually in a permanent settlement; and third, man the agriculturalist, turning cleared land into arable land and harvesting the crops.

The Bronze Age

It will probably never be possible to determine when Crawley was first 'settled', the land being used less for nomadic hunting and more for permanent farming. Evidence from Sussex as a whole suggests, however, that this occurred about 500 B.C., after the use of bronze had reached Britain. A succession of peoples came from mainland Europe to settle in the south of England.

In August 1952 some drainage work was being carried out at Langley Green. A small stream, the Polebrook, was being dredged at a point where it meets the River Mole. This is just north of Amberley Farm and to the west of Pole's Farm. A weapon was unearthed which turned out to be a good example of a late Bronze Age sword. It consisted of a long blade and a haft, altogether about half a metre long. The original wooden hand grip had rotted away. The New Town Commission had a replica made, showing how it may have looked when new. To the south of Broadfield, alongside the Pease Pottage to Colgate road, an old ridgeway can still be seen. From Cottesmore School entrance to past Shepherd's Farm the track runs alongside the present road, just a few yards to the north. There are low banks marking each side of the routeway. Along this track, and not far from it, are some round Bronze Age burial mounds or barrows, three of which were excavated during the late 1960s. A possible fourth was found on the north side of Bewbush Vale, near Ifield Mill pond. There is unlikely now to be anything of value in them, most burial mounds having been raided and robbed in the past. Their very existence, however, suggests settlement in the area, since people and organisation were necessary to construct a barrow. Almost certainly, they contained the bodies of local chieftains or settlement leaders. It would be stretching the imagination to suggest that one of them held the remains of the man who lost his sword in the Polebrook!

The Iron Age

Historians have for too long written about the Wealden forest area as one where little settlement took place until comparatively recently. The impression is given of an unpenetrated desolate forest which had no attraction for man. It is true that most archaeological

4. This case contains the original Bronze Age sword found during construction of the New Town and a modern reconstruction of how it would have looked when new.

discoveries have been made outside the Weald, and that north Sussex has been a 'no-man's land' for serious study. But the absence of finds reflects the absence of searching. From the time the Sussex Archaeological Society was founded, the coastal settlements seem to have dominated its efforts. It is obviously easier, and more immediately rewarding, to look for remains in an area where most early settlement took place.

Only in recent years has evidence been mounting which has changed the idea that when the Romans came to Britain they found a completely uninhabited forest area. The Downs have systems of trackways and roads which are obviously pre-Roman. More must also have existed in the Weald, though they may not have persisted in a clearly recognisable form. Most tracks or paths would have kept to ridges, if possible, for ease of progress. A few are well-known, such as the Pilgrims' Way on the North Downs. Others are less known, such as the long track which follows high ground from the Ashdown Forest area to West Hoathly, then to Selsfield Common, south of Turners Hill, and through the Worth and St Leonard's forests via Tilgate and Pease Pottage to Horsham. The fact that the 'Iron Age' was so named implies that iron was being made somewhere. To smelt iron requires iron-ore, lime to be mixed with it, a heat source and a container for the smelting process. Iron-ore was once readily available in small quantities near to the surface over a large part of northern Sussex. The heat source has to come into contact with the ore, and wood-burning in its natural state cannot produce good quality iron. Charcoal, however, is virtually pure carbon and this could be readily made in Sussex. It gives a higher temperature than burning wood, and results in purer iron. Lime was also widely available, either from the Downs or from the lime which is found in the clay. Finally, clay makes an excellent container when baked, ideal for crucibles or for furnaces. Since Sussex contained all the ingredients for iron-making and was close to the northern European iron-makers, it is not surprising that it became the first important iron-producing area of Britain.

Iron was not originally made as it is in a modern ironworks. The early iron-workers operated at lower temperatures with small hand-operated furnaces, which took longer. Such furnaces were known as 'bloomeries'; a 'bloom' was a small lump of rather impure wrought iron made in the small furnace, which then needed further heating and hammering to be usable. Bloomeries were usually close to a stream, the water being used to wash ore or to cool metal. What was the iron used for? From various finds in Sussex we can see that it was fashioned into domestic tools, agricultural implements, weapons, harness and even chains for slaves.

The Iron Age reached Britain when people with knowledge of iron-producing joined the cross-Channel movement, bringing their skills with them. It is known that people from northern Europe, the Belgic tribespeople, were moving to south-eastern England, attracted by both the farming and the iron-making possibilities.

Our area was part of the lands ruled during the first century B.C. by a group called the Atrebates, whose leader was named Commius. Commius had a mint in the tribal centre near Chichester. Some of the earliest pottery fragments found in the Crawley area are typical of Atrebatic pottery: it is black-burnished with an eyebrow pattern. Before the Romans arrived, however, the Atrebates had come into conflict with more belligerent neighbours to the north. Not surprisingly, the Atrebates welcomed the Romans, since at least they brought a promise of support.

The first bloomeries were sited near the east Sussex coast, but the search for iron ore and charcoal soon spread them inland north-westwards along the Hastings Beds, wherever ore could be mined. In this manner, throughout the central Wealden forest, small temporary clearances were made to exploit local iron ore. Here the iron-workers lived and worked. The history of the Sussex iron industry is now being studied by the Wealden Iron Research Group and eventually it is hoped that a clearer picture of this mobile industry will emerge.

It had long been known that some Roman ironworks existed in north Sussex and that 16th-century furnaces were sited in the Crawley area; in 1969, however, traces of much earlier iron workings came to light. That summer, work was in progress developing the new Southgate West neighbourhood, between the old Brighton Road and the Horsham Road. This ridge was occupied by Hogs Hill Farm. (Hogs Hill is now re-named Ditchling Hill.) Just to the west of the present primary school, at the highest point of the ridge, the first operation was to mark out the roads and then to clear away the topsoil. Nothing could be seen to suggest any former use of the land other than as fields. While the topsoil was being cleared, one of the workmen was interested to find some flints and decided to look further during his non-working hours.

What he found next was not, at first sight, very important. The earth-moving machinery had cut into strata which contained two long curved ditches filled with burnt earth, bone fragments and pieces of pottery. These turned out to be old refuse ditches which belonged to a settlement based on the ridge. The find was reported to the builders. Some of the pottery was sent to the Sussex Archaeological Society museum at Lewes, whose curator confirmed that it dated from the time of the Roman occupation of Britain, and covered a period of about two hundred years. Unfortunately, the discovery was not professionally followed-up. No immediate investigation was undertaken by any organisation and building work continued. There had been a history of interrupted work on building sites in Crawley New Town and anything which might hold up new building was to be avoided. People — especially employees — were actively discouraged from looking for archaeological remains. Luckily, several persons continued to spend time visiting the site and collecting fragments at weekends and during the evenings. These were recorded and plotted. A large debt of gratitude is owed to them for their work.

Later in 1969 the information began to be more widely known and outsiders became interested. A local archaeological group was founded and this site became one of their first investigations. In the meantime, the builders pushed ahead very rapidly with their roads and house footings. In the process most of the evidence disappeared, either bulldozed away or quickly buried under concrete.

The next year more discoveries emerged. In the summer of 1970, Springfield House in the Horsham Road was demolished and its grounds, on the edge of Goffs Park, were prepared for a small building development to be known as Goffs Close. Again refuse pits were uncovered, but this time, with the co-operation of the site developers, they were properly investigated. The pottery remains were definitely identified by appearance and by carbon-dating techniques as pre-Roman, and assigned to the early centuries B.C. Other finds, such as slag and evidence of clay crucibles, show that iron was being smelted and worked on the site at least one hundred years before the Romans came to Britain. The Hogs Hill site, a quarter of a mile away, was a later continuation of this industrial activity. There were also criss-cross marks caused by ploughing seen in the clay. Here, at last, was the first firm proof of a small British settlement in the Crawley area. Domestic pottery, a long period of occupation and a local industry needed organisation and a distribution network. Crawley — whatever its name at that time — was in existence, and the ridgeways were the routes by which iron could be distributed to customers.

The Romans

In A.D. 43 the Romans under Claudius invaded Britain, and proceeded to draw the whole of the country into the Roman Empire. The western area of Sussex was pro-Roman and one of the Atrebates, named Cogidubnus, was appointed local king. The Romans supported his rule over the land from the Meon, in the west, to the Ouse, in the east, and north towards the Mole, an area described henceforth as the lands of the Regni. The administrative centre was at Chichester, known then as Noviomagus Regnentium, where a palace was built at Fishbourne. The eastern area of Sussex was ruled from Canterbury. The absence of fighting in the area, and the rapid development by the Romans of commerce and building, gave an increased impetus to the demand for all sorts of raw materials. This meant a boost for the exploitation of mineral and other resources.

The Romans built two main roads to link London with the South Coast. They pass either side of Crawley. When first laid down, these would have not only provided communication links, both for the military and for trade, but would also have helped further to open up the important iron-working areas of Sussex. The most well-known road is undoubtedly Stane Street, joining Chichester with London. This road was built in the first century A.D., and its nearest point to Crawley is where it crosses the Surrey-Sussex border at Rowhook, about ten miles to the west, north of Horsham. The nearer road, though less well-known, is the Brighton to London way which went through Clayton, Ardingly, Turners Hill, Felbridge, Godstone and Croydon. Its nearest point to Crawley is where it passes through the grounds of Fen Place, six miles to the east. It was probably constructed slightly later.

These roads were easily accessible for the Crawley iron-producers. To the east it would be simple to follow the low ridge from Hogs Hill which continues towards Three Bridges, past Blackwater Farm, Worth church and along to Turners Hill. Alternatively, one could strike south to the higher ridge at Pease Pottage and use the old ridgeway to reach either road.

Both roads were built when north Sussex was still an uncharted area, because of its scarcity of settlement. The recently examined remains of a fort at East Grinstead contain evidence of occupation by tribesmen from the Thames Valley area moving southwards. The pottery from Hogs Hill points to settlement northwards from the South Coast. Probably after the pacification of Britain and the building of the roads, Crawley became more clearly defined as an area of land belonging to the Regni; that is, it looked southwards for its rulers rather than northwards. Trade could have been in either direction; until the 12th century it was disputable as to where the north of Sussex ended and the south of Surrey began.

To return to the Hogs Hill site, three possible iron bloomeries were identified, dating from early in the Roman period. Some of the pottery was of good quality and had been brought a long way from where it had originated. Pieces of roof tile were found, so it is reasonable to infer that a substantial, well-built building had been put on the site. No trace of a farmstead, however, came to light. Once it had been proved that Roman iron-works existed in Crawley, those interested kept their eyes open when other developments took place. From the Hogs Hill site it was possible to look down the grassy slope, across the by-pass to the open ground at Broadfield. Could there be more evidence there?

The findings exceeded all expectations. That Roman remains had been discovered at Southgate West was almost unbelievable. When Broadfield was to be developed, a cursory examination had shown evidence of iron-slag and so a few more bloomeries were expected. In fact, when the earth-moving machinery started work and the topsoil was removed many remains of furnaces came to light. These were found particularly along a small stream which flowed northwards across the site.

The quality and the quantity of iron-slag and pottery, and even a badly corroded coin, showed how important it had been. So far over 100 furnaces have been traced and though each was small the total number is enormous. The earliest are pre-Roman, but the majority date from the last quarter of the first century A.D. onwards. The whole smelting process could be identified: ore-roasting pits, shaft-type furnaces, slag heaps, a water-reservoir, a puddling pit and a blacksmith's workshop with a stone-built forge. This must have been a very important settlement.

There must have been a large farming community nearby, although the main aim of the Broadfield site was to make iron, not to run a commercial farm. Soldiers would have been stationed to protect (or to coerce) the iron-workers. It is clear that the army had a large rectangular site here, measuring approximately 76 m. by 63 m., and surrounded on four sides by a ditch and bank. This enclosed a barrack building, a bath house and a temple; outside the camp were the workmen's quarters — timber-framed buildings measuring 11 m. by 5 m. containing an oven. Dating the pottery suggests that the site produced most of its iron in the early years of the Roman conquest of Britain. Once the army had extended its conquest northwards, then the iron-making at Crawley became less important. More convenient areas became major producers and, after a hundred years of production, Crawley, like many American frontier towns, declined as the frontier moved away. It is unlikely that Roman immigrants had come to Crawley: more probably the workers were native Britons, who overwhelmingly outnumbered the Romans. The absence of nearby sites would seem to suggest that the Crawley settlement itself did not have an extensive farming population: the absence of huts, storage pits or other 'village' evidence supports this interpretation.

Crawley produced more iron than could have been consumed locally, and needed a distribution network. The Weald bloomeries produced bars of iron; iron goods were probably produced elsewhere (there was a gild of iron-workers in Chichester). Much iron production was destined for military use. By the late second century A.D. the Roman fleet seems to have taken control of many ironworks in the Weald, though it withdrew during the third century. Another Roman bloomery has been found in the east of Worth parish and is sited exactly on the present county boundary, to the south of Gibbshaven Farm on Felbridge Water. This is a smaller site, but stands on the Roman road, and would have been well placed for sending its output to market. The last group of bloomeries at Broadfield dates from the fourth century, and shows that the work continued even when Roman demand was waning.

The other 'industrial' product which interests us in this period is pottery. Many of the potsherds found in Crawley are judged merely as 'local' rough earthenware of no particular merit. Much is grey in colour and of little artistic style. Some is of better quality, white or red-brown, including Nene pottery and Samian ware, which had to cross the Channel. Remains of very large oil containers, such as came from Naples, have also been found.

The impression we receive from some books that the Romans came to a dark, unorganised, uncultured Britain and brought civilisation at a stroke is an over-simplification. To this one can only say that, apart from a few places, the Romans did not transform Sussex. Excavations at Mount Caburn, near Lewes, show that the Britons there lived in well-built huts with door-latches and wore woven clothes; the men shaved and the women wore glass beads, brooches and bronze rings. They kept dogs, horses, pigs, sheep and cattle, and used implements which included ploughs and sickles. They had money, a system of agreed weights and measures, and used knives, saws and hammers. There was an assortment of pottery. Was this an uncivilised, unorganised community?

When, in A.D. 410, the Roman legions finally left Britain to its fate there was a twilight period before more tribes from northern Europe invaded and settled this island; we now move on from the Romano-Celtic Britons who inhabited Sussex and turn our attention to the next group, who assimilated them.

Chapter 3

The Saxon Settlers

The Anglo-Saxon Chronicle records much of what we know of early Saxon settlement in England. However, as a good deal of it was written quite a while after the events it might be as inaccurate as Shakespeare's history plays of English kings, written to please the successful Tudor dynasty.

> Aelle came to Britain and his three sons Cymen, Wlencing and Cissa with three ships at the place which is called (Selsey Bill) and there slew many Welsh and drove some to flight into the wood which is called Andreds Wood.

Thus the writer of the Anglo-Saxon Chronicle records the first Saxon invaders of Sussex in A.D. 477, telling of a small, armed tribal unit landing at Selsey, but meeting opposition from the native Britons (or Welsh as the Saxons called them). In 14 years this group and their reinforcements fought and overcame the Regni, laid claim to a large expanse of coastal plain and took and destroyed much of the Roman town of Noviomagus. Aelle proclaimed himself king of the South Saxons — or Suthe Sexe. Thus the name 'Sussex' was given to the region. The invaders came from northern Europe and comprised Angles, Jutes and Saxons. Those who settled in this area can be called Saxons; although we do not know where they came from, they called their territory that of the South Saxons and this is how they saw themselves. Their kingdom extended from the marshland of Pevensey in the east to the Hampshire borders in the west.

The northern limit was not delineated because the Weald was densely forested. The first settlers found enough good farmland for their needs south of the South Downs. The Saxons seem to have had little regard for the native British-speaking tribespeople. Those who annoyed were killed, and some were enslaved, though the majority were probably allowed to co-exist with the Saxons and — with intermarriage — gradually disappeared as a separate entity. The Britons who were evicted from their homes could move northwards to the safety of the Weald or westwards away from the invaders. It is likely that the British iron-workers of the Weald were allowed to continue their craft since the output would have been useful to the Saxons. Since iron was used to make weapons, however, it is likely that they would have been closely watched.

Whatever may have happened to the British who remained as independent settlers, little trace of Celtic place-names persisted. Saxon-based names became dominant. The pattern of Saxon settlement can be traced by looking at the place-names which they gave to the area. Although popular mythology makes us take sides with the noble Arthur and his Britons against the savage, boorish Saxons it was, nevertheless, the mixture of Anglo-Saxons who became our ancestors, and it is from these invaders that most of us are, in truth, descended. They became the 'English'.

Place-names in the Crawley area

Most of our place-names describe a settlement or a natural feature. It can be assumed that every place-name we now have is derived from words which, when given, were a normal expression in some language. Modern English is mostly Anglo-Saxon in origin, and the majority of place-names in Sussex were probably given before the Norman Conquest. Although these had a specific meaning when given, in a thousand years or more of use most have become unintelligible to us, and are now just 'words'. Sounds change, meanings fade, new words replace old ones. If, however, we believe that at one time 'Crawley', for example, meant something, then the problem is to find out what it was. We should start by going back as far as written records persist. Unfortunately, most early records date from after the Norman Conquest, and represent attempts to write down a sound at a time when uniformity of spelling did not exist: indeed, the original meaning itself may already have faded by then. Even when names were being copied, clerks could misread what they saw in another document. For many years the mass of people spoke an Anglo-Saxon derived language, known from about 1150 as Middle English, while the ruling classes, clerks and churchmen found a common language in French. Clerks and clergy included many native-born 'English', but Latin and French were the written languages of the masters. Place-names have had to survive many difficulties.

Since they give most of the evidence for the way our district was permanently settled, however, let us look at them. There is the usual mixture of settlement names and natural features. One of the earliest remains of human habitation, for example, is just to the north of Crawley at Thunderfield, near Horley, Surrey. This was named after Thor, the God of War, at a time when the area was nominally Christian. Nearby is Burstow, which is the 'place' (stow) by the 'fortified place' (burh). Most early settlements in the area would have been fortified in some way — by fence or with water — as a protection in the wild, wooded terrain.

Many local place-names refer to the forest. The Anglo-Saxon word 'leah' originally meant a wood, though the word eventually came to mean a clearing and finally was used to describe a field. In place names it can now be written -ley, -ly or -leigh, and it can have various pronunciations, which to our ears sound like lee, lie or lay. We can usually tell which meaning is meant by looking at the whole word. Therefore Crawley was the Crow's Wood; Langley was a Long Wood; Burleigh records the wood near to the fortified place. A second word meaning woodland is 'hurst'; although this is less common in our area, we do have Ewhurst Farm, which was the Yew Wood Farm.

The first inhabitants to live in the district were probably, as we have seen, the iron-workers. They required food, and needed to be part-time farmers as well as craftsmen. For such people, and indeed for subsequent inhabitants, the forest provided much of their sustenance. As previously stated, the timber itself was used for building, implement making, fuel and light. But there were also nuts, fruit and berries growing on trees and we see these in such names as Hazelwick (the farm by the hazel trees), Slaugham (the farm by the sloe trees) and Imberhorne (raspberry hill). Finally there was much wildlife which provided food, skins and furs, sinew and bone. This was marked by names such as Buckswood, Coneyhurst (rabbit's wood) and Broxmead (badger's hole). There are few names relating to bees or birds, however, except of course for Crawley itself.

After the forest names, we move on to names which show clearances taking place in the forest. The earliest word for a clearing is 'worth'. Interestingly, in this area the place-name Worth was given without an adjective to distinguish it. It was simply 'the clearing', apparently the only one at the time, and so needed no further identification. It must have been a very early place-name. Did the iron-workers live there? Later, there was a Deerswood in Ifield, originally Deersworth.

As more settlers came to the area, more trees would be cut down, and the next word we meet to describe the clearings is 'field' or 'fold'. It was much later that these words acquired their modern meanings: at first they simply meant places cleared of trees or open land. In this way we have Ifield, which was a clearing in the yew trees. Copthorne refers to copped, or cut, thorn trees.

Clearances became more common. Woolborough Farm was a very early farmstead. Its

5. The interior of the impressive aisled barn at Woolborough farm, over 400 years old. It was demolished with all the other Woolborough Farm buildings during the building of Manor Royal.

name is a corruption of wolf-borough, or the fortified place where wolves were to be found. Here is a useful reminder that the animals in the forest were not all benign creatures such as deer and squirrels. Incidentally, Woolborough Farm was Crawley's oldest known timber-framed building, dating from the early 14th century. Both farm and barn were demolished to make way for a corner of a factory sports field by Woolborough Lane. Luckily, not all of Crawley's past was so destroyed: Jordan's Barn is used as a social club by another Crawley factory.

After these clearances, it is not surprising that we get a number of names referring to farmsteads. We have already met the word 'burh' (which nowadays has become bur- or -bury or -borough). Place-names including the ending '-ham' were used early. The word is like our modern word 'village' and was used for a variety of places, which may have grown into a large village or shrunk to a small homestead. Slaugham is an example of this, and we are not far from the settlements of Horsham and Warnham. This suggests that Slaugham is an older place than Crawley. However, there is an element of doubt in this interpretation because of the possible confusion between '-ham' and the later and more common element '-hamm', a topographical term meaning river-meadow. Later the word '-wick' (or 'wich') was used to denote farms and this was more common in our area. It too had a width of meaning, but in this area was often used of animal/dairy farms; Gatwick was a goat farm, and reference has already been made to Hazelwick and Crabbett (crabbe-wick).

The nature of early settlement

What sort of life did these earliest Crawley settlers live? There was a strong family tie in their lives and much of their organisation was family-based. Our simplistic view of barbaric warlike Saxons has to accept that, having taken control of the land, they were concerned with farming it. After the initial settlement of the coastal areas, the settlers pushed into the Weald and its useful forest.

Coastal settlements were keen to claim control of inland areas, which became prized possessions. For example, the village of Beeding in the south, now Upper Beeding, claimed land to the north, which became known as Lower Beeding. The forest clearances may at first have been grazed only in summer. In particular swine pastures were valued and often appear in catalogues of land owned by the villages in the south. 'Pannage' was the right to keep pigs in the forest, where they could eat acorns or beech nuts (mast). Coastal settlements needed inland Sussex as part of an integrated farming economy. The coastal areas were good arable land, and the inland holdings in the forest provided both timber and pasture. Such forest land was suitable for both hunting and grazing. This wide use of the Weald made settlement uneven, but — in time — inevitable.

There is an early charter referring to Burleigh, standing on the Roman road from London to Brighton near to its crossing of the Medway. As long as there were road links Burleigh could survive once the Romans had left. The land there was closely connected to Lindfield. Later, both were owned by the archbishop of Canterbury and Burleigh became known as Burleigh Arches from 'Archiepiscopi' or 'belonging to the Archbishop'. In A.D. 765 Burleigh was named as part of a gift of land given by Aldulf (king of the South Saxons) to the archbishop and to the canons of South Malling, near Lewes. Burleigh and Lindfield were both outlying swine pastures belonging to the settlement of Stanmer in the south.

In 947 King Eadred granted to Eadric land in the village of Washington, near to Worthing. This land also had outlying holdings to the north and the charter refers to the 'wood pastures which belong thereto'. A later charter called them the swine pastures. Not all can be identified but they stretched north-east from Washington. The list reads (in modern words) 'Wynburgh's spear, and the three Crockhursts, and Horsham, and Yffels's clearing, and Hazelwick, and Gatwick, and the Redfold'. These are the first references to places in the centre of our area, Hazelwick and Gatwick farms.

How were such areas administered? The chief man in any settled area would be called the 'thane'. Freemen in the area would be known as 'ceorls'. The name still persists in the adjective 'churlish' and in the village name of Charlwood, which indicates the wood belonging to the freemen. At the bottom of the social ladder were the unfree serfs, who were virtual slaves, and who needed permission to do anything. It is easy to envisage the problems caused in Sussex as the population slowly grew. The ceorls could choose to be the frontiersmen who moved to the village-owned lands in the north, there to clear the trees and set up farmsteads. In addition, the 'unfree' men who ran away from their home village could move to a remote area to create a new life.

The Crawley area is not typical of the development of an agricultural community in England. We do not have the nucleated village surrounded by large open fields, where villagers held strips of land dispersed among the strips of others. In north Sussex the pioneers were those who stayed permanently in the forest areas. The Saxon settlers were the first to start large-scale clearance and settlement, but it is important to stress that this movement continued until the early modern period. Such settlers had to clear the trees, create their own agricultural land and live on a protected farm in the middle. Most would have built wooden stockades for safety; a moated site sometimes developed. Though we see that the landholdings in the north were valuable to the landowners in the south, the support of a settled community in the south must have been virtually essential to a northern settlement in its early years. We can envisage the Saxon farmstead, with its house, a byre, a storehouse, stable, sheds and pigsty, all surrounding a courtyard. A rickyard and a flaxyard might be adjacent, with an orchard, a garden and beehives. This would certainly need a large stockade. Even the smaller farmsteads needed a good work space. Incidentally, when we see timber-framed buildings today it is easy to forget that the Anglo-Saxons liked to paint their walls yellow (with ochre from clay) or blue (with archil, a dye made from liverwort and other lichen).

Obviously, animals were very important in forest areas. Most of Crawley's local farms are likely to have concentrated on animal husbandry. Horses were scarce; they were often turned loose and caught when needed. That they were bred locally can be seen in the names of Horsham (horse farm) and Warnham (stallion farm). Oxen were more common as beasts of burden than were horses.

6. Ewhurst Place, one of the moated farm sites in Ifield.

Land was traditionally measured by the number of oxen needed for ploughing. It is, after all, ploughed arable land which demonstrates where farmers have put their energy into permanent cultivation rather than forest and rough grazing. In all documents ploughed land is taken as a measure for taxation. A farmer with arable land could only expand its area by getting more oxen to plough it. The continued measurement of land with reference to oxen emphasises that arable farming was seen to be very important.

During the Saxon period the hide became a common unit of land area. Unfortunately for historians it was not a fixed area. It referred to the amount of land needed to support a ceorl and his family. This is roughly the amount a full plough team of eight oxen could cultivate, and also meadowland and pasture. On the whole it is taken to mean about one hundred and twenty acres, though it could be less. A ceorl who became wealthy enough to own five hides and build a church would become a thane. The hide is increasingly met in the later Anglo-Saxon period; there is a Hyde Farm in Ifield. No doubt it took a long time to build up such a substantial landholding in these frontier lands. Lesser men would have to make do with a yardland (or virgate) which required just two oxen; about thirty acres but enough to live on frugally. As an ox-team really required eight oxen, the smaller landholders may have had to combine to form an ox-team to plough their land adequately.

The other kept livestock included cows, goats and sheep. These all provided milk, butter and cheese, as well as skins. Pigs have already been mentioned; large herds were traditionally put out to the forest to eat acorns and beech mast, from the feast of St John the Baptist, at the end of August, until the New Year. Pigs were so common that they often gave their name to a settlement or a landscape feature, such as Hogs Hill Farm in Southgate. Geese, fowls, dogs and bees would have been kept in this area. The name of Gossops Green derives from the word goose; 150 years ago the map of Ifield showed also that land just north of what is now Ifield station was called Goose Green.

Arable farming provided both grain for men and fodder for animals. Animal feed was always in short supply in the winter months and surplus animals were slaughtered for meat at Martinmas. The oldest field systems in the area seem to be those on flat, alluvial clay in Burstow and to the north of Ifield church. It is only here that open fields may possibly have existed, but they have been most unusual in the area as a whole. Co-operative farming was a common feature of Anglo-Saxon society, but single, individually owned farms were the obvious result of the way the forest was colonised. There are traces of many lawsuits, until long after the Norman Conquest, where one person tried to exert his legal rights over a remote farm whose farmer had become used to his isolation and independence. The area bred an independent mind.

Even though place-names can illustrate the likely progression of settlement (woodland to clearings to fields and farms), it is impossible to give a clear chronology of settlement or to show a time scale. When the pre-Roman iron industry was being practised it is probable that rudimentary farming, too, was developing. The farms on the flatter clay lands around Ifield and Burstow might predate even the Anglo-Saxon settlement.

Then, at a time when the first growth of the Ifield/Burstow clayland settlements was taking place, there was another, older, farmed area on the upper reaches of the Medway in the Burleigh area. Here, in smaller valleys with alluvial deposits, was an arc stretching through Felbridge, Gulledge Farm, Burleigh Farm, Hazelden, to Standen and Whalesbeach. This area on the eastern borders of Worth was — in contrast — very uneven hilly land. Once a busy area, it faded in importance after the Norman Conquest.

The names of woods are not necessarily older than the names of settlements. Individual woods might not have been named until after the farms had been created and areas of woodland had been left. All that can be said is that people have lived in and farmed this area, even without a large settlement present, since before the Roman invasion. During all this time there would have been a *mélange* of well-established farms, newly-established farms, and men still clearing the forest waste (or 'assarting' as this activity was known). As described earlier, the Saxons penetrated this far inland within a few hundred years of their first appearance in Sussex, and doubtless very much increased the pace of assarting. As we have seen, Thunderfield in Horley got its name from the Saxon god Thunor. It would have been a place of worship, so relied on local residents. St Wilfred arrived in the kingdom of the South Saxons in A.D. 681 and travelled around preaching and converting the people. The South Saxons were one of the last groups of the English to convert to Christianity. They were never in the forefront of English history, and the area remained insular for many years. Worship of Thunor could have continued in the forests for a long time. It is possible that the Thunderfield site was established late, in a remote area, as a last defiant gesture to the steady encroachment of Christianity. On the other hand, Christianity did pierce the northern lands, although it did not necessarily make life more peaceful. Within a hundred years of the arrival of St Wilfred in Sussex, both Canterbury and York cathedrals had been burnt down. But Sussex people did start to build substantial churches from the eighth century onwards, and this gives more evidence of Saxon settlement.

Early organised government and administration

Once people have decided to settle a piece of land, they are eager to make their boundaries known. Much of our knowledge of early history comes from records of disputes over land ownership. The Surrey-Sussex border was late in being precisely defined. We have already seen references to Hazelwick and Gatwick as being connected with Washington in the south; similarly Charlwood, Burstow and Worth were outlying lands connected with Merstham to the north.

A vital component of the administrative system evolved by the Anglo-Saxons was the hundred. It is not known precisely how it developed, but areas containing a number of settlements with a population of about a hundred families of freemen were grouped together. These then became local government units, and also law-keeping and defensive units. The area which comprised a hundred could be compact or very extensive, depending on the quality of land and its settlement pattern, and on how much forest or waste was included.

In Sussex local government was further complicated in that the hundreds themselves were further grouped into larger units, known as rapes. This word is peculiar to Sussex, and nobody knows what it really means or how it was derived. Sussex was grouped into five rapes at first, each with a major castle guarding its southern coastline. The Crawley area was near the conjunction of three rapes. Ifield was in the Rape of Bramber; Crawley and Worth were in the Rape of Lewes; part of eastern Worth and East Grinstead was in the Rape of Hastings. When we look for references to this area in old documents, it is essential to know in which rape we are to look.

At the same time as a secular administration was being set up in the hundreds, so too an ecclesiastical one was developing. As a result of St Wilfred's ministry, several churches were built, the number increasing as settlement widened. At first these would have been simple timber structures, but if the settlement grew into a village and the population became richer, it would have been considered right to build a stone church. This could serve as a place of worship, a place for general assembly, and a place of safety. With any threat of war, a strong church became a place of sanctuary. Even after the various Anglo-Saxon groups stopped fighting one another, soldiers from Europe still posed threats. In A.D. 994, for example, an army led by Olaf of Norway and Sweyn of Denmark was beaten back from London and turned to Sussex for plunder.

Churches were founded to serve a local community, often by the major local landowner who retained the right (advowson) to nominate the priest and perhaps kept some of the tithes for himself. The diocese would normally be content to have yet another church in its ambit. Both secular and spiritual authorities had a vested interest in getting an income from the land. The developing parish structure was useful for both Church and landowner. The hundreds of Sussex contained a number of settlements (or vills as they are called in old documents) which became the nucleus of future parishes. It was eventually the definition of these parish boundaries which allocated land firmly to Surrey and Sussex.

Our main concern is with two of the hundreds. The one which eventually contained Ifield became known as the Hundred of Burbeach, in the Rape of Bramber; the one which contained Crawley and Worth became the Hundred of Buttinghill, in the Rape of Lewes. Occasionally other names will be referred to, and these will be explained where appropriate (*see* Ill. 7).

As can be seen from our maps, the parish of Worth covered an enormous area. Before Turners Hill, Copthorne and Crawley Down were separated from it in the 19th century the parish contained over 13,000 acres. Though large, it never contained a nucleated settlement: in other words, there was never a Worth village. Ifield, too, was large, in time the parish contained over 4,000 acres, and had just a very small settlement around the church. Ifield village was a recent development.

Compared with Ifield and Worth, Crawley was the odd parish out. Firstly, the parish was very small, less than 800 acres. Half of this was in a detached area south of Pease Pottage, which only comprised a few farms in a woodland area. Secondly, as we will see later, when the village of Crawley developed the parish boundary ran up the High Street so that the east of the High Street, with the church, was Crawley parish, whereas the west of the High Street was in Ifield parish. A settlement at Crawley may not have existed in the Anglo-Saxon period; if it did, it was very small.

What comprised the two hundreds we are mostly concerned with? As with most of the

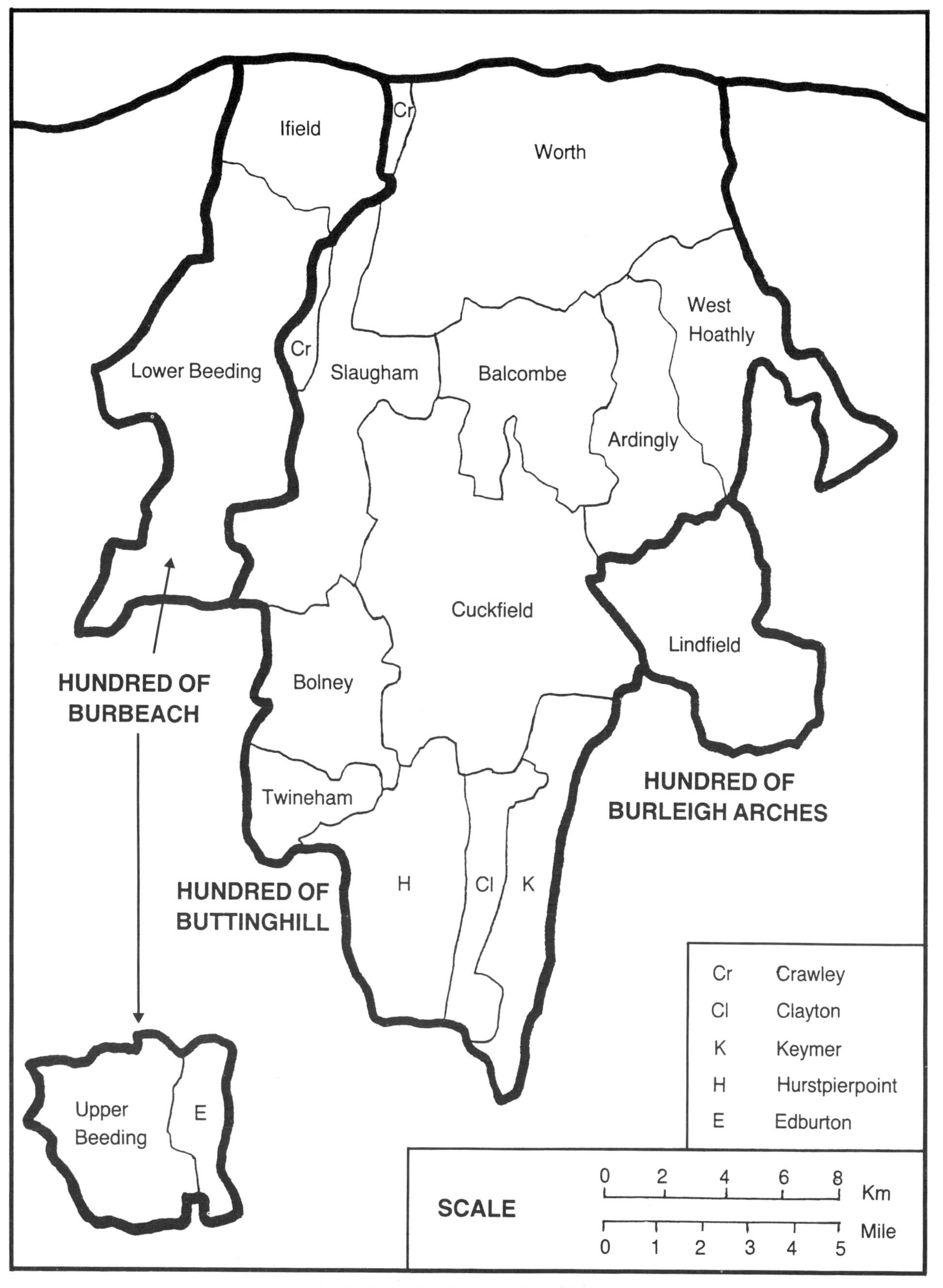

7. Local hundreds and parishes.

hundreds of north Sussex, they were elongated from north to south, which fits in with our ideas of how the north was claimed by the south. The Hundred of Buttinghill was first listed as comprising the richer and older settlements of Hurst, Clayton and Wickham as well as Crawley. By the 14th century the hundred was said to comprise the vills of Hurst, Keymer. Clayton, Wyndham, Cuckfield, Worth and Crawley. This is clearly not an exhaustive list of the settlements which existed in late Anglo-Saxon times. No separate mention of places like Ardingly, Balcombe, Bolney, Slaugham, Twineham or West Hoathly is made until the 16th century in the hundred records which survive, yet some of their churches have traces of Saxon work. The meeting place of the hundred court was originally at Butting Hill, a mound at Ham Farm in Clayton. By the 13th century it had been moved to Cuckfield to take account of the northwards shift in importance of settlement in the hundred.

An early reference to a Hundred of Ifield survives, which is surprising, but before long Ifield was part of the Hundred of Burbeach in the Rape of Bramber. This hundred was much smaller than most in extent, suggesting a more densely settled area. It comprised Upper and Lower Beeding, Edburton and Ifield. The original meeting place is unknown but is likely to have been in the Lower Beeding area, perhaps near the Priory of Sele. Burleigh, like Ifield, was also occasionally quoted as a hundred itself, but the east of Worth parish and beyond was normally shown in the Hundred of Streat. Streat is just a small village now, near Plumpton, but the hundred included Chailey, Wivelsfield and Lindfield. Finally, Worth was originally a part of the Hundred of Churchfelle (now Reigate) and appears in the Surrey return for Domesday Book. Not long afterwards it was taken to be part of Sussex and started to appear in the Hundred of Buttinghill.

We can conclude from this that in late Anglo-Saxon times the area was still rather poorly defined. Ifield was an important early settlement area which later diminished in importance as more land in the area was settled, and Burleigh was once important, but was declining long before the Normans came. Worth was, for many years, an ill-defined forest area in terms of settlement, though when it was given to the Earl de Warrenne after the Conquest it became a hunting forest and important for that reason. Crawley was a potential growth point which eventually forged trade and communication links with outside areas, but had little importance during the late Anglo-Saxon period.

The Saxon Church

Some Sussex churches, even those which are not mentioned in Domesday, still have traces of Saxon stone work. In some cases there is no documentary evidence for the village, let alone the church, before the 14th century. Although it is impossible always to be completely certain, it is thought that there are Saxon traces in the churches of Clayton, Bolney, Slaugham and West Hoathly yet, of these four villages, early references to the Hundred of Buttinghill only mention Clayton. At Worth itself we have a gem, though a puzzling one.

Worth church is an example of the problems historians face, since logically it should not be there at all. According to its Domesday entry there were few inhabitants and the existence of the church is ignored, which is not uncommon. As we have seen there are several old settled areas in the district but Worth church is not convenient to serve any of them. It may have been a central church to serve an isolated, scattered, forest population, but why then erect such a large, extremely expensive stone building? Who would pay for it? What income would maintain it?

Nobody knows exactly when the church was built, though there is a general agreement among architectural historians that it was erected early in the 11th century, just before the Norman invasion. The style of the building is in general typically Saxon, but not completely so. It was built in the shape of a cross (cruciform) with two side aisles forming the arms of the cross, though they are not symmetrical. The rounded end of the apse, behind the altar, looks like a Roman basilica, which was a model recommended by King Alfred. The building material is local sandstone and the structure's size is impressive. It is not so grand as the older Saxon church at Bosham, but its isolation has led to it keeping many of its original features.

Worth never developed, so there was no need to make the church larger. Many churches have had side aisles added which destroyed the original walls, and strong towers have been built. This is not so at Worth. Obviously there have been changes, and the present apse with its apparently ancient windows surrounding the altar is mostly Victorian rebuilding; the 'restoration' of 1871 caused much controversy at the time. Other walls show signs of having been repaired and rebuilt in the 13th century. It is nothing new for churches to be 'improved'. The nave measures about 18 m. by 8 m. It is impressively tall. The evidence that it is Saxon lies in the 'long' and 'short' stone columns of the wall, the shape of the chancel arch, the fact that the stones of the arch match the thickness of the wall, the two tall, narrow doorways, the shape of the high windows on the north wall, and its general plan. Other evidence, however, might indicate that it had Norman origins, since its shape is that used also in early Norman architecture and it seems to be no earlier than the 11th century.

The late Anglo-Saxon period saw a revival of monasticism, and the Benedictines who settled and worked in unoccupied lands were well supported by the crown and aristocracy. The great Abbey of Chertsey had long roots which linked it with the south of Surrey, and was rich enough to have borne the cost of building Worth, as too were royal and noble families. Perhaps it is significant that according to the Domesday entry Worth belonged, at the time of King Edward the Confessor, to a man called Oswald who is known to have been a brother of the abbot of Chertsey. It is unlikely that we will ever know the truth, but it is certainly possible that the church at Worth was built by an abbey. For what purpose? It may have been a place for quiet contemplation, or a base for 'missionary' work in a frontier area. Certainly a stone-built substantial building would have its uses in a forest, although the walls of this church are not very thick. Early inhabitants would have had to risk spasmodic attacks by animals, marauding soldiers or armed men of various nationalities, outlaws, vagrants or even neighbours.

There is one final point that can be made concerning Worth church, and that arises from the consideration of the choice of site. Very many early churches were sited quite deliberately on pagan holy sites. As the local population would be used to worshipping at a particular location the pre-Christian meeting-place would simply be used for a different religious activity from its original one. Throughout Sussex there are churches on top of or adjacent to barrows. A walk around the church grounds at Worth gives a strong impression of a barrow site, and there appears to be a circular pattern of ditches. I surmise that Worth church may occupy the site of a barrow or perhaps even an associated Iron Age camp. There are churches in England where, a barrow having been levelled off, the large stones which had been used to build the barrow were then used as a foundation upon which the church was built. The plinth on which Worth church still stands may have originated in this way. Though this is not put forward as a complete explanation there is evidence to support the theory, and it would provide a plausible reason for the church being built on a prominent, hilltop site deep in the forest beside a pre-Roman trackway. The church is not an early church, but there could have been strong pagan worship surviving in the remote forest long after the area had become nominally Christian. Indeed, if the worship of Thunor was strong in this remote area, then the church could have been deliberately built to counteract it.

It is strange that most local parishes were subject to external religious influence. Charlwood was one of the archbishop of Canterbury's 'peculiars'. This means that it was

8. The exterior of Worth church, a view drawn in the 1780s and now in the Burrell Collection at the British Museum.

9. Worth church. The Saxon features visible here include the windows high in the nave and the stone pilasters, of alternate long and short stones, strengthening the walls of the south transept.

10. An engraving showing the interior of Worth church about one hundred and fifty years ago, when high-backed pews and a rood screen were still in place and the apse had not been rebuilt. Note the Saxon arch.

not part of the diocese of the local bishop but owed allegiance directly to the archbishop. Burstow was in the same position as Charlwood, and at one time both churches were given to the Abbey of Chertsey, which exercised local control via Merstham — which also belonged to the archbishop of Canterbury. Worth we have already mentioned, and Burleigh was an area which, together with the neighbouring Lindfield parish, was owned by the archbishop although it never became a parish. Ifield contributed to the income of the nuns at the Priory of Rusper, who had the 'tithes of corn and hay and all portions, pensions and rents arising from all . . . lands in Ifield not assigned to the Vicar'. Finally Crawley was, as we will see, originally an outlying chapel of the mother church at Slaugham which still claimed control of Crawley church in the 16th century, though in practice had long lost it.

We have now reached a turning point in our local history. So far, much of what has been written about the origins and growth of Crawley has been speculative. The 'harder' evidence has been obtained from archaeological digs, a few scattered references in Saxon charters (which are themselves often only known from medieval copies) and the structure of one church. The 'softer' evidence comes from place-names, and from observation of the land. The speculations have been based on what, from general historical knowledge, we could reasonably have expected to have happened. The arrival of the Normans, however, brought about an important change. Their administrators kept good records, many of which have survived, and wrote copiously about ownership and possession of land. They went to law and recorded taxes. The story of our locality now becomes clearer.

Chapter 4

The Normans

In 1064 Harold sailed from Bosham in the west of Sussex and his voyage ended in shipwreck on the coast of Normandy. As an enforced guest of Duke William of Normandy, he agreed to support him as future successor to Edward, King of England. Later, safely back in England, he changed his mind. After King Edward's death, William made his claim to the English throne and landed accompanied by a large army in the east of Sussex, near Pevensey, on 28 September 1066. Harold was at the time fighting a Danish army in Yorkshire. He defeated the Danes and marched south, calling on reinforcements from other parts of England and passing through Sussex. North of Hastings the two armies met and the Normans were the victors.

There are local stories of soldiers from the fleeing English army passing by Worth church, and warning the local inhabitants of Harold's defeat. This is not unlikely. Those who wanted to return north or west would have had to travel through the Weald before crossing the clay vale between Crawley and the North Downs, where the main routes to the rest of Britain ran.

Once William, still not 40 years old, was declared king on Christmas Day, 1066, the south-east of England was quickly pacified. It is likely that everyday life for the people living in this area changed very little. They would only be aware of new overlords claiming their feudal dues. The south-east was spared much of the fighting and despoiling experienced elsewhere. William is remembered for setting up firm government, and for establishing the rule of fixed law, with justice — though it must be pointed out that the Saxons already had fixed laws and justice. Just how they were enforced depended on the local administrators. We must thank their records for most of what we know of our local history for the next 500 years.

Sussex stood between London and the invaders' homeland of Normandy, and William was anxious to safeguard the area, by now organised into six rapes. He therefore entrusted the government of each one to a noble whom he thought he could trust. Chichester and Arundel rapes were given to Earl Roger; the Rape of Bramber, a new creation, was given to William de Braose. A distant relative of the king, William de Warrenne, who was later made Earl of Surrey, was given the Rape of Lewes. The coat of arms of the de Warrennes was a chequer pattern, and one can be seen carved on the wall of Worth church. There are a number of old inns in the area which are known as *The Chequers*, the nearest to Crawley being those at Slaugham and Horley. To complete the picture, the Rape of Pevensey was given to the Count of Mortain and the Rape of Hastings to the Count of Eu. Each of these nobles owned land in Sussex and was given control over the other landholders in the rape.

Domesday Survey

The king in theory owned all the land. Anyone who claimed to possess land was said to be 'holding' it with the permission of the king, and would be called the 'tenant-in-chief'. This person in time simply became known as the owner, and he could sublet or sell to anyone. As part of his position, each noble who was given a rape of Sussex to govern was also tenant-in-chief of much of the land in the rape. With the passing of time, much was sold off or sublet to minor Frenchmen, who became known as lords of the manor (or estate). The king also possessed all the feudal customs and services of the people who lived on the land, a valuable source of labour and income, and these rights were passed to the tenant-in-chief. The local residents were either freemen or they lay under one of the varying grades of bondage.

Early in 1086, royal commissioners came to Sussex after having held an enquiry in Kent. They had a number of questions to ask regarding who held the land. Then they listed all the landholdings in Sussex, showing who the landholders were. The various holders of estates (or manors) were eventually listed in order of precedence, beginning with the king, followed by the archbishops, the bishops, earls, barons and so on, right down to the humblest tenant-in-chief. Some villages, especially in the south , comprised more than one manor. Others, especially in the north, away from the coast, were parts of a larger estate and so their names are not separately shown in Domesday Book.

As the county had long been divided into rapes, hundreds and vills, these were convenient administrative units for the Normans to continue to use. But the estates recorded in Domesday did not necessarily coincide with the vills or parishes. This causes some confusion when looking at early documents. If, as seems likely, there was settled land at Crawley, even though there may not have been a nucleated settlement, it would have formed part of the holdings of a larger estate elsewhere. Ifield and Worth are specifically mentioned in Domesday: Crawley is not. This does not mean Crawley did not exist, but that it did not then comprise a clearly separate estate.

The woodlands of north Sussex were being colonised slowly. Any tenant-in-chief who held a large tract of forest would want some of the forest for hunting, but would welcome a man who was willing to clear and settle on part of this land. Such a man provided a rent income and a source of labour, increasing the value of the holding. If enough people settled in an area, eventually a separate estate or manor could be formed and somewhere like Crawley could appear at last in legal documents. The commissioners called together the Sheriff of Sussex, the barons and their Frenchmen, and a jury of representatives from each hundred (a priest, the hundred's bailiff, and six commonfolk from each village). The tenants-in-chief who were listed could say what they believed there was in each manor. The illiterate hundred juries who heard this could testify as to ownership before the Conquest. Much had been simply taken over by the new French nobility, and Domesday helped to settle the question of who now held what.

The Domesday record refers to land areas measured in hides. As already mentioned, this was an old unit of land area measurement. By the time the Normans arrived it had been taken as a standard assessment area for tax purposes. Most villagers would have had a good idea of how many hides their community was worth. If the number of hides varied over a period of time, it may have reflected changes in a place's wealth and prosperity, rather than in the actual area settled and farmed. The number of ploughs given was used as an indication of the amount of arable land. This in practice also pointed to wealth for tax purposes, and was not necessarily a real number, as can be seen in references to 'half a plough' in Domesday.

One could speculate, too, on how accurate the returns were for remote estates on the northern boundary. A suspicious jury of local men forced to travel to Lewes would not be over-eager to agree that their area comprised a large number of hides. If they suspected that the information was to be used for taxation purposes, human nature would tend to under-value the amount of cultivated land to be taxed.

What do the Domesday entries tell of this area?

(i) Ifield

The entry for Ifield appears almost at the end of the Sussex list. The new Rape of Bramber is the last rape to be dealt with. The survey's first entries relate to the Hundred of Burbeach (including Beeding and Shoreham), but Ifield is not mentioned here. At the end of William de Braose's land is listed what the Domesday writer referred to as 'In Tifeld Hundred, Ifelt'. The spelling is phonetic, but Ifield was in fact then shown on its own as part of a hundred called Ifield Hundred. Translated into modern English the entry reads:

> William Son of Ranulf holds IFIELD from William. Alfwy held it from King Edward. Then and now it answered for one Hide. In lordship, nothing. There are five villagers and four smallholders with one plough. Meadow, six acres; woodland, six pigs. The value is and was 20 shillings.

In such simple words we are given our first glimpse of Ifield. The Domesday entries are given in order of precedence, and the owner of Ifield is virtually at the end of the Sussex list. It is a wonder that the entry appears at all since the northern half of Sussex is almost completely ignored by Domesday Book — at least by name. You would need to travel 10 miles to the east, 10 miles to the south and 25 miles to the west to find the nearest named settlement. Yet it is inconceivable that the north of Sussex did not contain any valuable, occupied land. It is obvious that the northern estates were still being claimed by — and settled by — landlords based in the south of Sussex.

To be given a specific entry for Ifield suggests that it had, by Domesday, established an identity separate from the southern influence. The first landowner of this area whose name we know is Alfwy, a Saxon. As a result of the Conquest, he had been superseded by William, son of Ranulf, a Norman. The area was assessed at one hide; in the north of Sussex this would suggest something in excess of 120 acres. This was likely to be mostly farmland, unless the forest was also valued and assessed. No land in lordship implies that the land was not farmed directly by an owner in residence, but had been let to tenants.

The nine men (and their families) suggest a maximum of nine small farms and smallholdings. For taxation purposes, they were assessed as having one plough, suggesting the hide was likely to be arable farmland, with some animal grazing. It also suggests that clearances had taken place some time earlier. The six acres of meadow (along the brook by the church, no doubt) would provide winter grazing. The wood provided 'pasture' for about forty pigs, since the reference to 'six pigs' relates to the tenant-in-chief's share (about a seventh).

There is no reference to freemen in the Ifield entry. Under the Normans, the previous idea of various degrees of 'freedom' continued. The native Englishman of lower status was usually described as a villein (translated above as villager), with his virgate of land, or as a cottar (translated above as smallholder), with his small personal plot, who was employed as a skilled farm worker. The lowest group was the serfs, men with few rights or possessions, who were employed as labourers and servants. So the five villagers counted by Domesday may have had small farms. The four smallholders were likely to be low-status labourers who had a small plot of personal land but little wealth; they were valuable as a source of labour, however, and so were recorded. They could have been occupied looking after animals or working in the forest.

William, son of Ranulf, had other land further south in Sussex: in Sakeham, Morley, Woodmancote, Kingston and Shoreham. We know little else about him; we simply know he was favoured with the grant of land stretching from the northern boundary in a line to the coast: in fact, the whole of the eastern boundary of the Rape of Bramber. It is as if he were given the job of protecting the route to the sea. He is always referred to as 'William, son of Ranulf', and this Ranulf could well be the man who was the favourite court clerk of King William. By many means, mostly underhand, Ranulf amassed great wealth. It seems possible that the Ifield entry refers to the same Ranulf: the land given to his son was very strategically placed.

(ii) Burleigh

The reference to land in Burleigh which formed the eastern portion of Worth appears in the list of lands belonging to the Count of Mortain. He held the Hundred of (East)

Grinstead, which was almost entirely in the Rape of Lewes. There had been, as has been described, a Roman road through Burleigh which led to Brighton. The Roman roads had not survived intact after the Roman withdrawal from Britain, however. There was unlikely to be much road repair in the Weald and, indeed, the local inhabitants were unlikely to want to make it easy for coastal invaders to reach inland. In fact, by the time Domesday was written there was scant trace or memory of the Roman roads, and nobody would have known how or why Burleigh had come to exist. Within a few hundred years it was virtually forgotten except as a farm.

Grinstead's main link by 1086, as now, was with Pevensey (Eastbourne). Shortly after Domesday the hundred was transferred to the Rape of Pevensey. Oddly enough the hundred is known as Grinstead, but no lands are listed as being in a settlement of that name. The list of places in Grinstead Hundred is familiar to us now mainly as farm names, for example Burleigh, Hazleden, Standen, Whalesbeech and Brambletye. We are constantly told in Domesday that these used to lie in land belonging to estates near the South Coast such as Ditchling, Bevenden or small places near Lewes (Allington, Warningore, Wootton and Tarring Neville). We see yet again that the very old Saxon settlements near the South Downs had colonised and then claimed land in the north of the county.

It is, perhaps, surprising that the estate of Whalesbeech, now mainly occupied by a reservoir, was said to be in lands owned by Lavant, just north of Chichester. This long link may possibly, however, be explained by the fact that Lavant was also an estate held by the archbishop of Canterbury, who claimed ownership of much land in Sussex,

The entry for Burleigh (referring to the place as Berchelie) says:

> In BURLEIGH, William holds $1\frac{1}{2}$ Hides from the Count. It is outside the Rape. It did not pay tax. Before 1066, Alfhere held it from Holy Trinity in the Manor of Wootton, as the Hundred testifies. Land for 4 ploughs, 3 villagers with 1 plough. Value before 1066, 20 shillings. Now 10 shillings.

The estate at Burleigh is 50 per cent larger than the area of Ifield or, rather, taxed at 50 per cent more, which may mean the same thing in the northern areas. There is no mention made of meadow, woodland or animals. In King Edward's time the owner was Alfhere, who also had land in the south-east of Sussex, at Selmeston, Sidnor, Ewhurst (by Bodiam) and Tilton (by Alciston). There were, in 1086, just three families shown as living at Burleigh though there was land enough for four ploughs — which should point to a large, arable-based settlement. Rather larger farm units are suggested than those at Ifield — there is four times as much arable land mentioned — but that might be accounted for by its ownership. Lands owned by the Church were often farmed extensively. The leading agriculturalists were churchmen, and they were keen to ensure maximum return from their holdings. Before 1066, Burleigh was part of the manor of Wootton, an important estate owned by the archbishop.

The value of the estate had fallen since the Conquest from 20s. to 10s. which indicates some decline or disruption in the isolated area. To underline this, the land is assessed now for one-and-a-half hides (180 acres) whereas there is land for four ploughs (480 acres). A similar decline is also recorded for the values of Hazleden, Whalesbeech and Brambletye. In the 12th century, both Worth and East Grinstead began to supersede these small estates. East Grinstead became a borough and dominated the area. Worth took over as the general name for the area between East Grinstead and Crawley.

(iii) Worth

The entry for Worth is found in the Surrey lists, where in the Hundred of Churchfelle (later known as the Hundred of Reigate) there is a reference to 'Orde'. At first sight, the words Orde and Worth may appear dissimilar. If you consider, however, that our word 'one' is pronounced as if it began with a 'w' and that a 'd' and a 'th' sound can be interchanged in dialect, the two words can be shown to be the same. Thus the place was always known as Worth but the scribe wrote this sound down as Orde. The entry reads:

> Siward holds WORTH from Richard (son of Count Gilbert). Oswald held it from King Edward. It answered for ½ Hide, then and now. 1 villager with ½ plough. Value before 1066, 30 shillings; later 2 shillings; now 20 shillings.

This is a curious entry. Worth had a reported area (or value) of half a hide, which is about sixty acres. That is confirmed by a similar measurement of half a plough. Indeed, there is only one family shown, so a sixty-acre estate is about right. This is a small, and, one would assume, unimportant estate. But its value was 30s. before the Conquest, and after a temporary disruption, was back to 20s. in 1086. That is double the value of Burleigh with its far greater area of farmland, and the same as Ifield with its far larger population. What could have made it so valuable? One family working sixty acres is unlikely to be worth 20s. Could it be that the forest provided an income from timber, iron or its vast hunting reserves? In that case why are no people mentioned? Was there land let out to forest workers or to monks or laymen working for a church who would owe no allegiance to the landowner? In that case, why was there no forest mentioned in the entry? And why did the value of the land plummet after the Conquest but regain its value later?

The sparse yet contradictory entry for Worth raises far more questions than this book can attempt to answer. Perhaps the important missing entry relates to the fact that there was a church at Worth (attached to the Abbey of Merstham), but the church did not belong to the landowner and therefore did not appear in the records as a potential form of income. In this case, what made Worth so valuable a landholding? Perhaps we shall never know.

(iv) Burstow

Though not strictly within the limits of this book, it is worth adding the information that a reference to Burstow, immediately to the north of Worth, exists. In about 1100 the draft records which the Commissioners had used to draw up Domesday were once again consulted, in order to draw up a list of all the lands in England owned by the archbishop of Canterbury. The resulting document is known as Domesday Monachorum (or the Domesday of the Monks). The entries in this are similar to the final entries recorded in the king's Domesday Book, but sometimes include extra details. The entry for West Tarring (just north of Worthing) repeats that the land there was held by the archbishop, but in addition it mentions that there is outlying land at 'Buresto' (or Burstow).

This is yet another example of how the settlements in the south claimed land in the north. Washington originally claimed Hazelwick, as we have seen. Here West Tarring (five miles south of Washington) claimed Burstow. There must have been much argument when the wilderness to the north was in process of being claimed by people up to 40 miles away in the south, especially when there was no practical way of recording the boundaries.

(v) Crawley

What then of Crawley? Like many other local places, this name does not occur in Domesday. Another entry, however, states that Washington was assessed at 59 hides in the time of King Edward — over 7,000 acres of usable land. This must include very many northern outliers. Similarly, Hurstpierpoint (in the same hundred as Crawley) was originally assessed at 41 hides (about five thousand acres); by the time the commissioners came it was much reduced. Where Crawley's land was actually listed in Domesday we cannot say: it must have existed, though not completely separated from the south of the county. It was probably included somewhere among the Earl de Warrenne's lands. The fact that many southern villages had lost their outlying settlements between 1066 and 1086 does suggest that the north Sussex borders were then undergoing changes as revenue-hunting nobles were actively seeking to establish just who paid taxes to which lord. Independence from the south could have been bought in return for giving allegiance to the lord.

After Domesday

Clearly, the Crawley area was not simply a wild and deserted place in the 11th century. There may not have been a large number of inhabitants living 'village' life, but there were many family units working on farms and continuing to clear the forest. If, as is likely, there were also forest workers and a few iron workers, they would need feeding and looking after. The area was already 'named' which shows it had been well explored, and there would have been a network of paths and tracks connecting the places where families lived and worked.

One curious fact about Crawley is the relationship of West Green with the High Street. It seems that the crossroads at West Green should not be there; surely the east-west and north-south roads should logically cross just in one place — the High Street. A map of Crawley in 1790 shows a pattern of roads and paths (*see* Ill. 11). To understand them, it is only necessary to consider the information already given. The land in Crawley was claimed by communities near the coast but to the south-west. We must expect to find a track system connecting these estates, which would have a north-east to south-west alignment. There would also be a local east-west route connecting Burleigh with Ifield via Worth and Crawley. These tracks can easily be seen on the map.

The conclusion is that the original local crossroads was at West Green. Here, the track came from the Horsham Road, continued along Smalls Lane, crossed the High Street at a narrow angle, kept going towards Black Dog Lane and then became the footpath going across the field shown as The Cobbles. Today, south of West Green the Horsham Road still remains. Northwards, most of Smalls Lane has vanished, except for a few yards at the end of St John's Road. (St John's Road and St Peter's Road mark the edge of the original green.) Smalls Lane — before it disappeared when West Green Drive was constructed — was somewhat sunken, as would be expected for a lane over 1,000 years old. Older residents who still remember it would have thought it a pointless road; indeed its reason for existence did disappear a long while ago, though the lane remained. At the top of the map, the track is marked by the rear of the gardens of a row of cottages (recently demolished) built along the main road. Further along it becomes a footpath which still exists. When Cobbles Crescent was built on Cobbles Field, the builders had to retain the old footpath. This is another fragment of the original main road which has lost its point, though at first it would have been taken by travellers going north-eastwards towards Woolborough, Hazelwick and Gatwick Farms. The original east-west road is still used, though the lane alongside the church became so restricted by building that it is now only a small path.

Until the Conquest, then, Crawley was marked by a crossroads at West Green. When the Normans came, this pattern was changed. The local farms and estates were already becoming detached from their parent settlements in the south, and though the east-west link continued the new communication links were between London and the South Coast. The main road had to cross the Weald clay from Reigate, through Horley, to Crawley. At Crawley, the new main road rose from its clay base and took a harder and drier route along the present High Street, superseding the original track through West Green.

In the town centre, therefore, we see two very early settlements side by side: the Saxon crossroads at West Green and the Norman High Street. Crawley became a staging post. Here, travellers would stop for a while, either preparatory to making the awkward journey northwards across the wet clay or to rest after having successfully negotiated it southwards

11. West Green and the High Street. From early documents we know that there was a south-west to north-east alignment of forest holdings and their parent villages on the south coast. The original trackway linking them can be seen in this map, based on tithe maps. This route crossed the old east–west track at West Green. After the Norman Conquest the routes needed were more directly north–south, and the new High Street and its settlement became more important than the old crossroads.

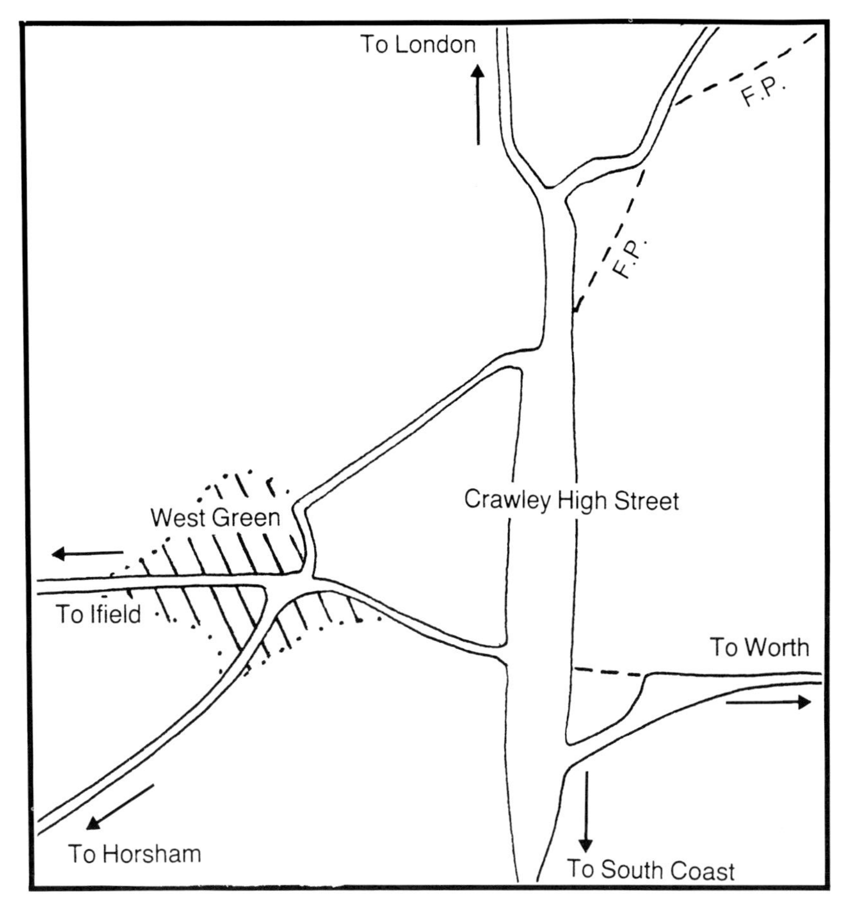

12. Hazelwick Mill, Pound Hill, the only local water mill not constructed for the iron industry. The railway passed close by. The site is now occupied in part by a supermarket and in part by a secondary school.

from the Downs. Alternatively, they gained breath before or after climbing the High Weald to the south, with its dangerous road passing through St Leonard's Forest. The settlements east and west continued to be based on farming. Both Ifield and Worth were good sources of income, mainly from agriculture. Crawley, however, occupied an important site on the main road, and became an 'urban' site comparatively quickly. Ifield and Worth remained areas of scattered population with no real village centres. Even Ifield Green never became a compact village. It was Crawley that built up the non-farming employment which looked beyond its own boundaries for customers, and became the local market. We can see this happening during the next 300 years.

This is not to underestimate the importance of the rural nature of the area. Changes took place from the 12th century. Horses were increasingly used as draught animals. Rabbits became an important source of meat and fur, and the king would grant 'free warren' to protect the lord's rights. This meant that rabbits were allowed to breed and burrow where they wished, just as deer were protected animals — at least, from all except the lord. The spread of rabbits and deer became a cause of alarm to farmers when they saw the damage these animals could cause to their crops; when they were hunted even more crop damage resulted.

Parts of Bewbush Vale, St Leonard's and Worth forests were in the hunting reserves kept by the Norman overlords. In the 13th century ducks were introduced to many areas, and pigeons and doves were bred for winter meat. Geese became more important for a number of reasons. They laid eggs and acted as watch-dogs, goose-down made excellent quilts, their wing feathers were used as pen quills or for arrow flights, and goose fat was a basis for much medicine. No wonder geese figure so widely in nursery rhymes and folktales.

Within the manor men were elected to carry out a part-time unpaid office. A woodward looked after timber; a hayward looked after hedges and fences; a messer was in charge of the harvest; the pindar or pinfold collected strays in the pound. Craftsmen carried out specific jobs: carpenter, smith, miller, baker, weaver, leatherworker, brewer, charcoal burner, furnaceman. It is instructive to look at local surnames, which have persisted in the area for many years, that reveal some of these trade-names.

Finally, is it possible to explain how Worth became part of Sussex? Shortly after the Domesday survey William de Warrenne was made Earl of Surrey, though most of his lands were in Sussex. Worth Forest became subject to his control as hunting land, subject to forest law and, as lord of the Rape of Lewes, it could have been tidier to administer it as a part of his Sussex estates than to leave it as a remote, detached part of Surrey. Whatever the reason, Worth was, from the 12th century onwards, included in Sussex documents.

Chapter 5

Medieval Beginnings
Twelfth and Thirteenth Centuries: the Pioneering Years

We have little information about our area in the 12th century. However, there is a variety of material for the 13th century. As we shall see, that in itself may provide a clue to the development of the local area in general, and to Crawley village in particular.

Crawley

(i) A market-place.

In 1202, early in the reign of King John, a royal charter was granted to one of the Poynings family. In return 'Michael of Poynings gives one good Norwegian osprey [or goshawk?] for licence to hold one market at Crawley one day in each week on Wednesday'. This is a surprising development. Though we have seen that a small settlement is likely to have developed at Crawley in the 11th century, and that the present Brighton Road became important in the 12th century, no other documentation has survived which would prepare us for the chartering of a weekly market at the start of the 13th century.

During the 13th century, over 3,000 new markets in England were chartered by the Crown, especially in 'new towns'. In 1889 a list was published, drawn up from manuscripts in the Public Record Office, of markets and fairs which had been given charters by Letters Patent from the Crown. Some were listed by county, and others were named without a county. The following local places were given:

Horsham (fair only)	1232
Burstow (market and fair)	1246
Grenestead (market and fair)	1246
Cokefeld (market and fair)	1254
Craule (market and fair)	1271
Grensted (market and fair)	1284
Cukefeld (market and fair)	1312
Lindefeld (market and fair)	1343
Horsham (market and fair)	1448

The list is somewhat confusing in that some places are listed twice. The earlier charter from Crawley is not included, but for 1271, at the end of the reign of King Henry III, a second charter is listed, granting an annual fair. The fair was held in August to coincide with the Feast commemorating the decapitation of St John, to whom the local church is dedicated. The villages named (Burstow is a surprise) show that the 13th century saw the burgeoning of weekly markets on the north Sussex borders.

Not all trade took place in a market, but the local landowner would try to make sure it did since he could then tax it. For a weekly market to be set up suggests that trade locally had become, or was hoped to become, large enough to be able to benefit from one. A fixed site and a regular day would encourage the local people to use the market, and permanent structures would follow soon. In Crawley, the wide High Street became the market area, near to the church. That it was on a through road was to its advantage. The market served two functions for the local people. First, it was a place for households to sell small quantities of surplus food and to make their purchases. Second, it was a place where goods manufactured in the home could be sold and where goods from outside the area (salt, fish, ironware, earthenware, pitch) could be bought.

No mention is ever made of a market being held in the Ifield or Worth areas — only Crawley ever appears. Few references to Crawley market are recorded, however, which suggests that it was not very successful. But the evidence of the High Street suggests that the market probably continued for several hundred years. Until the 20th century, the wide High Street was interrupted in two places by buildings in the middle of the road, which forced traffic to pass either side. The road areas each side of, and between, these buildings were known as Upper, Middle and Lower squares. The origins of such buildings in English settlements are usually that a market stall area has become fixed in site, and a permanent building has subsequently replaced the temporary stall.

(ii) A church.
Our earliest buildings give us visual signposts to our past. All three local churches possess architectural features dating from the 13th century.

Worth church, as we have seen, is very much Saxon in design and structure. The walls of the two transepts were rebuilt at some time in the 13th century, and larger windows were inserted. More light could then enter the church. Both transepts had side chapels. In one stood a statue to Our Lady and another to St Nicholas, to whom the church was dedicated. In the other chapel was a statue to St Stephen, much later to be accompanied by a statue to Henry VI (who was treated as a saint after his death). The extra windows and the flickering lights from candles before the altars may have dispelled some of the gloom from such a large, dark building. There was local wealth to pay for these building works.

In Ifield, the oldest part of the church is the chancel (the altar end), which dates from the early part of the 13th century. The original walls of the nave (the body of the church) were subsequently removed to widen the building but the basic shape of Ifield church was that which still exists. It was never a small church, and there must have been a good number of people living locally to justify the building. It is likely that a wooden church would have originally stood on the site until a growing population led to its replacement.

During the 13th century Crawley church was built. The south wall (with its small doorways and a little window) is all that remains of the original stone building. Although it was the most recent of the local settlements, by the later part of the 13th century Crawley had also grown large enough to have its own stone-built church. At first it was a daughter church of Slaugham, and early references mention a chantry. What does that mean?

In the north of Sussex, the most valuable settlements were at Cuckfield and Slaugham. One of the owners of the larger settlement to the south, almost certainly a Poynings, must have arranged for an outlying chapel of Slaugham to be built. In any large parish, if parishioners found it difficult to attend the church, a local chapel, known as a chapel of ease, could be provided. If subsequently a person endowed it to provide a chantry chapel within the main church buildings, this would be a subsidiary function. (Chantry chapels were common. A rich man would leave a large sum of money so that prayers and candles could speed his journey through purgatory; a cathedral might have dozens of chantries.) In a taxation list dated 1291 the church at Slaugham is listed as *Slaugham cum Capella de Crawle* — or Slaugham with the chapel at Crawley. In 1408, there is a reference to 'the chantry in the chapel of St John the Baptist in Crawley'. Two years later it is referred to as 'the Free Chapel or Permanent Chantry of Crawle'.

For whom was the chantry built? In 1444 it was being referred to as 'the Chantry at Crawle for the Soul of Lucy Poynings'. Here we get another mention of the family whose name is closely linked with Crawley's development and growth. The de Warrennes were the major landowners, or tenants-in-chief, of the Rape of Lewes. The Norman family of

13. Ifield church. This photograph taken in 1860 shows the wooden bell turret, beside the entrance, which stood for about thirty years until the present tower was built in 1883.

14. Crawley church, a watercolour made in the 1780s and now in the Burrell Collection at the British Museum.

Poynings, whose name persists in the name of the village outside Brighton, became the tenants of the earl and took possession of much of the land along the line of the present Brighton Road, including Slaugham. Eventually they bought it from one of the de Warrennes. There was a Lucas (or Luke) de Poynings who fought with his men for Richard I at the siege of Acre in 1191. Another Lucas left a will in 1267. A third was called lord of Crawley at his death in 1294. There are three Poynings men recorded who were known as Lucas, but no women named Lucy are known. Who, then, was the Lucy Poynings previously named?

The will dated 1267 points to an answer: it states

> I, Luke, son of Thomas de Poynings, for the salvation of my father and mother, grant to the chapel of St John Baptist of Crawley for the keep of Thomas de la Brewere, Chaplain, and his successors a house in Crawley . . . [much rent in Crawley] . . . also pannage for six swine in my wood of Crawley and three four-ox loads of wood. I and my heirs and whoso holds the Manor of Slaugham shall warrant this. I and my heirs shall present to the diocesan a chaplain who, on admission, shall make oath unto the Rector of Slaugham.

The chapel existed already in 1267. Either Lucy was a wife of one of the Poynings or, more likely, the name is a corruption of Lucas. Though the will makes it clear that the chantry was set up for the parents of a Lucas, it is probable that the chantry itself became known as Lucas' chantry after the donor. In time the chapel became a church in its own right and its 'chantry' function was secondary.

The Poynings family held the manor and lordship of Crawley from some time in the 12th or 13th centuries until the death of the last of them, named Robert, in 1429. He fought in France for both Henry V and Henry VI, and was killed at Orléans. His father, Richard, had fought with John of Gaunt and died in Castile. The last Poynings had provided 60 men-at-arms and 180 archers for the war with France from his lands in Sussex. Though they are nameless, it seems that men from Crawley were fighting in the Crusades, in Spain, and in France — including the battle of Agincourt (1415), and the Battle of Orléans, against Joan of Arc (1429). The longbowmen of the Weald were well-known from the 13th century onwards.

By the mid-13th century the Crawley area was obviously thriving. Building work was taking place in three churches only a few miles apart, and the land was becoming valuable enough to fight over. Local farmers were flexing their muscles and getting into disputes with their overlords.

(iii) Court cases.

Disputes arose about the way law was being administered, so much so that in 1275 King Edward I had to appoint commissioners to inquire into the way men were abusing royal authority. His father, Henry III, had inspired little respect and many people — from nobles to the lords of single manors — were exercising judicial authority without reference to the laws of the country. Complaints were made in the Hundred of Buttinghill, in 1279, that the Earl de Warrenne had taxed all manner of people, from knights to tradesmen. His 'warrens' were so extensive that it was alleged that the animals protected were destroying much grain, especially in Cuckfield and Slaugham. (A 'deer park' had been built at Cuckfield in about 1218.) However, the earl was a close friend and supporter of the king. Not surprisingly, he won the case, which confirmed his right to do as he wished in his lands.

Some of the records of court cases for the Rape of Lewes, heard at Lewes in the middle of the 13th century, have survived; these include references to Crawley. They concerned attempts by the Earl de Warrenne to obtain his rightful dues from the heirs of deceased local people who should have paid a 'fine' in order to inherit the occupancy of the property or to impound the belongings of serfs who had run away from their land. Occasionally the immediate tenants — Lucas de Poynings and Thomas de Poynings — were also involved. It appears from the repetition of some of these cases that it was not easy to exercise control over the remote northern areas, like Crawley.

Statements abound like '. . . has been distrained to give answer, but has not come to court . . .', or '. . . has an adjournment . . .' or '. . . another warrant has been issued . . .'. At one point, '. . . the bailiff has been instructed to compel the tithing at Worth to attend'. However, '. . . the tithing did not attend . . .'. Although we nowadays usually believe that the power of life and death exercised by these lords must have been very oppressive to the common people of the time, it seems that the people did not always react as we would expect. The claim of the Poynings to the lordship of Crawley manor took a long time to establish. The earl also had to put up with it!

There are a number of people named, some of whom we meet again later in the comprehensive tax returns. These include Nicholas the White, Gilbert of Woolborough, Osbert the Clerk, Peter the Dauber and Roger of the Garden. At one court, the nine jury men of Crawley actually attended and declared that the deceased local resident, Reginald, had held a workshop in the settlement ('*unam fabricam in predictava vill*'). His holdings had been taken over by William David, a smith ('*Willemus David faber*'). Here is a clear reference to a local blacksmith. Also we can read of Godfrey, an arrow maker ('*Godefridus factor sagittarum*'). All these people had land and cattle — part craftsmen and part farmers.

Other complaints which are of interest are that 'Robert de Lynde impeded the men of Luke de Poynings of the vill of Crawle in the use of their common rights in the Kings Street from Frythcote to Alexander's Cross in the said Hundred' (unidentifiable places). Also, 'Maurice de Hewekene closed the King's Street in the parish of Worth from Selasle to Crawledun' (Selsfield to Crawley Down).

There are two other interesting snippets from these records. One relates to the chief tither of Worth taking possession, for the earl, of 'all the goods wherever they might be' of Henry and John de la Hale, both villeins of the earl '. . . who have fled from his land . . .'. This emphasises that people were a source of wealth to landowners; they were not allowed to leave their birthplace without permission, and if they did they could be hunted and compelled to return. In reality, this did not often happen. Someone who reached a large town would be welcomed as an extra worker, and someone who moved to another rural spot to offer his services as a farmworker is likely to have been taken on willingly. Even in a period of comparatively rapid population growth, there was an unfulfilled demand for labour.

The other references which give an insight into the life of the time are those which name an Assize of Bread and Ale in the vill of Crawley, to be held by the steward of Lord Thomas de Poynings, brought before successive courts in June, July and August 1266. From 1266 onwards, throughout England, the civic authorities met, usually annually, to lay down the price of bread and ale, which was based on the current prices of corn and malt. This was often accompanied by the appointment of an 'aletaster', whose duties included proclaiming the permitted prices in the area and sampling the quality offered for sale. The Lewes courts referred to complaints that the assizes had not been held in Crawley. It may seem odd that Crawley was the only place in the rape to be complained about. Was it really the only place not to hold an Assize of Bread and Ale? If Crawley was becoming a thriving routeway village with a market, it was more likely to have bakers and brewers wanting to sell to travellers passing through the village. Perhaps they wanted to fix their own prices and standards of production: does this suggest that the local bakers and brewers were persons of standing locally who could determine what should or should not occur?

The parish of Ifield was in the Hundred of Burbeach and so offences committed here were tried at the Chichester assizes. All manner of people are met with in the court records: in

1288 the vicar of Ifield was himself accused of having killed an archdeacon, but acquitted. In 1305, another local brawl ended up in court:

> Roger Atte Watere indicted that he beat and ill-treated Adam Le Hunte, servant of John de Ifeld, in the church of Ifeld, and likewise beat and ill-treated Henry Atte Welle servant of the said John on the heath by the vill of Horsham. Taken, asked how he will acquit himself of the said trespasses, says he is in no way guilty thereof and for good and ill puts himself on the country. The jurors say an oath that the said Roger in the church at Ifeld twice struck the said Adam Le Hunte with his fist without any weapon, because of contumacious words there had, and likewise with his bow twice hit the said Henry on the said heath by reason of a certain contention then being between William de Brewosa (Braose) Lord of the said Roger, and John de Ifeld, Lord of the said Henry. Therefore the said Roger to be remitted to gaol.

Some ideas of the value of the lands can be gauged from inquisitions post-mortem, the enquiries into the value of men's wealth after their death. When a Thomas de Poynings died in 1339, his income from Crawley was valued at just over £12 per year. Most rents were paid at religious festivals (e.g. the Feast of St Thomas the Apostle, the Purification of the Blessed Virgin Mary, the Nativity of St John the Baptist), but he also had income from '. . . the pleas and perquisites of the court there . . .'. Not only were the Crawley men called to Lewes to face accusations, but there was a manorial court at Crawley itself.

(iv) An oddly-shaped parish.

The old parish of Crawley was a very odd shape. It looked as if someone had been shaving the eastern edge of Ifield parish and cut off a long sliver which began just below the parish church, where the present Haslett Avenue leaves the High Street, and moved northwards to the county boundary, getting slightly wider all the time but never having much width. At the county boundary it bordered what was for centuries common land. The detached portion of the old parish, in the south by Pease Pottage, doubled the area of the parish but basically comprised just one farm. This section once contained a small chapel and may indeed have been the first part of the old parish of Slaugham to be separated from it, later to be joined with Crawley to form a new, very small, parish.

The 1836 tithe map of Crawley parish shows the shape of the village plots. They are strikingly even, and extend the width of the parish, from the High Street to the eastern boundary. The plots to the south are approximately rectangular and would have been the first to have been laid out when the settlement was 'planted'. As the population started to grow, further building would have been contained within the land designated for the settlement. The newer houses would have to occupy the gently curving strips to the north of the village. These were originally field strips, set out when the settlement was created, and are slightly longer and wider as the parish widens northwards. It is as if the land which was set aside for the new market town was narrow at the base, because only building plots were required, but widened where arable strips and pasture land were needed. This suggests that there was a large open field to the north, where a limited strip system operated. The area bordering the county boundary became the Manor Farm.

(v) Crawley — a 13th-century new town?

We now have a collection of evidence for the prosperity of Crawley in the 13th century — a weekly market, a stone-built church, a court for disputes. In 1279 there is also the granting of an annual fair to be held on the feast of the decapitation of St John the Baptist (August 29), the patron saint of the church. For the Poynings family, this was a lucrative form of income, jealously guarded! In addition, we have a series of apparently unconnected facts. The village church began as an outpost of Slaugham church. The High Street is extremely wide through the village, but is of a more normal width to the north and south, away from

15. Crawley High Street. Taken from the 1836 tithe map, this diagram shows plainly the original plots of the settlement which was first established 600 years earlier. The southern end of the parish had straight-edged plots, and the church was built behind them. Former market stalls became permanent buildings in the middle of the street. As the settlement grew it expanded northwards along the High Street and the later houses were built on curved plots formerly strips in an open field. The houses stood square to the street, but the plots curved away behind.

the old village core. The plots of land are all regular in size. The first reference to Crawley itself is in 1202, with the mention of a market.

As an explanation of these facts, the work carried out by Professor Maurice Beresford and published in his book *New Towns of the Middle Ages* is pertinent. He drew attention to the large number of deliberately planned new towns, or plantations, which were set up on previously unsettled sites, especially between the 1190s and the 1230s.

16. Crawley High Street, looking north. This photograph was taken from outside the *George* in the late 1890s. It shows the width of the High Street provided to accommodate the market. The large house on the left is Terry's *Temperance Hotel*, now the site of the cinema. The small bushy tree on the right of the roadside in centre picture was all that remained of the famous Crawley Elm.

Though for most places the documentary evidence of a new town actually beginning is absent, he writes about the characteristics they shared. Often they were built on the edge of a rural parish on common land. If their plan was of a ribbon pattern, along a road, then the former country lane would be widened along the limits of the settlement. Tenement plots for these new towns were of standard lengths and breadths. If their creation infringed the existing rights of a parish, then they could be forced to accept a chapel which depended on a church elsewhere in the locality. Many of these new towns were inevitably small in size and served an unsophisticated local population.

To read this list of characteristics is to read a description of medieval Crawley as we know it. The fact that the earliest references to the place are in the first half of the 13th century adds emphasis. It seems certain that Crawley, and probably East Grinstead and Horsham as well, are examples of the new towns about which Beresford wrote (though he did not include any of these three in his book). Crawley, however, never achieved borough status, with a royal charter, as did the two adjacent towns.

Why did the new town of Crawley not achieve borough status, even though, as we shall see subsequently, it became modestly prosperous in the following few hundred years? There was local population and wealth, but the common progression is absent. Beresford makes the point that there was no unwillingness on the part of the kings and the chief landowners to create new boroughs if there were commercial prospects. Would the landowners willingly turn down the opportunity to increase their income? The answer to these questions must be speculative. It is possible that those who wanted success for Horsham and East Grinstead did not want competition from Crawley. Their markets became successful; Crawley's apparently did not. Furthermore, the area seems to have given the landlords in the south some problems. The population was not easy to govern. To give them more freedom and independence with a borough charter might not have been perceived as sensible. The people needed a firm hand and discipline, not more autonomy. So Crawley must be included in what Beresford would call a failed new town, but not for the usual reasons.

One puzzle which probably dates from this time, and cannot satisfactorily be explained, concerns the discrepancy between Crawley village and Crawley parish. As has been mentioned, the High Street divides the village between two separate parishes. If, as seems probable, Crawley was a 'planted' village, it was almost certainly created from the start on both sides of the road. The village plots on the Ifield side of the road are almost as regular as those on the east side.

Crawley parish church was endowed by a Poynings and our first reference to the Poynings family as lords of the manor of Crawley occurs at the end of the 13th century, even though they are mentioned in connection with the village much earlier. The Poynings family were also lords of the manor of Slaugham at the same time. Finally, in the later years of the 13th century they were lords of the manor of Ifield as well. If members of the same family were the local landowners and lords of the manor of all three places, why should Crawley village be split between two parishes? It just does not make sense. The explanation may lie submerged in the fact that Crawley and Slaugham (and Worth) are in the Rape of Lewes, whereas Ifield is in the Rape of Bramber. If this is so, then perhaps Crawley parish was not taken from the edge of Ifield parish, but from the edge of Worth parish? Whatever the reason, there is much room for speculation.

Ifield and Worth

Successful or not, Crawley — rather than Ifield or Worth — became the name which was known by most people outside the area, and references to it dominate later history. The wider use of the word can be seen in relation to the other two local churches in Worth and in Ifield. In 1278 an entry in the assize roll at Lewes reads:

> Walter Curleu and Odo son of Christiana Snelling were in a certain tavern in the vill of Worth and there the aforesaid Odo struck the aforesaid Walter with a certain pike in the head, of which he died. Odo was captured and led to the prison of Lewes, and there was in the custody of Hamelin the porter of Lewes, who holds the prison, and he escaped from his custody and fled to the church of St Nicholas of Crauele and there confessed to homicide before the coroner, and abjured the realm. He had no chattels and was in the tithing of Robert of Kissmere in Worth, therefore he is in mercy.

Here we see an example of the old law of 'sanctuary'. If a felon could reach a church and confess to his crime, his life was spared. In return he had to give up all his possessions and leave the country for ever. But at least he was promised safety by the Church from the wrathful relatives of the dead man and from the punishment of the law. Imagine the fearful Odo, breaking out of prison and finding his way through woods, evading his pursuers — especially the kinsfolk of the poor Walter. At last, before the altar of St Nicholas in Worth, he confessed his crime, said a tearful farewell to his family and then, wearing only sackcloth, he left the church for the last time. He would have had to go directly to the coast and board the first available boat. Whether he made it safely to the port and what became of him thereafter we will never know. The story is strangely modern in its outline — it almost sounds like a quarrel over a game of darts! Where the tavern stood is unknown. Soon after

17. Ifield Green. This watercolour of 1814 shows the small settlement which slowly grew around the church. Small plots were nibbled from the green, with the approval of the lord of the manor.

this event, the family of Curleu are found in Strete Hundred and the Snellings are found in Lindfield. This suggests that the tavern was in the east of Worth — the place we have so far called Burleigh, perhaps at Turners Hill.

On the other side of our area, in 1247, an endowment was recorded whereby much of the income of the vicarage of Ifield was given to the prioress and convent of Rusper. Just as previously the church of St Nicholas was said to be in Crawley, so in this document the agreement was made by 'Alan, Chaplain of Crawley', who was clearly the priest at Ifield. The endowment is long, and much of it of little interest. But there are one or two statements which throw more light on our history. Alan, the priest, was to be given tithes of corn and hay from three named local men. Clearly, arable farming was as important in Ifield as in most places. The nuns were to reserve for themselves the tithes '. . . of all lands which shall at this time be cleared or shall hereafter be cleared of wood . . .'. This is a specific reference to the continuing process of carving out farmland from unused woodland (known as assarting), which was the way the area developed. Later in the document, the priest was given '. . . all the tithes of the mills which are now built or shall hereafter be built . . .', which is our first reference to the mills which had to be built to grind corn into flour for the district.

Ifield was the centre of a corn-growing area and needed a mill. Worth was still the more wooded area, since the lands along the river in Ifield parish were better farmland than the sandier soils of Worth. More scientific farming than was possible then was needed to improve the soils in much of Worth. There was however, a mill serving Worth farmers. The tax return of 1327 lists 'William at the Mill'. The mill past Fen Place on the road to East Grinstead was perhaps the first in the parish.

The best illustration of Worth at this time can be given by referring to a post-mortem inquisition held in 1268. Richard de Playz held much land — his family were the first subtenants of the earl of Surrey to hold Worth. This included:

> . . . in his demesne in the vill of Worthe 60 acres of arable and poorer land, each acre of which is worth 2d. a year . . . On the day he died he had 14 tenants there who pay 52s. lld. annual rent, . . . and for reaping and threshing crops they give 3s. 8d. a year. Carrying service is worth . . . a year. Also there are 12 cows there put to farm by ancient custom from time without memory, and they produce a rent of 12s. a year.

De Playtz was the local 'lord of the manor'; he had tenant farmers who owed him labour services, to avoid which they were willing to pay; some of the land was recognised as poor; the custom of grazing cows on common land was of very long standing. This all fits in with the image of Worth we have acquired.

The development of a successful local mixed economy led to, and in turn benefited from, Crawley's creation. When the local community simply consisted of frontier farmers, clearing the forests for farmland, there was little need for a local market. But once the farmers supplemented their living by making basic items at home for retail, however, we see the change from a purely agricultural to a partly commercial growth. Some farmers became bakers, or brewers, or butchers, in addition to farming. Few men pursued a single trade, such as millers, smiths, tailors, carpenters, potters, cooks, tanners and clothworkers, without involvement in farming. Slowly, however, specialists emerged, and such men had to buy some of their food.

18. These fragments of a 13th-century decorated pot were unearthed just off the High Street in the roots of a tree blown over in the 1987 hurricane. They are thought to have come from the pottery at Earlswood, eight miles to the north along the London Road. They are decorated with faces and a bluish-green glaze.

Occasional, but recurring, references to the iron industry continue during this time in north Sussex. Iron-workers must have been numerous, since in 1300 the Gild of Ironmongers of the City of London was complaining about the smiths of the Weald. Competition was ever threatening. Richer men could give up farming and become traders; poorer men became wage-earners. All needed the services of a market, and the village of Crawley became a focus for non-agricultural life. This was new in our rather remote northern area, and explains why Crawley — as has been shown — became widely known, and its name was applied generally in the district.

The heading to this chapter referred to the 'pioneering years' in the 12th and 13th centuries. Throughout the whole of the Weald, older settlements were growing and newer ones developing as population growth gave an impetus for increased food production. Farming was becoming a lucrative activity and marginal forest land was being brought into cultivation. From this time on, local wealth was accumulating.

Chapter 6

Medieval Growth
Fourteenth and Fifteenth Centuries: the Evidence of Local Wealth

Tax returns

Fascinating snapshots of the local population are recorded in the taxation returns. From time to time the king raised a tax on people's movable goods, which meant trade stock for those engaged in industry and commerce, or farm stock and produce for those engaged in agriculture. Whenever a tax was made, the returns were listed. In Sussex we are lucky to have three tax returns for virtually the whole of the county which were made in 1296, 1327 and 1332, and have been printed in Vol. X of the Sussex Record Society publications. From these can be seen the oldest farm names and occupations.

Once again the lists were made by rapes, and then by hundreds within the rapes. The smaller units in each hundred were each called in Latin *villata*, which can be translated as township, although the term vill is often used. Some of these are names of a town or a village, whereas others are names of a district. Later, when documents were written in English, the word 'tithing' was used for the smaller areas, especially the outlying areas. A tithing was responsible for maintaining its own law and order, and would elect a constable each year. Justices of the Peace, an office created in 1361, would administer the law in the hundred.

Let us now take each *villata* in turn.

(i) The Rape of Bramber, the Hundred of Boughbeach, the Vill of Ifield
The three tax lists record many of the farms which we now know, though the phonetic spelling may be difficult at first to decipher. (In the lists, 'de' means 'of' and 'atte' means 'at the'.)
The following farm names are of interest:

Jordan de Langely	Langley Farm
Nicholas atte Naubele	Amberley Farm
John de Shullygh	Shelley Farm
Thomas atte Hyde	Hyde Farm — now Ifield Golf Course
John de Ifelde	(Ifield Court)
Thomas de Hywhurst	Ewhurst Farm
Felicia de Stereford	Stafford Farm
Peter de Stombelhole	Stumblehole Farm
Gilbert atte Blakehulle	Blackhill Farm
William de Bonwyk	Bonnyck Farm

There are also names referring to places which cannot now be identified, for example Sandersfield, Beechley; names which indicate the occupation, for example Godfrey Parker — Deer-park keeper; and personal nicknames, for example William Skorpheyn — 'Scorpion'.

These are not our only references to people and places in the Ifield area. From other legal documents we get other names which cannot be identified from the tax returns. It is worth remembering that at this time a person would be given a 'Christian name' when baptised, but the identifying 'surname' would be given as he grew into adulthood. A person might be named after his homestead, his occupation, his father or from personal

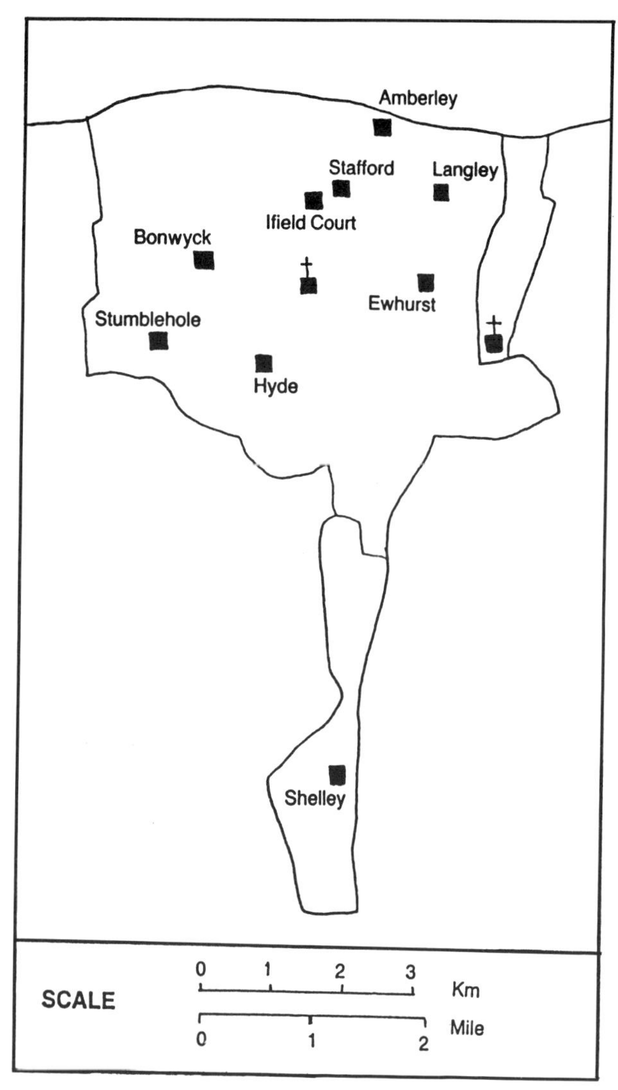

19. Farms recorded in tax returns in the 14th century.

characteristics. Indeed, he may be named in different ways in each legal document. The same person could, at various times, be called John by the Brook, John Carpenter, John son of William and John Little. It still took some years before family surnames were fixed.

(ii) The Rape of Lewes, the Hundred of Buttinghill, the 'Villatae' of Crawley and Worth

Although it is comparatively easy to pick out the Ifield inhabitants, we encounter more problems when we reach Crawley. The area we are looking at is variously named Crawley, Worth and Burleigh, or combinations of these names: In 1296, there is a list for the '*Villata* of Crawle'. Later in the tax roll, under the Hundred of Strete, is a list for the '*Villata de Lyndefeld et Burle*'. In 1327 there is a list for the '*Villata de Crawle, Worth et Borle*'. Under the Hundred of Strete is a list for Lindfield only. In 1332 there are two lists, one called '*Villata de Werth*' and the other '*Villata de Burle*'.

These lists show that administration in the remote north was still rather haphazard. The places were known to exist, but those in the south put them into convenient groups. Burleigh was, in fact, still oscillating between two separate hundreds, and there must have been many disputes as to who had the feudal dues.

Once again, we can see the farm names appearing:

Walter de Brenteregg	Brantridge
William Yllegate (or de Illegate)	Tilgate
William le Hog	Hog's Hill
William de Wolbergh	Woolborough
Philip de Heselwyke	Hazelwick
Richard de Tyntesle	Tinsley
Richard de Ketebrugg	Kits Bridge
Adam de Ronferth	Rowfant
Roger le Shephurd	Down Park, once Shepherd's Farm
Roger le Fronke/Le Frensh	Frenches
Geoffrey atte Smithforde	Smithsfield, by Gibbshaven

William de Culleslee	Cuttinglye
Richard le Hunte	Huntsland
William de Burle	Burleigh
William atte Sandhille	Sandhill
John atte Fenne	Fen Place
Edward de Selesle	Selsfield
William le Dokel	Duckyls
Bartholomew de Gravethye	Gravetye

Second, there are names referring to places which cannot now be identified, but only guessed at, for example, Woodgate, Gore; and finally there is a group of names which indicate the occupation of a taxpayer or a personal nickname, for example, Chapman or Petyt.

Fifty per cent of the names describe the individual's place of residence. Of the other 50 per cent, about half describe the work he did. We already have a local community where a number of people in the area earn a living, in part at least, by providing goods and services. For example, there is a group of names for specialised workers on the land: deer-park keeper, sheepman and forester.

Some men work with wood (Turner, Forester, Fletcher); some with metal (Smith, Farrier, Blower — or bellows-man); some process food (Baker, Miller); others build (Dauber — a plasterer); there is a travelling salesman (Chapman) and a carrier who transports food or goods on longer journeys (Porter). All this suggests a growing, prosperous community. The baker had an important role in the village, and had opportunity to mis-use his power. In 1357, at Crawley, a court found 'Robert Baker who had three times been convicted of breaking the Assize of Bread is adjudged the judgement of the pillory'.

Another reference to the local iron industry at this time is that in 1327 the sheriff of the county was allowed £4 3s. 4d. to buy 1,000 horse-shoes, and 3s. to pay for their carriage from Le Rougheye (Roffey) near Horsham, where they were made, to Shoreham. They were for use by soldiers in the war with Scotland. At a time when warfare was never far away, arrows made locally would find a ready market. In 1338, 6,000 arrows were purchased from Roffey. Edward I ordered that all males of a certain rank were to practise shooting with a bow. Indeed, bows and butts had to be provided in each settlement. There was a field called Butts Field along the Ifield Road, just past West Green; the first local sportsfield, perhaps?

In the 1379 poll tax returns for Crawley there is reference to William Rokenham, an iron-maker ('*Factor Ferri*') who was quite wealthy, and to William Danecombe, another iron-maker. In addition, two smiths ('*faber*') and one farrier ('*ferour*') were named. The iron industry continued to flourish.

One final point about the tax returns is that most of those named locally paid a small amount of money because their landholding was low in value. The impression is not of large land-owners with estates in the district, but of many small farmers and craftsmen who were still actively colonising.

What estimate of population can be made from these lists? If we look at the number of people named, then the lists show:

1296	Ifield :	24 names, and 3 tax-collectors
	Crawley :	34 names and 4 tax-collectors
1327	Ifield :	17 names, and 1 tax-collector
	Crawley, Worth & Burleigh :	39 names, and 3 tax-collectors

1334	Ifield :	14 names, and 1 tax-collector
	Worth :	31 names, and 1 tax-collector
	Burleigh :	25 names.

There are three points to make about this list. Firstly, some of the tax-payers were in fact absentee landlords, who held land in a number of settlements in Sussex. Secondly, the lists show a remarkably varied set of names, and people seem to appear in and disappear from the lists rapidly. The population was very mobile. Thirdly, the Ifield list shows a steady decline whereas the Crawley/Worth area shows a steady growth. It would be easy to accept that the very wooded Worth area was being colonised and that Crawley village was growing at this time, but it is not really credible that the population of the agricultural parish of Ifield was declining.

If, therefore, one were to try to assess the state of the population in the 1330s, using a multiplier of four for each taxpayer, the figures would be as follows: Ifield — about seventy people; Crawley and Worth — about one hundred and seventy people.

Land Transfers: the 'feet of fines'

When land ownership was disputed it was necessary to go to law. However, even when land was sold or leased without dispute it was still a good idea to use a lawsuit. Court records were kept safely, and the best way to prove land-ownership would be to produce a legal judgement which stated who the owner was. By the 13th century we start to see these fictitious lawsuits appearing. The final agreement — or 'fine' — of both parties to the land transfer would be written in triplicate on a single membrane of parchment, which was then cut into three sections. They would both keep one part while the third part, or 'foot' of the document, was sent to Westminster and filed. Many of these 'feet' of fines are still in existence, and have been transcribed. They contain names of local people, not all of whom were listed in tax returns, and a description of the land. The latter gives an idea of the type of agricultural activity taking place. Sometimes the land is named, and we may find names of farms or areas which are not given in the surviving tax returns.

A brief survey of these documents, from west to east, gives the following picture. In 1315, we meet with the first reference to the manor (or estate) of Beaubusson. By 1413 the spelling is being amended to Beaubussh, and we are on the way to the modern spelling of Bewbush. The French phrase 'beau buisson' means literally 'beautiful bush', either from the healthy appearance of the property or because the building was surrounded at first by a fine hedge. The name is not unknown in France, and this is one of the very few French place-names we can find in north Sussex. The first owners — the de Braose family — were Normans, and it was likely to have been hunting land, with a hunting lodge which later became a farm. The farm was certainly valuable. When the main farmhouse was constructed, it was on an extremely large moated site.

Ifield itself appears in a transfer between Robert de la Brok and Helewisam, son of Alwin, of half a virgate of land in Ifield (Yfeld). This was signed in Lewes in 1236. From the 1250s onwards we get an increasing number of references, either to the whole manor of Ifield when the large landowners are concerned with their ownership of the feudal dues and services of the local population, or to individual smallholdings of land, meadow and woodland. In 1273 a smallholding was sold which was adjacent to '. . . a mill which is called Gilbert's Mill . . .', (*'illius molendine quod vocatur Gyleberdes Mylne . . .'*). Early in the 14th century Sir John of Ifield was the major tenant-in-chief. In August 1325, when Edward II feared a French invasion, he ordered the bishop of Chichester to assist the king's four marshals in Sussex in levying forces. One of the four was John of Ifield: he was responsible for raising troops from north Sussex.

The 14th century, with, at first, overpopulation and, after the Black Death of 1349, recurrent plague, saw a fall in the national population. One result was that many landholdings were amalgamated and the market in land became more active. Although it is an important landmark in British history, there is no direct evidence of any major outbreak of plague locally. There probably was one, but because settlement in the three parishes was dispersed it is likely to have been less devastating than in other places. Any references to a plague at Crawley refer to the Crawley in Hampshire, near Winchester. It is not surprising that other settlements in southern England were also called 'Crow's Wood'. By the 1400s there was clearly trade in much larger parcels of farmland. People from London started to buy land for investment purposes. For example, William de Neudegate sold Simon Ungram of London, draper, '2 messuages and 46 acres of land in Rousparre and Ifeld' in 1376.

Crawley itself is also mentioned in early documents. Lucas de Poynings was an early buyer in the 1270s, not surprisingly, but the main difference in Crawley is that we read mostly of the transfer of houses and small plots of land. In old documents, the word 'messuage' is usually given. This meant a house, its yard, outbuildings and garden. Whereas Ifield was a rural area, where smallholdings were traded, Crawley was by then a village with a market, and commercial premises were involved. In 1262 Walter Baker and his wife took on a messuage and six acres of land 'in Croweleye' — perhaps as a baker's shop? Though prices are not always given, it is clear that the village properties were more valuable. For example, in Ifield in 1330, an area of about thirty-five acres was sold for nearly £7, and in 1356 an estate of about one hundred and seventy acres fetched £33. Compare this with the sale of one house and just one acre in Crawley in 1352, which cost £3, and a similar sale by Roger Burstow in 1372 which cost the buyer £5.

The Sussex Record Society has printed transcripts of many of these 'feet of fines'. There are occasional errors in transcription which anyone who knows the Crawley area may discover. One problem is that in the writing of the time, the letter 'n' looked much like the letter 'u'. Thus what appears to be the earliest reference to Crawley (or Craule) actually refers to Cranleigh (or Cranle).

When we pass to the Worth area, it is similar in character to Ifield. In 1342, William atte Mille of Burleigh and Isabel his wife sold land in Worth to John Le Marscal of Burleigh and Isabel his wife: a messuage, 28 acres of land, two acres of meadow and 10 acres of wood. There are far more references to woods, gardens and heathland in Worth when smallholdings are traded. In 1426, as an example of the larger-scale dealings which developed, John Gladwin of London, gentleman, purchased from Henry Haunshard, clerk, and Thomas Crofton, clerk, (two priests) '. . . 8 messuages, 242 acres of land, 32 acres of meadow, 4 acres of wood, 150 acres of heath, in Lindfield, Cokefield, Wyvelesfeld, Turnours Hill, and Lewes . . .'. This is our first reference to Turners Hill, and it was part of a large speculative land purchase by a rich Londoner.

Previous mention has been made of the three churches in the area. To be accurate, a fourth church once also existed. The area of Shelley Plain, to the south-west of Pease Pottage, was (as previously mentioned) until recently a detached portion of Crawley parish. The name itself means the 'shelf-clearing', because it occupied a shelf of flattish land with valleys sloping away to each side. Now an isolated area of farmland, its name appears in some of these early land transfers. In 1291 there was a chapel mentioned, worth £4 13s. 4d. a year. In 1341 there was a sale of '. . . the advowson of the church of Shulflegh . . .', which was traded again in 1354 and 1357.

So a small chapel stood on Shelley Plain, and its value was akin to that of the church at Crawley at the time. This chapel could even have pre-dated the building at Crawley, and was probably the first chapel of ease set up as an outpost of Slaugham. By 1408 the chapel was reported to be vacant and Crawley chapel had become the northern outpost of Slaugham. References to it virtually cease, though it was still in occasional use in the early

16th century. Its site was discovered in 1898 when its sandstone foundations were uncovered 50 yards from the south-east corner of Shelley Plain.

One reason why we know about the churches in the 1400s is because the bishop of Chichester's records show the names of priests appointed. In this area they appear to have moved every couple of years, presumably to more remunerative livings. This was not unusual. The bishop's registers make many references to the habit of '. . . chopping and changing . . .' and in 1391 the archbishop of Canterbury had condemned these '. . . chop-churches . . .'. The vicar was sworn to perpetual residence. In reality, up until the 18th century and beyond it was not uncommon for a well-connected priest to be appointed to a church living, to take most of the income, and to pay a poor curate a much smaller sum to perform the job for him. A good late example of this locally was when John Flamsteed, the first Astronomer-Royal, was given the living of the church at Burstow in 1684 to supplement his meagre pay. He tried to attend the parish for two weeks a year.

Wills, bequests and other legal documents

A sign of increasing wealth is seen in the number of wills which mention the area. They were invariably made by local residents who were landowners or by those who became wealthy as merchants, either in Sussex or in London. The richest were the London merchants and in their wills we see the attachment they had to their roots. William Blast has a brass memorial plate in Crawley church. He died in 1438. John Blast, son of Thomas Blast, died in 1445 and asked in his will to be buried in the chapel of St John the Baptist in Crawley, before the altar of Our Blessed Virgin Mary. This was a popular place for the rich. When Richard Jay died in 1467 he wanted to be buried '. . . in the middel place of the rome there, betwene the auter of the chauntrie of our Blessed Lady and the auter of St Thomas the Martir'.

Much information about the state of the village in the mid-1400s comes from the will of this Richard Jay. He left money to a number of Sussex churches, but in particular left money 'to amende the foule weyes next to Craweley'; 'to the amending of the weies of the new cawcie bytwene Crawele and Reygate'; and for the church at Crawley, 'I woll and ordeigne that if the werk of the steple of the chapell at Craweley be not fully perfourmed up in my life, that thanne it be performed up fully by myne executeurs after my decease . . .'.

We learn from these and other wills that Crawley church tower was built in the 1460s (the hinges for the original door can still be seen inside the church on what was once the outside wall), and that there were three altars in the church — the high altar in the centre and two side altars (dedicated to the Blessed Mary and St Thomas à Becket) — and a font. The roads, a vital connection for the village, were always in need of maintenance. This would be because the drainage was poor and the traffic was becoming heavier. A causeway (still called a cawsey in some parts of Britain) had been constructed for the ten miles or so between Reigate and Crawley. No doubt stone, iron slag and timber were used to provide a firm base on the wetter areas. In 1490 John King of Horsham also left money to build and repair the road called Goffs Lane from Crawley to Horsham.

Proofs of Age

When a young man reached the age of 21 he could inherit his deceased father's estate. Before there were birth certificates it was necessary to prove a person's age by getting local people to testify to the date of birth. The witnesses had to say why they remembered the birth, and often did so by reference to an event which took place near the time. To give an example of this, one proof of age, taken at Chidham in the south of the county, produced four witnesses who remembered the birth of a baby in 1404 because on that day:

> One man was playing at football directly after the baptism and broke his leg; one man had his servant taken by the French and carried off to Harfleur; one man had his house burnt down; one man was driving a haycart and fell off, breaking his left arm.

So many of these were catastrophes that one is tempted to think that a rich man marked the birth of a son and heir by terrorising his neighbours!

Four proofs are recorded as having been taken at Crawley. The first relates to a man named William de Fifhide who was born in Shirmanbury, owned much land in central and southern Sussex, and was sponsored by the prior of Shoreham. Why should his proof of age be taken at Crawley on 19 June 1363? Some of the witnesses were local men, but there seems little real connection between the man and Crawley. Probably the people who took the proof had to travel from London and, after crossing the clay lands south of the Downs, stopped at Crawley. The others could then travel north to the county boundary and meet at a convenient half-way point. Perhaps they would have met in the church or a local house after a comfortable mid-summer journey across the dry, clay plain.

Six months later, on 7 December, another journey took place. This time it was for John Lillebone, also of Shirmanbury, sponsored by Kingston church, near Shoreham. Again, everyone was asked to meet in Crawley — obviously a place well-known to all parties. The journey in winter across a waterlogged clay vale could not have been so convenient or so comfortable. If the ground was frozen enough to travel across easily, it would have been very cold. Whatever the weather it could not have been very pleasant.

Seven years later one of the Poynings family, Thomas, had his proofing ceremony at Crawley and finally, in 1383, there is the record of the proof of age of a local man, William Changeton, born in Ifield. In each case about a dozen people were produced to recall something which had occurred 21 years earlier. John Jay, for example, an ancestor of Richard Jay, remembered buying a house from Richard Young and, another time, the birth of his daughter Alice. About half the names of the witnesses relate to where they lived, and these are often less detailed than the names given in the earlier tax returns, which took great care to identify correctly each tax-payer. The names in the proofs of age are less specific, and leave tantalising glimpses of local people who have no other memorial. Just to read their names is to evoke lives of hardship, opening up the new settlements in the forest borders of Sussex. In the 13th and 14th centuries Crawley was a new town and still growing.

The Buildings

The last evidence of the growth of wealth in the area can be seen in the quality of building which survives (or survived until recently) from the medieval period. Though this is not as large as the heritage of buildings we still have as a result of the national boom in building and rebuilding which marked the opulence of Tudor society, there are still remains of the 15th century to be seen locally.

The local churches show that they were enlarged and embellished during this period. Builders were learning in the 13th century to deal better with the loads and strains of walls and roofs. Consequently the simple box-shape of early churches (still seen at Worth) could be extended by building side aisles, as happened at St Margaret's in Ifield during the 14th century. First the north aisle and, later, the south aisle were added, doubling the capacity of the church. Windows were inserted in the upper part of the remaining nave walls to admit more light. There must have been a high population at that time to afford the cost of such an extension. The two tombs were added, though not necessarily on their present site. One is of a knight in armour, and the other is of a lady, presumably his wife. The armour worn by the knight puts the date of the effigies at about 1340 and it must have taken great efforts to bring these from the carver's workshops, almost certainly in London.

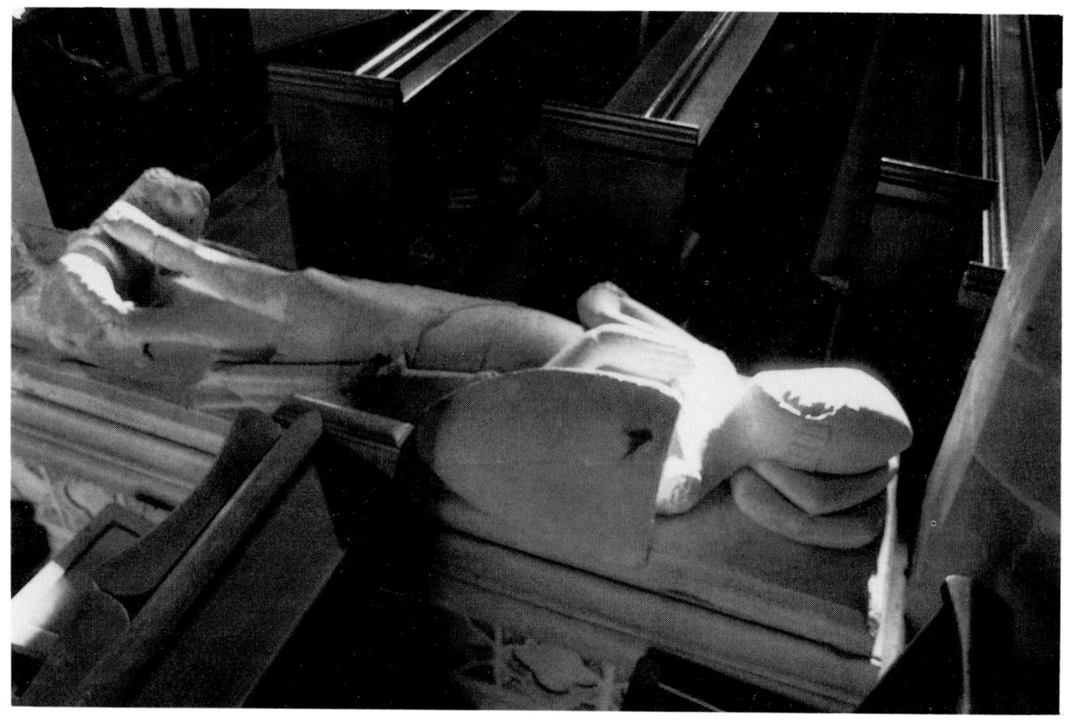

20. Thought to be a memorial to Sir John of Ifield, this 14th-century effigy is one of a pair of medieval monuments which have surprisingly survived all the upheavals in Ifield church.

There was then a pause in rebuilding. Though the Black Death did not seem to check the growth of the local population — its still relatively isolated position seems to have protected it, even though Crawley stood on the main road from London — there was a national shortage of skilled building craftsmen for the next fifty years.

In the 15th century at Ifield the original arch separating chancel from nave was at last widened so that an ornate rood screen could be added. This screen would have been either carved or painted to show the Crucifixion, or a crucifix would have been mounted on it, and was an important feature in medieval churches. The larger, more ornate screens had a narrow passage-way along the top for processions at Easter and other festivals. They would have had to be substantial to bear the weight of those in the procession and also the choir and musicians. Most churches in the 15th century were decorated by painting of walls, pillars and wooden screens: all were coloured, with reminders of the Day of Judgement painted above the chancel arch. Little was whitewashed at this time but the Protestant zeal of the Ifield clergy in the 17th century destroyed most traces of earlier decoration.

St John's church in Crawley itself was, perhaps surprisingly, not extended at this time though, as already described, the massive tower was built in the mid-15th century. Larger windows were inserted in the walls to give added light to the interior, however, and a rood screen was built. Though this screen has disappeared, as at Ifield, the staircase leading to the top of the screen is still traceable.

Money was therefore being spent to embellish the church though it was not considered necessary to increase its capacity. Why should this be? The parish boundaries were probably decided by the 14th century, and so only those who lived on the eastern side of the High Street would have St John's as their parish church. A small parish might not have needed a larger church, but those who lived in the thriving village might have wanted to spend some of their wealth on improving the fabric of the building. The church roof dates from about the same time as the brass memorial tablet to William Blast. It seems that the 14th-century village was prosperous enough, but not growing very much in population.

At Worth church, the Saxon building was given more interior light by the insertion of larger windows. Those in the transepts are 13th-century, the window to the right of the porch is 15th-century. The nave at Worth was not extended but, since the original building was so huge, no increase in size would have been necessary if the parish was not greatly populated. Some traces of medieval wall-painting can still be seen in the south transept's east window. Of the three churches, this one was changed the least. A new window was inserted behind the altar — this was replaced during the 19th century with copies of Saxon windows.

21. Nobody knows the origins of these three figures, nor who they represent. They are fixed to the tower of Crawley church, just above the main entrance, and appear to have been carved at different dates.

As the land was being settled by the colonists, they built themselves houses as soon as they could. It would take a while before the families were sufficiently established and wealthy to erect substantial timber-framed buildings of a sort which has survived to the present. The oldest local house which survives is probably Burstow Lodge, just outside our area to the north-east, parts of which date from about 1350. There were until comparatively recently, moreover, a number of local timber-framed houses which included parts of what were undoubtedly 14th-century buildings. Many were destroyed in order to build Crawley New Town, including Woolborough Farm and some houses in Crawley High Street. The Tree House, in the High Street, was the original manor house and is late 14th century in origin. Many of its timbers are now hidden behind more modern brick walls and roof (*see* Ill. 28).

Behind the Tree House stood a building known as Crawley Barn which is now re-erected in Singleton Open Air Museum. This is possibly early 15th-century and was originally a very long four-bay building, jettied completely along one side, and with a single long chamber on the first floor. It is now described as a Moot Hall, a village meeting-place, which might also have been a large workshop for local smiths and metal-workers. It was amusing for the author to attend a meeting some years ago of the Wealden Buildings Study Group at which historic building inspectors from the Department of the Environment were present. They all concluded that the building was of such advanced construction for its time that it ought not to have been erected at such a remote, backwoods place as Crawley! Crawley's history certainly needs more publicity.

22. Crawley Moot Hall, now restored and re-erected at the Weald and Downland Museum, Singleton.

There are many books which describe the evolution of timber-framed buildings but for examples of diverse local styles it will be enough to direct the reader to two buildings in Crawley High Street which provide silent evidence. The Ancient Priors is ornate and in many ways untypical of the north Sussex building style. This could have been the priest's house. The Punch Bowl, now a bank, is to the north of the Ancient Priors, and shows the usual local design. Both were built in about 1450. Though less well-known there is still much medieval building in the High Street. The busy village has always updated its buildings and so modern facades have been added to most of them. The Ancient Priors and the Punch Bowl have been restored in recent years to show what they may have originally looked like.

Of the six moated sites in Crawley, only Ewhurst Place and perhaps Gatwick Manor (originally Hyders Farm) retain a timber-framed building. The original houses are missing at Bewbush Farm, Ifield Court Farm, Pound Hill moat, and the small moat to the east of the Balcombe Road by the foot of Church Lane, Worth.

The settled community

Although much of the evidence we have considered is from legal documents, we must not imagine that it affords a full picture of medieval life in the area.

23. Ancient Priors, *c.*1904. A building that has had a variety of uses during its 500-year history. It is likely to have been built as the priest's house, beside the church. Later it became the *White Hart Inn*, and then was used by a variety of tradespeople. In the early 20th century it was what we would now call an antiques shop. Note the fake timber-framing, now stripped away to reveal the original timbers.

24. The Punchbowl, High Street. Originally a farmhouse, the building was later divided into labourers' cottages (as shown here). It was renovated in the 1920s and became a tea shop; now it is a bank.

During the 15th century the title 'gentleman' was applied to those just below the rank of knight. From the end of the 15th century such people could be granted coats of arms. There was a rebellion in south-east England in the summer of 1450 caused by financial and political mismanagement by the government. This rising was much concerned with seeking redress from the heavy taxation imposed by king and parliament, and the general failure of justice in the country. It was the emerging, moneyed classes who provided the support for what was known as Jack Cade's Rebellion. Though much came from Kent and east Sussex, some came from central and west Sussex. After the collapse of the rebellion, most of the rebels were pardoned. The list of their names includes a description of their status; labourers, husbandmen, tradesmen, yeomen and churchmen. Among them was 'Henry Lecheford, of Crawley, gentilman'.

As the settlements developed, society seems to have been strongly concerned with titles, as well as with wealth. Tradesmen occupied a somewhat undefined position and we see different types of society developing in the area. The Ifield and Worth areas were agricultural districts with gentlemen, yeomen, husbandmen and labourers. Crawley village contained more craftsmen and traders, probably with a different social structure. This was a division which continued until the 20th century.

Some of the craftsmen would have been smiths: the description occurs from time to time in lists of inhabitants. Iron-workers are of two kinds; there are those who smelt and produce the metal itself, and there are those who fashion it into useful shapes. Although the direct evidence is scant, it is likely that iron bloomeries persisted in the area. The raw materials and skills were available, and a market — local and regional — was there. In 1371, John Neil and others were accused of having dug the highway in Horley (just to the north of Crawley and over the county boundary) to get iron ore. An excavation on the site of Crawley Barn revealed a lined underground water channel which could have driven a small water-wheel for the workshops there.

We have now reached the end of the 15th century. Wealth was accumulating in the locality, and was displayed both in new church buildings and in a large number of timber-framed buildings. Some of the local farms were small and worked by one family, but others had substantial farmhouses set among extensive farmlands which needed wage-earning labourers. Large estate holdings rented to local people were being built up by absentee landowners in London.

The local people were of an independent mind; the original links with the south coast were disappearing from memory. There was a deal of mobility during this time. Moving goods by horse or by carriage may have been slow but, despite what we may believe about an immobile population, travel on foot was common. References to local people can be found in documents relating to places far away. Large numbers of Sussex people were recorded as marrying in London churches, for instance; priests, merchants and lawyers travelled long distances for their work. Any village on a busy road flourished.

East Grinstead and Horsham were important market towns with Members of Parliament, but Crawley did not really have much need of them. It is noticeable that over the centuries, for Sussex people Crawley was simply a place on one's travels to London. In return the local population of any social grouping did not pay much attention to what was going on in Horsham or East Grinstead. They were busy making their own living and looked more to London for progress than to the local small towns. The part played by the London market in this area's growth cannot be over-emphasised, and especially its voracious demand for food. In return, it was probably just as easy for Crawley folk to get goods from London as from local towns.

We have seen that Crawley shows all the signs of having been a new town in the early 13th century. It must also be recorded that references to a weekly market are noticeably absent after the 1280s. True, there is evidence for local prosperity in the 14th and 15th centuries, but no evidence of Crawley developing as a market centre. Indeed, it was the Horsham and East Grinstead markets which developed. Local prosperity did not hinge on possession of a market, but resulted from Crawley's unique routeway position, between London and the coast, and from local farming. The twice-yearly fairs remained to show what might have been.

Chapter 7

The Sixteenth Century: the First Building Boom

When we reach the 16th century, local history becomes both easier and more difficult to write. It is easier because the sheer quantity of surviving documents rapidly increases and we can refer far more to records and need to rely less on imaginative reconstruction. It is at the same time more difficult because one can be buried beneath an abundance of data, in danger of losing the thread of the story of the Crawley area's development.

National events played their part. In 1500 all local churches preached the Catholic faith. By 1560 they were all preaching the faith of the Established Church of England. This transformation was not easily achieved. Although Henry VIII took the English Church away from loyalty to the pope in the 1530s, its ritual did not change. The Dissolution of the Monasteries was not altogether popular: too many people saw greedy king's men making money from what had been ecclesiastical wealth and a local source of relief for the poor. When Mary became queen in 1553, and the national church returned to Catholicism, it was welcomed at first by many people. Only the fear of Spain coupled with fierce persecution of the Protestants changed most minds, while the accession of Elizabeth in 1558 set the country finally on its Protestant track.

Locally, some people with strong Protestant convictions paid a heavy price. On 18 July 1556, two men and one woman were burnt at the stake in East Grinstead for rejecting the Catholic faith. One, Thomas Dungate, was a local man; it is said Martyrs Farm at Langley Green was renamed in his memory since he was arrested there.

International strife now created demands not only for armour and sharp blades but also for cannon and shot. This gave a dramatic impetus to new methods of iron production. The opening up of the New World introduced more gold and silver into the country. Industry and commerce expanded, and not only did a never hitherto experienced inflation occur, but more wealth was generated and much was spent on capital works in farming. New crops and new methods were introduced. A much closer contact with London and international events led to a modernisation of style and custom. The population of England continued to grow.

Local people

The tax returns (Subsidy Rolls) of 1524-5 supposedly list practically all the adult males and independent females in the area: in fact, most were probably heads of households. The returns for Ifield contain 29 different names; those for Crawley have 55 different names. There is no identifiable list for Worth. One very wealthy taxpayer, Thomas Culpeper, paid £100, and six paid either £20 or £10, including Edmund Lassheford, a successor to the Henry who took part in Cade's Rebellion. The majority, however, were men of modest means. Although only three are described as labourers in the Crawley lists, in total 20 paid the minimum tax of £1, which was that paid by wage-earners. The impression given is of a few wealthy land-owners or successful farmers, and a large number of smaller farmers (perhaps tenants), village craftsmen and traders, and labourers. All the names are given in the Sussex Record Society's Vol. 56.

If we assume that each named person headed a household, and that itself is doubtful, it suggests about eighty-four families in Crawley and Ifield parishes. This is puzzling. If one were to list for these parishes: (i) existing houses which are known to have been built by

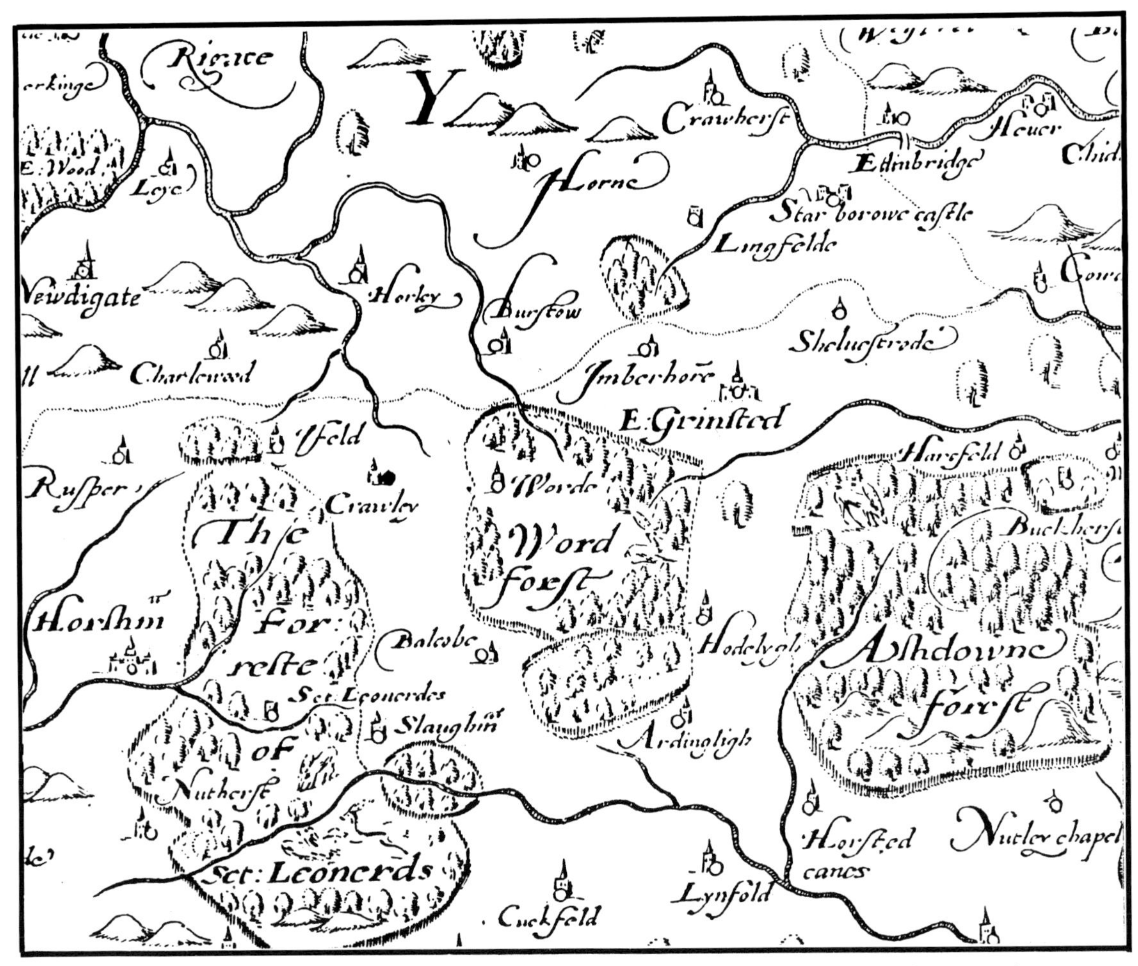

25. Saxton's map of Sussex, 1575. This was the first map of the whole county. Villages are shown by a circle and a steeple, towns have a larger church-like symbol. Though rivers are shown, roads are omitted. Note the phonetic spelling.

1524; (ii) known demolished houses which were built by 1524; and (iii) known farm sites which were in occupation in 1524, then one would be faced with at least 120 buildings — or 120 families. In addition, there are likely to have been other buildings which have since been demolished and of which no trace survives. There must have been a large degree of evasion in the area, which is not what one expects from tax returns. To rely on the tax returns, however, and to use a multiplier of four for the average household size, an estimate of population for the parishes of Ifield and Crawley for the early 16th century would point to about three hundred and fifty people. If we base our estimate on houses, then perhaps four hundred and fifty might be nearer the truth.

The evidence has suggested that the 14th and 15th centuries were times of steady population growth in this area. Farmland was still being cleared and brought into economic use and an urban-type population was being created in Crawley. Generally the late Middle Ages is seen as a period of static or falling population. What we had here is a local growth, which underlines the point that population distribution can vary greatly even in a period of little overall population growth. Though in Britain as a whole there was a large increase in population in the 16th century, Crawley was clearly growing before then. This would have been due more to inward migration than to natural increase. After 1500, the impression is that the 'frontier' town was settling down, the major farms were in existence and now more sophisticated outsiders were becoming interested in moving to a more settled village environment. Population growth may have slowed.

There are a number of recorded wills — frequent epidemics ensured this. From these, too, a picture emerges of modestly successful people with possessions worth bequeathing to their successors. There is still an emphasis on the Church in these wills — not too surprising given that it was the ecclesiastical courts where the wills were proved. People wanted to be buried 'in the parishe churche or churche yarde'. Usually the church was reserved for those of higher status; the testator who mentioned both in his will was hoping that at death his status would prove sufficient for him to be buried in the church itself. This was an outcome he was unlikely ever to be confident of unless he was very sure of his status. The major change in bequests was that whereas in the 15th century the testators left money for candles and for priests to sing a regular mass for their soul, by the middle of the 16th century with a reformed religion and the abolition of chantries they were leaving money for 'the pore men's boxe' instead.

26. The parish chest, used to store parochial records, Worth church.

It may have been a small society — bequests and witnesses show a regular repetition of some names — but what is striking is how often new names appear and disappear within a short time. This pattern certainly supports the argument that, however stable and unadventurous many people may have been, in a small urban settlement on a main road there was a steady turnover in residents. People's expectation of life may have been short, but it did not prevent many of them from leading an active life.

One further record of local people begins at this time. In 1538 Thomas Cromwell instructed each parish in England to buy a 'sure coffer' in which to keep church plate and church records safely. The priests were instructed to list on parchment sheets each christening, marriage and burial at which they had officiated. Later, in 1598, a further instruction ordered that these older documents should be copied into new books. The records of the previous 60 years had been somewhat haphazard, especially as Church organisation had changed several times. As a result, churches were given the option of transcribing only the previous 40 years' registers, those which had been made since the accession of Queen Elizabeth in 1558. An annual extract had also to be sent to the local bishop. This accounts for the fact that a large number of English parish registers begin in 1558. The registers of Worth actually began in 1558 and of Ifield in 1568. Those for Crawley only survive now in part from 1653 (though the transcripts sent to the bishop of Chichester survive from 1611 onwards). The coffer or chest purchased for Worth church is still in the church.

As a final comment on population size, between 1568 and 1600 the Ifield registers show an average of nine baptisms a year. If we assume a birth rate of about twenty-five per thousand, then this points to a population size for Ifield in 1600 of about three hundred and fifty people. Adding another hundred for Crawley parish leads to a population estimate of about four hundred and fifty for Ifield and Crawley combined. During the same period, the Worth registers show an average of 24 baptisms a year. Using the same calculation, Worth parish would have had a population almost three times as large, about nine hundred and fifty people.

Local buildings

The 16th century was one in which, throughout England, there was feverish housebuilding activity, both new houses and extensions and improvements to existing ones. The dates given to a house from a cursory outside look often need to be revised once a closer look at the roof structure has taken place. The 1944 Town and Country Planning Act ordered the first real attempt to make a national list of buildings of architectural and historic interest. The officials who drew up the list were warned that the occupiers might object to the listing of their houses and so care had to be taken. Much of what they wrote in estimating a house's age was based only upon an external viewing.

In recent years, local societies have shown a greater interest in trying to date a house's construction and establish its chronology. (In Sussex the Wealden Buildings Study Group is very active.) Occupants of old property are usually pleased to establish a construction date for their home. It is only those owners who wish to demolish the few remaining historic buildings who object to the listing of a house. A revised list has been produced following further legislation, and that for the Crawley area is dated 23 February 1983. It includes all buildings which survive from before 1700 in anything like their original form.

Over 20 of the medieval houses which were listed in the 1940s have since been demolished, as have some which were not on the original list. By looking at those which remain, however, and by plotting those which were known to have existed in the past, it is clear that by 1600 the High Street of Crawley must have contained at least 30 substantial houses. These were timber-framed and mostly built in the 15th and 16th centuries. They are likely to have had a larger occupancy than older ones, and so the village population was possibly about one hundred and fifty people. The oldest now remaining is the Tree House (facing the bowling alley), which was referred to in the previous chapter. After about a century-and-a-half, that is in the mid-1500s, it was rebuilt and added to, also in timber. This took place at a time when there was extensive building taking place in the locality. A similar story could be told of the Punch Bowl just across the road from the Tree House, built in the mid-1400s and extended a century later.

Most old houses show signs of alteration; each at the time was a modernisation. Traditionally, the fire occupied a central position in the living area, and smoke escaped as best it could through a gap in the roof rafters. The first improvements usually meant fitting a smoke hood to aid its dispersal. The major introduction in the 16th century was when houses were given a brick chimney. When a stone or brick fireplace was installed, and a brick flue and chimney built, although some space was lost safety improved, convenience increased and comfort was introduced. Brick became very popular and widely used. At the same time, with smoke being channelled out, the upper part of a large hall was no longer required for smoke dispersal. An upstairs room could therefore be inserted when the chimney was built. This can be seen at the Punch Bowl. In some houses the walls too had to be slightly raised making a new roof line, and this can be seen at Hazelwick Grange.

All of this was additional expense, and it took some time before all houses had a chimney, especially the poorer ones. The farmhouses and town houses in our area, however, all show signs of having had chimneys inserted from 1550 onwards. Brick was also now being used to infill the timber framing, in place of wattle and daub. Examples of this can be seen in the High Street of Crawley, at Brook Cottage in Ifield, and in Green Lane Cottage in Worth. Not until the end of the 17th century did houses appear in the area with completely brick exterior walls, such as Black Dog Cottage in Northgate.

The pressure in the 16th century of the various competing demands for timber gave an impetus to the use of brick, giving a new look to the landscape. One of the wills relating to a Crawley resident is that of 'William Foster, bricklayer'. He died in 1559 and was probably responsible for some of the chimneys still to be seen in the High Street. One of the problems of house-dating is that an early timber-framed house may have had a brick 'skin' added at a later date, as happened to the Tree House. When Deerswood House in Ifield was being demolished in the early 1950s, a timber-framed 15th-century house was revealed. In the High Street, No. 45 is also a timber-framed house which stands 45 cm. behind its present facade.

The forest, waste and heathland was still in evidence, despite the building activity. Land was still being cleared, though not all planned clearances took place. Magdalen College in Oxford was given the income from land owned by Thomas, Lord Seymour, in the 1540s. He wrote about his plans to his agent. It was recorded: 'There is communication that the Lord Admiral will build a town within the forest of St Leonard's where increase of private tithes may grow to the College . . . whereas we now have but 3 shillings for the herbage of the forest, and 8 shillings for the park of Bewbush . . .'. The site may have been selected but it was not built upon, Lord Seymour being executed in 1549. The new town had to wait for another four hundred years!

As for the heathland, in 1573 the justices of Sussex were charged with winkling out the many vagrants and lawless men who dwelt in the heath and woods of the Surrey-Sussex borders, especially near to Charlwood. The forests hid many acts. At about 3 p.m. on 20 July 1558, when John Hedlowe was at 'Chirchehill Greene' in Worth Forest, Walter Bocher of Burstow, a butcher, murdered him by breaking his neck with a blow from a stout staff. The Coroner's inquest reported that 'Bocher fled', and he was not heard of again. There must have been similar stories over the years, most unrecorded.

What is not clear in looking at these clearances and housebuilding is what led to the building boom. Was it just the use of newly acquired wealth, or was there population growth pressuring the locality? The only clues come from the parish registers but these are somewhat confusing. Take, for example, those of the parish of Ifield.

From 1568 to 1599 there are 251 infant baptisms recorded, but only 88 burials. Though some of the records are missing, there would appear on the face of it to have been a large natural increase in population over this 30-year period. On the other hand, baptisms were steady during the period at an average of nine a year. A large excess of births over deaths would suggest a population growth; a steady number of births suggests little change in the size of the local population. The missing statistic is the number of people who migrated from the area. On the whole, it does seem that there was some population growth in the area, but would that in itself account for the house-building boom? If we persisted in using birth rates as the sole population indicator, then in the early years of the 17th century the Ifield baptisms averaged 13 a year, showing some growth at last. It is worth pointing out, however, that from 1690 to 1740 the recorded Ifield parish baptisms averaged only 8.4 per annum. If we use the same assumptions, does this show a large decline? That did not occur.

Local communications

The growth of a capitalist economy, where inhabitants no longer are content just to survive but look to invest time and money in an enterprise to produce surplus goods for

27. Green Lane Cottage, Worth, the only thatched building left in the Crawley district.

28. The Tree House, Crawley, *c.*1925. Behind this somewhat bland exterior there is still the timber framework of a 14th-century house, originally Crawley's manor house. The Moot Hall stood in the gardens behind it.

sale, is shown in this area by increased agricultural activity, commercial and craft activity in the village, and industrial activity. This posed a problem for road users. The hundred was still responsible for the upkeep of the highway, and kept a close watch on those whose actions caused the roads to deteriorate. Upkeep meant expenditure. Increasingly in wills of the time people were leaving money for the upkeep of the road system. Examples of this are Henry Michell (1524) who left 'to the mendyng of Goffys Lane — if it be mended with synder — 40 shillings, or els nothing'; Richard Collyer (1533) who left £50 to repair the highway between Horsham and Crawley, and £50 to repair the highway between Crawley and Reigate; and Thomas Venner (1548) who left 10s. 'to the mendyng of iii bridges to Crawley way'.

Concern for the roads was, it seems, an abiding passion. The national increase in economic activity and the population growth increased the demand for food and for goods. Both local and through traffic increased. The iron industry locally, and the timber industry, both led to excessively heavy loads being carried on the roads, with disastrous effects on the claylands. The routeways were semi-fixed. Though the amount of waste land remaining was declining, landowners did not necessarily regard roads as completely public domain. It was the custom that if an existing road was too bad for use then the road users went around the bad spot, creating a new road alongside, and the farmers altered the field boundaries. This was another way in which farmers could reorganise their farm holdings, and at the same time improve the roadway.

In 1555 a law was passed ordering each parish to appoint a surveyor responsible to the parish for the upkeep of roads. The post involved surveying roads, bridges, water courses and pavements, removing nuisances, scouring ditches, clearing obstructions, trimming hedges and reporting offending parishioners. All inhabitants had to contribute labour or pay cash in lieu. The Worth furnace accounts for the late 1540s include 'new making up three bridges upon the wayes between the hammer at Worth and Crawley'. The increase in complaints about local roads does not show so much a deterioration in their upkeep as a sharp increase in their use. Trade — and road use — was booming!

As a reminder that an increase in trade — and so in travelling — was not without its attendant dangers, there is a report that in 1505 a merchant was killed in Crawley.

> About 11 a.m. on 20 April when William Gorney late of Ewell in Surrey, a pinner, was at Crawley, Walter Melers came and murdered him, giving him a mortal wound in the head . . . with two staves . . . throwing him to the ground and cutting his throat . . . Melers feloniously carried off his goods and merchandise worth 30s.

One last comment about local 'produce'. Much of the oak timber used in 1538 to build Nonsuch Palace in Surrey for Henry VIII came from Ifield. It is easy to overlook the fact that timber has always been a marketable commodity.

Local farms

Because of the increased number of records available it is possible to trace many of the tenants and owners of farms in the area. The well-known farm names, and family names, recur quite regularly. Thus places like Bonwycks and Priestwood, Woolborough Farm and Crabbett Farm, and the family known as Jordan, are often met with. Similarly Richard Covert, who died in 1579, left a tenement in Ifield called the *George*. When he died it was being rented at 14d. a year and was worth 40s. At the same time, Hyde Farm was also worth 40s. and Bonwycks and Priestwood Farms were worth a little more. The *George* was clearly valuable, occupying as it did a prime site in central Crawley on the main highway, and must have been an inn at that time.

Other farms had less settled names, depending on whoever occupied them at the time

29a. & b. Jordans Farm and Barn. Members of the Jordan family have lived in this area for 800 years. The barn is still used as a social club, having been turned into a restaurant before the New Town developed.

they are mentioned. It is difficult to recognise, for example, where John Saunders of Ifield resided at his death in 1560 when his lands are recorded as '. . . a messuage, a garden and land and meadow called Odworth and Rush Croft, and a piece of land bordered the old deer park at Ifield'. These names are not met with again. Where was 'Bullocks Mede at Thre Brygges', owned by Henry Jordan in 1560? These are examples taken from the manorial court held at Ifield before Lady Joan Amcotts (or Hamcot). They are a reminder that local names are not all irreplaceably fixed. On the other hand, the same court also made a firm record of many hedges and fences being constructed. It is clear that boundaries were much more important than names.

At the 1560 court, the mother of John Saunders (a minor) produced an old deed which supported her objection to some enclosures which had taken place 'so that the lands of the Lady are not all in the Park according to the ancient arrangement between the Lord and the Tenants'. Later an agreement was made that the bank around the deer park, particularly near 'Shermark Gate' (Shiremark means county boundary) should be closed and fenced off. It was also said that where the bank '. . . is by estimations of five furlongs, that John Washeforth and John Swain shall at their costs and charges make and kepe fencible the said banks for the space of two furlongs'. In 1565 it was noted that 'John Warford farmer of Ifield Park made a ditch and hedge below the bank . . . and that Robert Saunders made a hedge of fifteen rods length in and on the bank of the park'. The old deer park in Ifield, parts of whose banks are still traceable north of Ifield church, remains to be plotted.

Medieval society was now coming to an end. The old parkland was disappearing. Proper hedges and fences were being built and a new body of people was about to occupy the land. No longer did the Crawley area comprise large expanses of woodland with farms interspersed. Farms were now adjacent, land-holdings sometimes dispersed, but farmed as a unit. Small areas of woodland called shaws were retained as shelters for wildlife that was hunted and harvested, and only on the poor sandstone soils to the south did extensive forest remain.

One other remnant of a feudal society was still present, and persisted for many centuries. It was pointed out in Chapter Four that land possession was shared between an occupier, who probably rented it with annual payments to an owner in lieu of feudal duties; an owner, who was technically called 'tenant-in-chief' and who owed duties to the king; and the king, who in theory 'owned' all the land. Over the years a title of 'lord of the manor' developed, which entitled the holder to those feudal services originally owed to the king but later passed to the 'tenant-in-chief'. Though the lord of the manor might no longer own the land, he could still claim his feudal services as descendant or successor of the tenant-in-chief. He retained some rights over land even if it was now someone else's freehold. In practice this may have meant only an occasional payment and suit of court when land ownership changed.

We meet this in 16th-century wills, where all land-holdings of the deceased land owner are first listed. In legal terms, we are told, for example, that Richard Covert died 'seised' of a tenement in Ifield called the *George*, that is, he owned it. Later we are told that he held this property from John Shurley 'by fealty and rent of 14d.'. John Shurley owned the lordship of the Manor of Ifield and claimed 14d. a year in lieu of feudal services. Whenever land changed hands — for example, Richard Covert was succeeded by his son, Walter Covert — the incoming owner had to pay a fine to the lord of the manor. There were, of course, manors of Worth, Crawley and Ifield, since each of these parishes was originally an area of land held by a tenant-in-chief. Not surprisingly a number of 'manors' were created in an attempt to provide income. We read sometimes of the manors of Bonwick, Priestwood, Woolborough and Tilgate, but they were not ancient manors.

Local industry — the growth of the ironworks

It would be impossible to describe the local community in the 16th century without referring to the iron industry. At the end of the 14th century a new method of iron production evolved in Europe. Instead of a short furnace producing a small 'bloom' of iron as a result of three or four days' work, a very tall, large furnace was developed, continuously fed through an open top and kept burning at a very high temperature by a blast of air. From time to time molten iron was 'tapped' from its base. This was the blast furnace. By the end of the 15th century this new method had been introduced to Sussex, where there were iron founders at Buxted in 1492. Many French workers at first were brought over to work in the enterprises.

What changes did these furnaces make? The new process had two stages. First a large, stone furnace was built which needed vast quantities of ore, lime and charcoal to keep going. The draught of air, the blast, was produced by means of a water-wheel driving a shaft attached to large bellows. Many furnace ponds were created to provide a regular supply of water for such wheels. A local example can still be seen at Slaugham Pond, and one used to exist at Bewbush. The high temperatures in the furnace produced cast iron.

Next a forge was built. Here the cast iron was reheated and hammered in order to turn it into wrought iron, a malleable metal which can be beaten into a desired shape by a smith. To deal with the large quantity of cast iron, another water-wheel was needed to operate a heavy hammer. Consequently, ponds, usually called hammer ponds, were also needed at forges. Local examples can be seen at St Leonard's Forest, Ifield and Rowfant, and used to exist at Forge Farm in Tinsley Green.

It is obvious from this sketchy description that the new industry required much capital to build a pond, a building where the water-wheel operated, and to make all the necessary equipment. It also needed enormous quantities of materials, especially charcoal, which speeded the forest clearances. To add to the expense, the furnace and forge were invariably on separate sites, often some distance apart, since each needed its own water-wheel, and thus its own pond.

In 1931 a book was written by Ernest Straker which recorded all the ironworking sites in the Weald which he had visited. He also gathered information from a variety of sources and his book *Wealden Iron* is an essential starting point for study of the local history of iron working. Recently, in 1985, another book has updated Straker's work and introduced more evidence, which has come to light particularly through the activities of the Wealden Iron Research Group. This book, by Cleere and Crossley, is called *The Iron Industry of the Weald.*

What do we know of Crawley's Tudor ironworks? It is difficult to estimate exactly when any of them began operation. In each case, the earliest reference describes a site which is already producing iron. It seems highly likely, however, that at least one of the sites was a long-established one. The growth of Crawley needed much iron and the area had always been one which was well-suited to 'bloomery' production.

To the west lay **Bewbush Furnace** and **Ifield Forge**. The pond at Ifield is still there, though now cut in two by the railway line to Horsham. In 1841 it covered 22 acres — much more than the present pond. Bewbush Pond was described in 1931 as 'larger than that of Ifield . . . still extant, and the resort of numerous wildfowl'. There are some Crawley residents who will remember that pond, which finally vanished about forty years ago. In the 1550s an ironmaster, Arthur Middleton of Horsham, leased Bewbush Furnace. In 1570 Roger Gratwyck and his son (also named Roger) had taken over the lease. It is likely that Bewbush Pond was built first, to provide water power at the furnace, when a low dam was constructed across the flood plain of the stream. Roger Gratwyck also leased Ifield Forge, which was probably built later. Here a narrow, shallow valley was dammed and the resulting lake fed by a number of convergent streams. Both the Gratwycks worked this site, and other local sites, until in 1599 another of the Horsham Middletons, John, and his son Thomas, bought the lease.

When Thomas Shurley died in 1579, he owned both the Manor of Crawley with its market and fair, and that of Ifield with its mansion called Court Lands. Among the long list of his

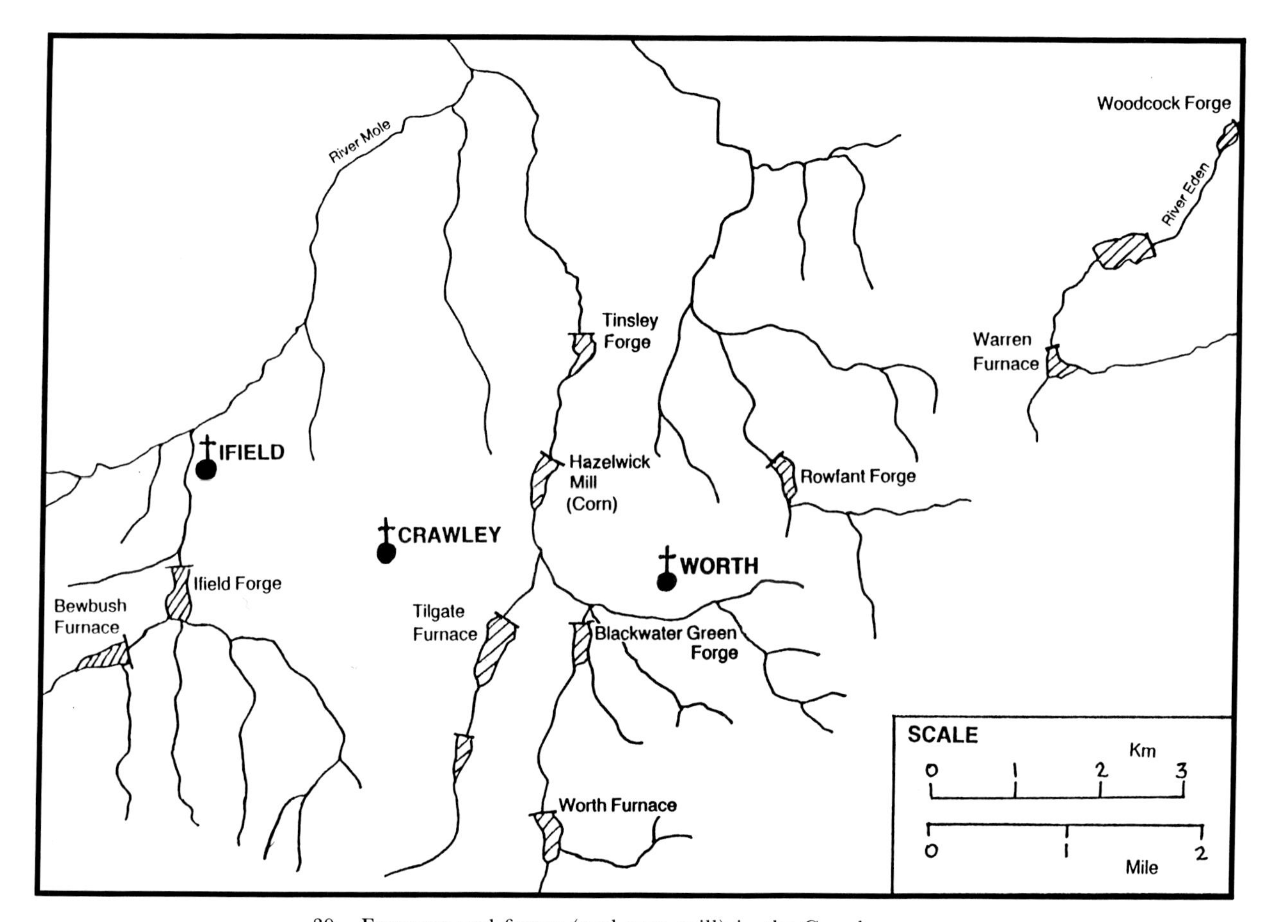

30. Furnaces and forges (and corn mill) in the Crawley area.

Ifield property was '. . . a watercourse running from a certain furnace to . . . the Court Lands, with free [access] for the digging and scouring of the same watercourse to ensure the sufficient drainage of the said furnace . . .'.

It is recorded that between 1589 and 1596 the Bewbush Furnace used 56,000 cords of wood, stacked and ready for burning or turning into charcoal. Each cord measured about 8 ft. x 4 ft. x 4 ft. The charcoal burners used young tree-shoots, from coppice woodlands, rather than established trees, and the forest had to be farmed for timber. Only if the wood was to be burned directly would mature trees be cut, and most of the wood was, in fact, required for charcoal, from which higher temperatures can be obtained. In either case, the forest areas would soon feel the strain of over-cropping, and furnaces and forges would call from further afield for their supplies.

Worth Forest Furnace was probably the most important local works. The site was much disturbed when the railway to Brighton was built. To see it today one would need to go to Pease Pottage, turn eastwards along Parish Lane and continue to where the road now only exists as a muddy path on a forest track across the railway line. This area is called

Cinderbanks, and where the pond used to be is now a swampy area through which the stream still flows. The furnace was developed in the mid-1540s, and by 1547 many cannons were being cast there. The ironworks was one of those owned by the Duke of Norfolk, but when he was accused of treason his property was given to Thomas Seymour, the man who wanted to build a new town in the forest. Seymour, in turn, was also accused of treason, and as a result an inventory of his lands was taken in 1550. This inventory included a description of Worth Furnace, which can be read in *Sussex Archaeological Collections* Vol. 13. It was at the time a large double furnace — since only a double furnace could produce enough iron at one firing to cast a cannon — with a stock of a large quantity of iron, 29 guns, six tons of shot and much raw material. There was also a forge, called **Blackwater Forge**, which is sited half a mile south of Three Bridges Station, by Maidenbower Lane. The Brighton railway line follows the river valley connecting Worth Furnace, upstream, with Blackwater Forge, downstream, and the trackway between the two is easy to trace. Because the Maidenbower site was to be developed, the forge was excavated in 1988. It was shown to be very large, with channels for two water-wheels.

The records show that 33 people were employed at this ironworks: charcoal makers, miners, skilled metal workers and gunfounders. There were wagons, and oxen to draw them. No wonder the local roads were badly mauled by the ironworks traffic; in two years around 1550 the furnace produced over 250 tons of cast iron, and a greater weight of raw materials than that would have had to be brought in.

The accounts of Worth Furnace were kept by 'John Sheriff, Clerk' who was the priest at Worth church. As one of the very few men in the area likely to have known how to read and write, he obviously had a skill which enabled him to supplement his income. His employer at first was Thomas Seymour. In 1549, 'Sir [a courtesy title for a priest] John Sheriff confesseth that he hath not accounted for the furnace and mills in Worth since the Nativity of our Lord in 1547 and now desireth to come instantly to his account'. How modern this sounds!

The third pairing was **Tilgate Furnace** and **Tinsley Forge**. Tilgate Furnace has left its name with us where Furnace Green neighbourhood was built upon Furnace Farm. The original pond (shown in an 1842 map) disappeared in the late 19th century. As with Bewbush, a pond which occupies a site on a plain rather than in a narrow valley is likely to be a shallow one and when the bay holding back the water is breached then the pond rapidly disappears. The present Tilgate Lakes were supply ponds, holding back water further upstream to ensure that the furnace pond did not run dry. All traces of the pond and the furnace are now buried beneath the houses along Furnace Drive.

The iron from the furnace was taken to Tinsley Forge, where the site is now Forge Farm. The route taken by the bars of cast iron is still walked every day by many people who use the path behind Furnace Green shops, across the railway by the footbridge and continue northwards to reach Three Bridges station. The route then ran along what is now North Road and Tinsley Lane. Both Forge Farm and Black Corner (on the Balcombe Road) recall the nature of the industrial site which occupied the land in the mid-16th century. Tilgate and Tinsley were leased by Henry Bowyer in the 1570s and 1580s. He was a Cuckfield man and also operated a number of ironworks in the Ashdown Forest. 'Tillgates' was part of Thomas Shurley's estate. 'Tynsley' was owned by the Culpepper family.

A fourth pairing can be briefly mentioned; it lay to the far east of our area, in Copthorne and out into Surrey. The furnace was called **Warren Furnace**, and lay near Little Frenchies Farm, to the south of the main road to East Grinstead. Associated with it was **Woodcock Forge** to its north, and near Newchapel. The sites are marked today by three ponds which were formed on the stream. The pond by Furnace Wood served the furnace. Next downstream came the Hedgecourt Pond which was almost certainly originally constructed as a retaining pond to keep a water supply available. (Later, a corn mill was built here.) Finally came the Woodcock Pond, which became known as Wire Mill Pond when the forge turned to wire-making. This pairing was worked by John Thorpe in the 1570s; he lived at Gibbshaven in Worth.

Although the records show pairings as being usual — a furnace which made cast-iron bars needed an associated forge to reheat and beat the iron into usable wrought iron for sale to smiths — **Rowfant Forge** does not fit into this pattern. The large, picturesque lake served an iron forge, owned by the Whitfield family. It was in use in 1574 and continued so until the Civil War. It is not known which furnaces provided it with pig iron. The journey from Warren Furnace to Rowfant would have been easier than that taken by iron from the Worth Forest or the Tilgate furnaces, but logic does not always explain what actually happened.

It would seem that Worth Furnace was probably the first to be built; Bewbush Furnace followed, then Warren Furnace, and Tilgate Furnace was perhaps the last. Similarly Worth Furnace was the first to be abandoned, as its remote and inaccessible site was not conducive to long operation. The Bewbush Furnace was abandoned in about 1642, but Tilgate Furnace was still in operation when Leonard Gale, senior, moved to the area in the 1640s and may have continued working until the late 1600s. Warren Furnace, perhaps surprisingly, outlived them all, and was still casting cannon until the 1770s.

The ironmasters of the 16th century often had to bring in skilled workers from overseas. The Worth registers record the burial, in 1588, of 'a frenchwoman' and of 'a foreigner being a traveller falling sick at Worth Hamer'. In 1589, there was the burial of 'the wife of a collier working at Strodgate' (**Strudgate Furnace** was by Wakehurst Place, to the south). Finally, in 1590, it lists 'a frenchman being the servant of Michael Jarrett of Tinslye'.

Local churches

For about four hundred years, the church itself would have been a major centre for community life. The local people were inevitably insular in outlook or rather Sussex-focused. National affairs are unlikely to have had more than a passing effect on everyday life and the church was the place where news was dispersed. The major landowners were rarely local residents, and so the dispensation of law necessitated an outsider coming in to deliberate and adjudicate. The minor clergy were often only poorly educated, but occupied a rather important part in a community from whom they may not have been far removed in status. After the death of Elizabeth I we hear less of the local clergy except in the matters of denominational dispute. A more fluid population developed; people could move away, and more outsiders could come to live in the area. At this time also we see the beginning of the division of local affairs into those of the landed gentry (with whom the Church sided), agricultural workers, including tenant farmers, and the tradespeople living on the busy highway.

In the 1530s the Crown took over the monasteries' wealth: their lands were sold and their treasures dispersed. When John Bysshe, gentleman, died in 1582 he owned a barn, lands, meadows, pasture and wood in Worth called 'Burley' comprising 100 acres. This was all that remained of the old boundary farm of Burleigh. It was said that he held this land, and other '. . . of the dean and chapter of South Malling now suppressed'.

We shall conclude our survey of the 16th century by considering the changes revealed in Crawley church. As already shown, in the 15th century Crawley was still technically an outlying chantry church of Slaugham. By the 16th century, Crawley had clearly forged ahead in importance and the Slaugham link ceased in fact if not in memory.

Like the monasteries, chantries were another potential source of royal income. In 1549 they too were suppressed. Commissioners were appointed in each county to survey the chantries, and the king was empowered to take over their possessions or to let them remain, as he thought fit. In 1547 a survey had shown that Crawley church — still technically a chantry — had a small income from rents received from a number of local farms, land and tenements. Much was in Crawley itself, but there was also property (bequeathed to the church) in Balcombe, Southwick, Ifield, Cuckfield, Alburton and Slaugham. The annual value of the income from these properties was assessed as £5 3s. 5d. The list recorded '. . . the names of all . . . Free Chappells . . . and the clere yerlie value of the same . . . as also the names of the . . . Incumbents'. (It can be read in *Sussex Record Society* Vol. 36.)

Crawley is recorded as 'The Chappell of Shelley with Crawley . . . David Chirke, Incumbent of th'age of 48 years . . . value £4 9s. 11d. besides £2 in tithes'. Then 'The said Chappell of Crawley is called and reputed the parishe churche of Crawley and hath sacraments ministered [to] above 100 houselying people'. Since it was now not so much a chantry (which it might legally be) but a parish church for about one hundred and fifty people, nothing was done about the so-called chantry lands. When Stephen Borde of Lindfield died in 1567, part of his estate in north Sussex included a large farm called Brocksmead which he '. . . held of the late Chantry of Crawley . . .'.

Some years later commissioners were again appointed to look into the position of lands which should have passed to the Crown in 1549 but had been kept hidden. Crawley church was investigated. On 22 April 1585, three men questioned, in Chichester, a very old Crawley parishioner who had lately moved to Cuckfield. Richard Smallam claimed to be 97 years old, or thereabouts, and was therefore born in 1488, only three years after the Battle of Bosworth. The commissioners interrogated him to discover what they called 'concealed landes within the Countie of Sussex'. (The questions and answers are also recorded in *S.R.S.* Vol. 36.)

From the interrogation the following picture emerges. Smallam knew 'the village or streate of Crawley

31. A 16th-century memorial brass in Crawley church, to an unknown resident. The inscription has long since disappeared, though it may have been for one of the local Culpepper family, who were wealthy enough to have been able to have afforded such a memorial.

for he was borne there'. He declared that the parson and parishioners of Slaugham had long challenged the inhabitants of Crawley to come to Slaugham as their head church. He remembered very well that the parson of Slaugham sometimes sang mass in the Crawley chapel yearly on the day of St John the Baptist, but that was more than 60 years previously. He recalled by name the priests of Crawley, known as chantry priests, who served from 1511 to 1542. They lived in a house in Crawley called the Chantry House (probably the Ancient Priors). Finally, Smallam recalled a chapel on Shelley Plain which was known as 'Our Lady Chapel of Shelley'. There had been 'greate offringes' there before it had been pulled down. He himself had assisted in singing mass in the 1520s; he remembered that Our Lady's coat was decked with silver and gold sewn onto it, and that the offertory box sometimes contained 5s., a great sum.

So we see, the final emergence of Crawley as a parish church in its own right had taken place in the 16th century. By the late 1580s Crawley was a settled parish with its own identity, and the only recollection of its former dependent status lay in one old man's mind. But it was never a rich church. There were 13 priests during the 16th century. Men soon moved on, if they could, to better endowed livings.

Chapter 8

The Seventeenth Century: the Uneasy Century

Throughout Crawley's history, the nobility have been conspicuous by their absence, with the exception of a short period in the middle of the 17th century.

Denzil Holles, who was born in 1599, was the younger son of the earl of Clare and a childhood friend of Charles I. In 1624 he became an M.P., though as a result of opposing the king's actions he was fined and imprisoned in 1629. For the next 11 years Charles I reigned without summoning parliament, but when it was recalled Holles was once again elected and became a popular Member. He often represented the House in negotiations with the king. Holles was a Presbyterian, and later was again forced to leave parliament because of a political quarrel, this time with Cromwell. He returned to the House in 1659, and was part of the deputation which persuaded Charles II to return to England. Then he was a member of the court which tried those people who had themselves tried and sentenced Charles I.

On 20 April 1661, he was raised to the peerage and took his title of Baron Holles of Ifield. He owned land in Sussex as a result of marrying Jane, widow of Sir Walter Covert of Slaugham. He had become lord of the manor of Ifield and owned the advowson of Ifield church. Holles lived in north Sussex, though when he died he was buried in Dorchester. His land eventually passed, via his daughters, to the Pelham family after his son, the second baron, died in 1692 with no heir.

So much for our mention in the House of Lords! What is of interest here is that we have an example of a noble gentleman, a younger son of the peerage who had no previous associations with the area, marrying into local land ownership. Secondly, Holles was a Presbyterian in his younger days and we see the intrusion locally of the split between the Established Church and the Nonconformist Churches which recurs in our local story. After the religious conflicts of the 16th century, we get a different form of religious controversy in the 17th century.

Local churches and religious movements

The Established Church of England was very much a reflection of the social order, with its hierarchy of archbishops, bishops and local clergy. But there were at the other end of the spectrum the Independents who, from the 16th century, believed that the Church should be congregation-centred and not in need of other authority, organisation or many of the trappings of worship then used. Such churches as the Congregationalists and the Quakers developed as democratic organisations. Between the Established Church and these were the Presbyterians, wherein though each church elected its own minister and elders, the district organisation had to confirm the selection, and there was a national General Assembly. The Church of Scotland continues this practice. The Baptists could also be placed at this point in the spectrum.

Ifield became a centre of Dissent. Benjamin Browne was the vicar of Ifield from 1596 to 1638. (His father was vicar of Horley, to the north, from 1561 to 1613.) For 42 years he kept his parish register in a neat copperplate handwriting. He probably kept his church in an equally neat and proper manner.

His successor, however, was Robert Goddin, quite a different person. Goddin was given the living of Ifield by his father-in-law, one of the Coverts, who was a member of the committee in Sussex which during the Interregnum investigated offences 'by scandalous clergymen and others'. This meant those who still favoured the episcopacy, the Prayer Book and its rites. Those found to be guilty were usually thrown out of their livings, and a 'Minister of the Word' was installed. Robert Goddin was such a minister; strict Presbyterians were very antagonistic towards the pageantry of church life. Denzil Holles was at that time still a Presbyterian and so, one assumes, approved of Goddin.

Goddin was obviously a strong personality. In 1639 he was accused at the Chichester diocesan court of neglecting his church and of absenting himself. From what we know of him, this was probably a deliberate act to show the strength of a Presbyterian determined not to knuckle under to the local bishop. In 1641 the House of Commons resolved that every parish should make a return listing all males aged 18 years and over who swore to a 'protestation' in support of the Anglican Church and against Catholicism. Of the 118 males in Ifield parish, only one refused to swear, and Robert Goddin helped to administer the oath.

Then in 1644-5, by parliamentary decision, the Prayer Book was abolished, and throughout England stained glass windows were removed, the holy table and the font thrown out, walls whitewashed, marriages performed by magistrates, burials took place but no funeral ceremonies were carried out, men wore hats in church, nobody knelt in prayer and Christmas was a fast day. The intensity of these actions varied widely, depending on the local situation. It is not certain how many of them were carried out by Goddin, but it is obvious from the bleak appearance of Ifield church that the congregation must have espoused the fierce beliefs of their pastoral leader. It is a wonder that the two medieval memorials survived. The only decorations which the Puritans allowed were the tables of the Commandments behind the altar. In 1646 Goddin was accused of assaulting a parishioner; you disagreed with him at your peril!

Strong Nonconformity in Ifield obviously dates from the first half of the 17th century. It is strange that we know of much turmoil in Ifield church when Goddin was vicar, but very little open conflict is reported when his replacement, Henry Halliwell, senior, was vicar from 1651 to 1660, even though Nonconformity was growing. This is in marked contrast to the experience of Horley church where there were nine ministers between 1647 and 1661, and many problems with the Nonconformists. One of the unsuccessful applicants for the living of Horley church in 1648 was 'Henry Hollywell'.

Henry Halliwell, senior, moved to Ifield in 1651 from Crawley church; Ifield would have paid better and in any case he may have wanted a quiet life. But his son, Henry, who took his father's place in 1660 at the close of the Cromwellian period, was a different kind of person. He was presented to the living by Denzil Holles who seems to have wanted to demonstrate his loyalty to the new king by putting into the church at Ifield a man who was a strong upholder of the Established Church.

A famous preacher of the day with great powers of oratory and authorship, Halliwell, junior, wrote and published much, particularly against the Quakers. When William Penn published in 1673 *Wisdom Justified of Her Children from Calumny of Henry Hallywell*, Henry wrote back against the *Impertinent Cavils of William Penn.* The parishioners were evidently split. For some years they had been led to believe in the very strict, almost dour, Presbyterianism of Robert Goddin which had been approved by the local gentry. Now they were faced by the neo-Catholicism of a Church responding to Charles II and his brother, later James II.

It seems, in retrospect, almost inevitable that a branch of the Society of Friends should have been established in Ifield. In 1676, a religious census reported that there were 110 conformists in Ifield, but also '. . . 40 dissenters . . . which either obstinantly refuse or wholly absent themselves from the Communion'. That was the year in which the local

32. The interior of Ifield church.

33. Ifield church pulpit: an early 19th-century watercolour.

group was so strong that they built the meeting house which is still in regular use. 'This Henry Hallywell, priest of Ifield, was the First Persecuter of Friends for Tithes in that place, Taking from Severall poore men severall poundes worth of Goods For a few shillings demanded . . .', as a Quaker document put it. A history of Ifield Quakers was published in 1976 to celebrate the 300th anniversary of the building of Ifield meeting house. In fact, the Quakers had first met in Ifield in May 1655 in the house of Richard Bonwick, a weaver. At that time, too, there were Baptists in Horsham. In 1656, Thomas Patching, a former Ifield churchwarden, was sent to prison for the first time for refusing to pay tithes. He lived in Bonwyck's Place, though actually died in prison in 1660. The ideological struggle was well rooted in Ifield.

After this picture of intense religious fervour in Ifield, that of Crawley church is strangely dissimilar. In 1599, a new man named Thomas Bide was installed in Crawley. He had been ordained in 1587 and when he moved to Crawley he must have been in his early thirties. In 1608, at the age of about forty, he married Alice Terry, a younger woman from the Bolney area. It does not appear to have been a satisfactory marriage. In February 1620 his wife was accused at the archdeaconry court of Lewes of 'grossly misconducting herself'. Was that the cause or effect of her husband's slovenly habits? In 1619 he himself had been accused before the same court of neglecting the '. . . parsonage and chappell houses'. In January 1625 we find Thomas Bide was once more hauled before the same court

> . . . for not preaching nor reading any monthly sermon, no not a sermon in the whole yeare; for giving himself to base and servile labour; neither is his apparrell grave decent or comely; hee weareth no surplice in tyme of divine service or ministering the sacraments; he catechizeth not at all; his houses are in decaye, the chancel untyled, and is much decayed and in tyme will come to utter ruine.

A year later he was replaced. Poor man! He was certainly not another Robert Goddin. Yet it is no wonder really that he gave little time to the church and tried to earn money elsewhere. The living at Crawley was meagre. In 1650, when Worth and Balcombe churches provided £100 each for their parsons, Crawley was only worth £20 a year, virtually the lowest valuation in the whole of the Rape of Lewes.

The balance of wealth seems by then to have moved away from the village, with its craftsmen and service-based industry, to the rural-based industries, especially the iron industry. Merchant wealth was being brought into the rural area as new estates were formed. We can see the change of emphasis which had occurred. The first wealth of the area was in the smallholdings which were carved out of the forest in Ifield and Worth. Then, as the village grew, wealth and influence moved from the rural area to the growing village. At that time Crawley dominated the area. But in the 16th century we see the decline of Crawley in local affairs and the resurgence of Ifield and Worth.

Strangely enough, the poverty of the church is not reflected in the parish itself. In a tax return made in 1621, seven men are listed in Crawley who in total possessed lands to the value of £191, including William Dodd, gentleman, and Thomas Jeale and John Jordan, farmers. Yet the 14 men of Ifield listed — farmers, innkeepers and shopkeepers — were in possession of land to the value of only £202. Obviously, all was not well in the local community. Perhaps Thomas Bide was not liked by the parishioners, who refused to support him? There are doubtless the ingredients of a good story here.

Both Ifield's and Crawley's manorial rights and church advowsons were in the possession of the Covert family of Cuckfield. In the case of Crawley, when Thomas Covert married a younger daughter of Lord Goring he gave Crawley as a wedding settlement to his wife.

Worth church was enlarged whilst Crawley languished. When Anthony Lynton, the rector, died in 1610 he left money to build the large west gallery. Later in the century the chandeliers were hung and new silver-gilt church plate was provided. Nicholas Whiston was rector from 1610 to 1640. He married a daughter of the Whitfields, who were the local ironmasters. He was also the vicar of Horley from 1618 to 1626, enjoying a double income, when he resigned in favour of his son. The impression given is that Worth lived up to its name as far as the clergy were concerned.

In 1643 the manor and advowson of Worth were sold. Although little is ever heard of Worth as a manor, the right to nominate the rector was a good, saleable commodity. Included in the transaction were other properties, including 'Hasselwick Mill with the pond, floodgates and mill-dams in Worth'. The purchasers were two London gentlemen. This is another glimmer of interest in the area by London merchants. Was it as a result of their connection that the church was given good plate in the ensuing years?

As a postscript to this look at the three parishes, in view of all we know of Crawley it is strange that John Gratewick, who was appointed to Crawley church in 1661, should have stayed for almost 60 years, until 1718. Given the fact of the low value of the living, one wonders what kept him there. Did he have private means; was the endowment supplemented? All we know is that the man came from a prominent family in the Crawley-Horsham area.

One last reference to religious activity will show how, though in a small way, Dissent was being spread in the area. The Baptists were strong in Horsham in the mid-17th century, and their prominent leader was Matthew Caffyn, of Broadbridge Mill. Despite occasional imprisonment he preached widely in Sussex. A 'house church' system developed in which worshippers met in private houses and farms. There was a strong commitment which led, in the eastern part of Worth parish, to the founding of a congregation around Turners Hill and West Hoathly, with another further north in Bletchingly, Outwood and Horne. These congregations were never large and their own members ministered to them.

The one in the Turners Hill area met in a number of places. Among those recorded are Tanyard at Horley in 1668, Hogs Hill Farm at Crawley in 1675, Turners Hill in 1698, and Copthorne in 1702. The outstanding local organiser, selected by his congregation as minister, was a Turners Hill resident named Griffle English. The church met at his house from 1709 to 1761. It was, after all, a long way from Turners Hill and Copthorne to Worth church. We know that some Worth parishioners attended Burstow and West Hoathly churches because it was a shorter walk. Was the parish church's influence less strong in the east of the parish? That would not be surprising. We can tell from the monuments that the well-off farmers in the east of the parish were buried in Worth church. As for the poorer members, perhaps the rector did not mind too much if they stayed away, and left the gentry in comfort in the church.

Local people — population

Once again the parish records give clues to population changes. Although Crawley's registers only commence in 1653 for baptisms, in 1676 for burials, and in 1688 for marriages, the parish also had to send a copy of its register to the bishop each year; as a result we have the bishop's transcripts from 1611 onwards to help fill the gap. For Crawley there are 83 recorded baptisms in the 20 years from 1611 to 1631, averaging about four a year. The following ten years show only 30 baptisms, about three a year. Then in the 47 years from 1653 to 1699 there are just 95, two a year. This is a steady decline. Whilst the iron industry and associated employment were at its peak, there was an increase in the birth rate. Then for many years the birth rate was low, only picking up at the end of the century.

This may give another view of the local parishioners' reactions to all the changes in church life around the mid-century. Absence of baptisms may be due to absence of births: it may also be absence of interest in giving a child a church baptism. There were few recorded dissenters in Crawley parish, but to register as a Nonconformist meant that you had a strong belief. The impression given for Crawley in the 17th century is not of active religious beliefs but of a lack of interest. It is unlikely that the population fell.

A religious census, previously mentioned, of all above the age of 16 years was taken in 1676. Of the 150 parishioners of Ifield, 40 (or 27 per cent) were Nonconformist. Of the 300 parishioners of Worth, 20 (seven per cent) were Nonconformist and 16 (five per cent) were described as Papist. Of the 70 parishioners of Crawley, just three (four per cent) were Nonconformist. This certainly shows the strength of Dissent in the Ifield area. Altogether, in the three parishes 15 per cent did not subscribe to the Established Church's doctrines. It should be noted that the figures for each parish are suspiciously round.

It is usually stated that north Sussex was an area where Dissent was strong. The evidence here is inconclusive. In Crawley parish, and the part of Ifield parish which included Crawley village, there were low numbers of Nonconformists. Much of the church income came from tithes. This may explain why the Quakers were so persecuted by the Ifield clergy. It was one thing not to believe in what the church preached; it was another not to put money in the collection plate and not to pay tithes. It makes one wonder to what extent religion really played a part in everyday lives. There is even the suspicion that some may have joined the Nonconformist groups to avoid paying tithes, rather than on dogmatic grounds.

The Ifield parish registers show that until 1630 baptisms averaged about thirteen a year. From then onwards they fell to about seven in the 1650s before recovering somewhat to about nine-and-a-half in the 1690s. There is a constant relationship between Ifield and Crawley in the proportion of 3:1 judging by the entries in the parish registers.

Meanwhile, at Worth the baptisms from 1600 to 1650 averaged just over 26 a year, less than in the 16th century. Thereafter they declined to the low twenties until a revival in the 1690s. The proportional relationship between Worth and Ifield was about 2.5:1, once again judging from the parish registers. It is worth mentioning that the increase in the 1690s may be due as much to the zeal of the clergy in recording and officiating at baptisms as to any real increase in the birth rate.

Just to illustrate the problems which the historian faces, it can be seen that if the figures of the 1676 religious return are used, then Worth:Ifield is only in the proportion of 2:1 and the Ifield:Crawley proportion is also only 2:1. Over the whole of the 17th century, in Ifield and Crawley there were about two hundred more recorded baptisms than burials. In Worth the figure is nearer four hundred. That does not mean that the local population grew by that amount. Our locality always exported people; they were virtually one of the local crops. An estimate of the population at the end of the 17th century would give figures of 350-400 for Ifield, 120-130 for Crawley and 900-950 for Worth. There does not seem to have been much change in population size over the century. Few new buildings or farms appear.

Finally, another look at population size is possible as a result of the hearth tax, imposed in 1662, whereby every dwelling was charged 2s. for each fire, hearth or stove in the house. Only the poor were exempt and, since they were not listed, we do not know how many of them there were. There is a return for the Rape of Lewes which gives the names of Worth, Crawley and, surprisingly, Ifield (surprising because Ifield was not in that rape). In the Rape of Pevensey there is a list of tax payers in the Hundred of Burleigh Arches, and under the heading for West Hoathly there is a long list, the last half of which appear from the names actually to be in the eastern portion of Worth.

The names of the areas are not, in north Sussex, necessarily the same as those for the parishes, and the boundaries may vary. In the lists we find:

'Borough of Crawley'	12 names (40 hearths)
'Ifield Parish'	9 names (25 hearths)
'Crawley'	7 names (8 hearths)

'Borough of Worth'	67 names (164 hearths)
'unnamed' (Worth)	35 names (84 hearths)

It is almost certain that the 'Borough of Crawley' and 'Ifield Parish' refer to the two sides of Crawley High Street, and comprise the village.

The 21 Crawley villagers comprised 18 men and three widows, the householders. There were three men described as 'gentlemen'. The houses averaged just over three hearths each, spread between one and seven. The 102 Worth residents comprised 96 men and six widows, the householders. There were one 'Knight', two 'Gentlemen' and one 'Esquire' — and one publican! Their houses averaged 2.4 hearths each. There was, however, a wider spread in Worth. Fifty-one of the houses (50 per cent) only had one hearth, whereas Sir John Smith's had sixteen. One of the men described as 'gentleman' was Leonard Gale, and he only had one hearth, which seems rather lowly. However, he had newly arrived in the area to take over some ironworks, and he did not marry until 1666.

According to this list, Worth (102 names) is about five-and-a-half times as large as Crawley (19 names), if these can be approximated to the parishes. The proportion seems too low but, given the large number of lowly dwellings in Worth, there were likely to have been a good number of poor also.

One determinant of population size relates to population health. From time to time there were severe outbreaks of plague or epidemics of influenza. The winter months usually took their toll with 'flu, rheumatism, or simply the cold. The summer months, on the other hand, were not necessarily more healthy since living conditions were generally insanitary. Flies and rats spread disease; the water supply became less pure; sewage was known to harbour dangers, but it was thought that the danger lay in the smell, not in uncleanliness itself. So midsummer could be as lethal as midwinter.

Though not specifically recorded, epidemics can be detected from the burial records. In Ifield, nine people died between March and May 1573 and seven died in December 1596. The worst outbreak came in 1610 when 44 people died in six weeks between 23 June and 4 September. This was about fifteen per cent of the population. For many families, the effect of this epidemic was catastrophic. For an illustration, take the experiences of the Ashen, the Homewood and the Swift families. William Ashen and four of his five sons died in a three-week period. George Homewood had married Eleanor Waller in 1597. By 1610 they were living with their four children, Anne aged nine, George aged seven, Eleanor aged four, William aged three. Between 12 and 14 August the elder George Homewood and his three youngest children were buried. (The widow, who was left to bring up her surviving daughter, remarried, espousing John Michell, in 1612 and Anne grew up to marry her cousin, Thomas Waller, in 1623.) Richard and Katherine Swift had five children. On 28 June they lost eight-year-old Peter; on 15 July they lost ten-year-old Joan; on 18 July they lost six-year-old Richard; finally, on 22 July they lost four-month-old Francis. Only three-year-old Nicholas survived. The parents lived on for many years, but had no more children. In Crawley parish, whereas for most years there were only between three and five burials recorded, there were ten burials between 30 August and the end of October 1638.

In Worth parish, there were 34 deaths between December 1558 and April 1559 at a time when the average was ten per year. There were other peaks between March and May 1570, March and June 1587, December 1615 and March 1616, December 1617 and March 1618, and March and June 1623. It is interesting that Worth and Ifield did not have matching periods of peak deaths. A few miles seem to have been enough to contain epidemics. This may reinforce the view that it was the water or food supply which was the potential source of disease, and that the winter deaths were also caused by epidemic rather than severe weather. Influenza and bronchitis have been lethal illnesses at times, but sufficiently common not to be classified as plagues.

The Worth register also provides us with two cameos. In 1593 two brothers were recorded as 'Dying of the plague' and each was 'buryed uppon the comon at Crawlies Down'. Then in 1603 it was noted that 'Some others died this yeare in the great plague but were not brought into solemn buriall at the Church and therefore are (not) . . . registered'.

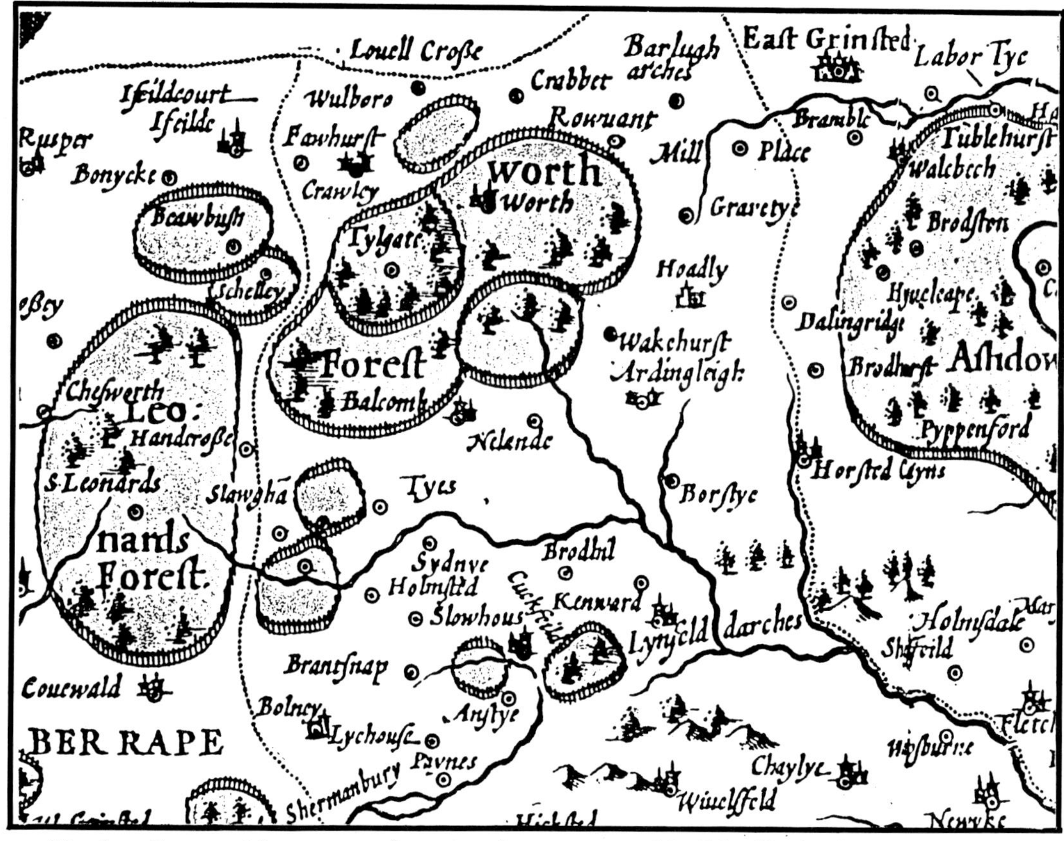

34. Speed's map of Sussex, one of a series of maps surveyed by John Norden in the 1590s, but published by John Speed in 1610. It includes greater detail than the Saxton map, showing the larger farms and estates as well as villages.

Local roads and trade

It is sometimes surprising how isolated sections of record from a long series come to light. There are records from the Buttinghill hundred court which show this old relic of early administration still meeting in the early 17th century after a 500-year existence. From 1613 to 1621 it met twice a year. What was its function? There were four constables for the hundred, and nine headboroughs who originally represented each tithing (but by 1613 each parish). Collectively these elected officers were ostensibly responsible for apprehending offenders, and this system persisted until a police force was formed. In reality each hundred court was more concerned with maintaining the highways of the area. They levied small fines on those who did not attend the court.

On 29 September 1613, for example, 'Ralph Willarde is to cleanse his ditches on either side of the King's highway leading between Slaugham and Crawley, and lying between Brodefilde and Tylgate, by the feast of St Andrew next under a penalty of 4d. for each perch uncleansed'. Farmers commonly cleared surface water from their land by channelling it onto the roads. Again and again, farmers are ordered to clean their ditches: 'opposite the Park Meade, near the three bridges'; 'between the three bridges and the meadow called the little Stubbe mead'; 'the north side of the King's highway leading between Crawley and Worth near le three bridges'. This road was particularly vulnerable to waterlogging, but that is not surprising when one considers the amount of iron-works traffic which used it. One entry requires the men of Worth '. . . to repair the bridge called le three bridges'. The original three were at last one! Finally, there were many references to farmers being required to clean out the common watercourse in Crawley. The drinking water was becoming too polluted.

That people were ambiguous in their approach towards law and order can be seen in the petty disputes taking place during the century. As an example, in the 1640s Henry Bowyer of Worth was elected parish constable. During the same period he was also appearing at Lewes court, where he was bound over to keep the peace.

Worth parish officials placed 51 pauper children in apprenticeships during the century; virtually all went into farming occupations. The exceptions were those who were apprenticed to tanners, a grocer, blacksmiths and, in the last 10 years of the century, a cordwainer, a carpenter and a stonemason. Worth was overwhelmingly rural.

A few of the local population were not farming, as we have seen. Those who applied for wedding licences at Crawley church, and their sureties, also show the sort of occupations in the village. True, many were described as husbandmen or yeomen, but there were others. For example:

1600	Henry Martin	Brewer
	Thomas George	Butcher
1639	John Hampson	Glover
	Richard Bashford	Mercer
1687	John Burt	Druggist

Moreover, in 1635 there was the burial of Thomas Truncheon, a tapster at the *George*. So we see people selling meat and beer, a glove-maker, a draper, a doctor even, all earning their living in the village High Street.

The parish registers continue to remind us that there was not a static local community. The main road still attracted travellers to the village, as well as providing a means of escape. In 1617 Robert Scholes from Aylesford in Kent married in Crawley; in 1625 Elizabeth Upton of Crawley married in Ardingly; Edmund Hunt of Crawley married in Lewes; and John Hampson of Ifield married in Cowfold. Obviously mobility was not uncommon; it definitely increased during the course of the century.

In particular, there was a growth of public scheduled carrying services between London and the provinces. Guides to carrier and coach services to Sussex were published. In 1681 there were 16 services; by 1715 there were forty-five. Packhorse journeys were being replaced by wagons, which allowed bulkier goods to be carried. Among the named destinations of the London services were Turners Hill, Crawley, Cuckfield and Brighton. Sussex journeys passed through East Grinstead, Crawley or Horsham, and the major staging post towards the end of the century appears to have been Crawley. The quantity of food going to London, and manufactured goods being sent from London, helped to improve living conditions. The wealthy gentry demanded good-quality merchandise. Hence the importance of the road system, and perhaps the reason why the hundred court was forever concerned with road upkeep.

In 1636 John Taylor published a catalogue of taverns — those places which were licensed to sell wine as well as beer. There were 61 listed in Sussex, six of them in the north. Two

35. The *George*, 1924. Over the years the original building has expanded each side along the High Street, taking in adjacent properties. Restructuring the roofs and tile-cladding the walls have now made it look an integrated whole.

each were in East Grinstead and Horsham, and the other two were shown as being owned by John Peake, one in Crawley and the other in Worth. We know that the one in Crawley was the *George*, but the other is not known for certain. It may have been at Worth but more likely at Turners Hill. Profits were good for the inn-keepers.

When Henry Waller, the inn-keeper at the *George*, died in 1689, his premises were described in some detail. The rooms were listed: 'Great Parlour, Little Parlour, Hall, Kitchen, Rose Chamber, Crown Chamber, 6 other Bedchambers, Bakehouse, Brewhouse, Cellar, Long-house, Stable, Barn, Yard'. There were altogether, upstairs and downstairs, 15 beds.

The increased road use, and the inability of many parishes to support the upkeep of a thriving through road, led to changes in the method of funding road upkeep. One of the earliest turnpike acts in the country was passed in 1696. Its preamble gave the reason:

> . . . Whereas the highway betweene Rygate in the County of Surrey and Crawley in the County of Sussex . . . are very ruinous and almost impassable for above three miles in length, insomuch as it is become dangerous to all persons that pass those ways, and for that the (law) of this realme . . . is not sufficient for the effectual repairing and maintaining of the same, neither are the inhabitants of the several . . . parishes in which the said ruinous lanes do lye of ability to repair the same. . .

Thus a toll road was needed. The worst part of the road was on the clay between Horley and Woodhatch, now known as Meath Green Lane, which was prone to flooding by the River Mole. The road itself was described as 'the road from Stenning, Horsham and other parts of great trade and commerce in the County of Sussex to London'.

Though the records are not clear, it seems that the road was not actually improved and turned into a toll road for some time: nevertheless later a toll-gate was built, known as the North Gate, as Crawley was approached. It stood just south of the junction of the present Ifield Drive with the High Street. The final toll house was only demolished at the beginning of this century.

Both physical and social mobility can be brought together in the lives of the two Leonard Gales. Leonard Gale, senior, was born in Sevenoaks, Kent, in 1620, the son of a blacksmith. In 1636 both his parents, three brothers and a sister died of the plague. He survived and worked hard for 20 years at his father's trade. Then Gale moved to Sussex to take over St Leonard's forge in Lower Beeding, later adding Tinsley forge and the furnace at Cowden. By the age of 46, he claimed to have been worth £6,000. At this stage of his life he married and had five children: the eldest son, also named Leonard, was born in 1673. Gale eventually died in 1690.

Leonard Gale, junior, had a very different life. Having a wealthy father he was educated privately, attended University College in Oxford from 1690 for four years, and followed this by studying as a barrister. He was called to the Bar in 1697 but did not practise. Having completed his education and having inherited his father's business, he purchased Crabbett Park and its estate in 1698 for £9,000. Now a wealthy landowner who had been well-educated, he was easily received into and became a leading light in local society.

The iron industry: decline and fall

It was not unique to enter local society with the profits from ironmaking, as Leonard Gale did. So, too, did the Whitfield family, originally from Northumberland, who took over Rowfant forge. They built an imposing stone frontage to the original timber-framed building called Rowfant House. Even though ironworking was declining, the decades of profit, both

36. Northgate Toll House. A picture taken about ninety years ago, shortly before its demolition. It stood near to the entrance of what is now Ifield Drive, near the *Sun*. (The word Crawley was written on the photograph by the printer.)

37. Rowfant House, a watercolour by S. Grimm *c.*1780, now in the Burrell Collection, the British Museum.

from civil and military demand for metal, left their mark. Astute ironmasters transferred their wealth into land, which generated a replacement income and gave a social position. They then built themselves fine mansions. Their children could marry well into established society; there were enough titled families who appreciated marrying their younger offspring into money. Each benefited from the transaction.

During the 17th century, the local iron industry had mixed fortunes, but was mostly in decline. **Rowfant Forge** was reportedly closed by 1664. **Bewbush Furnace**, according to a Parliamentary survey of 1649, went out of use in about 1642 and lack of wood was given as the reason. The survey stated:

> There is one old furnace standing at the lower end of the great furnace pond . . . but Mr. Thomas Middleton and his predecessors have so destroyed the woods and timber upon the several parks of Shelley and Bewbush . . . that it hath stood empty for about seven years last past.

Although Bewbush Furnace seems to have been working again in 1653 for a time, by 1664 it was recorded as 'ruined'.

Ifield Forge was one of the few which were destroyed during the Civil War. Colonel Sir William Waller was a leading Parliamentarian and, having captured Arundel Castle, he sent a force to the north of Sussex to seek retribution from those ironworks which had supported the Royalists. Thomas Middleton, the then owner, was a Horsham M.P. who had tried to play both sides, and his reward for backing the losing party of the time was that Ifield Forge was dismantled and the mill burnt in 1643. He was later suspected of complicity in the Royalist uprising in Horsham of 1648, and his estates were confiscated. The forge was never rebuilt, and the pond and watermill were used as a cornmill instead.

From 1660 onwards, and perhaps even earlier, the mill was leased by William Garton, a prominent Quaker. He would not have wanted anything to do with an ironworks with a munitions connection, and he may have been a safer tenant towards the end of the Cromwellian period. When Middleton got his estates back, the relationship between a Royalist landlord and a Quaker tenant could not have been easy. Garton spent much time in Horsham gaol for his beliefs. Eventually Leonard Gale bought the property from the Middletons. The present mill bears a foundation stone dating from the 1683 rebuilding when the first brick structure was erected by a later Thomas Middleton and his wife, Mary. It carries their initials.

Worth Furnace and **Blackwater Forge** had short lives. The furnace produced enormous quantities of iron in the 16th century, and their joint success was probably the cause of their failure. There was just not enough good quality iron ore and timber available to keep them going, and no reference to either remains in 17th-century records. They probably closed in the early 1600s.

Tilgate Furnace and **Tinsley Forge** both had longer lives. Each became the property eventually of Leonard Gale and were obviously very profitable. In a 1664 list, Tilgate furnace was described as being '. . . discontinued but repaired and stocked on account of the war', and was working again in 1665. At this time, Tinsley forge was also in use. Tilgate was casting shot for guns, and the roads to the furnace were referred to in 1685. The continuance of these two enterprises points to the fact that there was still enough local ore (at The Hawth) and timber to support one furnace. No closure date is known for the furnace, but it was likely to have been right at the end of the 17th century. Tinsley Forge, however, continued to be profitable; it appears in a 1717 list as one of 13 still remaining operational in Sussex, and again in 1737 when the Gales were buying in cast iron from Heathfield. It seems to have shut down finally in the mid-18th century.

Warren Furnace has enough documentary evidence to show its continued existence, though it may have been less active in the 17th century. Why this furnace continued while the other three closed down is a mystery. The furnace is somewhat remote, so the nearby forest may have been able to supply fuel more easily. It still required ore and limestone, however, and other local ironmasters were not able to find these in sufficient quantity to continue. Blast furnaces had a voracious appetite. There is a list of carriers' accounts for the 1760s which shows how much shot and cannon was carried to London for the then owners, Masters and Raby. But it was closed down finally by 1787. Mark Lower, the noted Sussex historian, in an article for *Sussex Archaeological Collections* Vol. 2 in 1849, reported that he had been told that cannon had been cast in Worth and conveyed to London '. . . within the last 70 years'. This must refer to Warren Furnace.

Woodcock Forge, which was associated with Warren Furnace, was working in the 1660s, in 1718, and again in 1736. When the furnace closed down, iron was still brought to the forge; in 1788 it was being referred to as the Wire Mill.

We now reach the end of the troubled 17th century, and one which saw large changes in Crawley. A postscript to the century can best be added with part of Leonard Gale's advice to his son, given in his will in 1690:

> . . . above all, hold fast to the ancient Protestant religion, for a better religion cannot be found out than that is. Avoid ill and debauched company, especially wicked and depraved priests such as Lee and Troughton of Worth . . . avoid swearing, lying, drunkenness, whoring and gaming, which are the ruin of all men's estates.

Presumably, anything omitted was allowable!

Chapter 9

Georgian England: the Peaceful Years at Home

The local area was, during the 18th century, developing a more varied character than hitherto. The three units — Worth, Crawley and Ifield — will be looked at separately, then be brought together again for an overall appraisal.

Worth

By the 18th century, Worth was potentially a very attractive area for a gentleman's country retreat. The forest still occupied a greater part of the parish and someone interested in hunting, shooting and fishing could find all these pursuits at hand. Because of the type of drainage pattern in north Sussex, there was never any good river fishing. The various lakes in the parish, however, mostly man-made and often for the iron industry in the first instance, were stocked to provide such sport.

As a farming area most of Worth had never been rich. Thus we find what may be the surprising portrait of an area which was about to blossom with modest but sound gentlemen's residences, yet with seemingly little local industry or agriculture to support them. The truth is that Worth has always had to rely on outside activities to bring wealth into the area. It was fortunate that London was only 30 miles away. The businessmen, bankers and merchants of the City were to bring their wealth and their acumen to their country homes.

In the 1705 election 23 parishioners voted. Most were farmers and just three were given an added title: 'Charles Goodwyn, Esq.; Leonard Gale, Esq.; Henry Gale, Gent.'. Leonard Gale's money was unusual in that it originated from local industry. Although the industry was itself declining in the 18th century, his wealth continued to grow. His son, Henry, died but his daughters married well; when he, too, died, in 1750, his eldest daughter — Philippa Clitherow — took the Crawley part of the estate, and the youngest—Sarah Blunt — inherited the Crabbett Park estate in Worth. The local gentry, who were then mostly well-to-do farmers, were a close-knit group and inevitably often intermarried. One of the Bysshe family of Fen Place married into the Shelley family of Horsham, and their son who was born in 1792 was named Percy Bysshe Shelley. He wrote much about nature, and a feeling of north Sussex can be experienced in his lines:

> Away, away, from men and towns,
> To the wild wood and the downs —
> To the silent wilderness . . .

The majority of the residents were still working in agriculture or in forestry, often with another part-time craft to supplement income. These occupations were very labour intensive until the 20th century. As the 18th century progressed the number of full-time craftsmen increased, but the persistence of Warren Furnace in the north-east corner of the parish was atypical. Few children had any schooling until Timothy Shelley provided the money for a school in the latter part of the century, as his memorial in the churchyard records.

When a child was apprenticed for seven years to learn a skill, the fact was recorded in the Lewes Assize Court records. These show the sort of local crafts which existed. The parents had to pay for the privilege of having the child apprenticed; in return the child lived with his or her master and learned a trade. Local examples include:

1713 Henry Carpenter was apprenticed to John Dew of Worth, weaver.
1716 Sara Blunt was apprenticed to Jane Beadle of Worth, mantua maker [women's gowns].
1721 Joseph Simmons of Burstow was apprenticed to John Ridley of Worth, blacksmith.
1726 John Pilbeam was apprenticed to Robert Ridley of Worth, tailor.
1738 Thomas Woodgate was apprenticed to John Morley of Worth, wheelwright.
1742 Thomas Mitchell of Charlwood was apprenticed to Thomas Potter of Worth, cordwainer [shoemaker].

The blacksmith and the wheelwright were semi-industrial, providing goods mostly for the agricultural market, and transport in particular. The horse and cart was the typical road user. But the workers in the clothing trades — tailor, dressmaker and shoemaker — suggest a ready market of those willing and able to buy new clothes. They could be making for local people or be out-workers for the London market.

For the children of the gentlemen in the area, more desirable occupations could be found, even those which required apprenticeships. Thus in 1716 Thomas Shelley, son of John Shelley, Gentleman, was apprenticed to Job Wilkes, Citizen of London and Haberdasher. The four sons of the Rector of Worth, William Hampton, were also well provided for. In turn they were allocated:

1716 James, to William Pearce, Citizen of London and goldsmith.
1717 John, to John Hill, Citizen of London and apothecary.
1718 Robert, to Edward Luxford, Citizen of London and mercer.
1718 Ambrose, to William Goddard, Citizen of London and vintner.

These 'Citizens' were all, of course, citizens and Freemen of the City of London. Admission to this honour was by membership of a City Livery Company. For all these sons of the well-to-do the future was pretty well assured, though the father had to pay a price, or 'consideration'. Local apprenticeships usually cost the parents between £5 and £10 each. John Shelley had to pay £74 for his son, and considerations for the four sons of William Hampton cost him £140 in total. These favoured young men are early examples of residents of Worth becoming 'something in the City'.

The comparative calm of the parish was both the consequence of and the reason for what was probably its most flourishing industry; one which by its very nature left virtually no record, except when a mistake was made. In 1743, a book was published about Britain by George Bickhem, and it found the following to say about Sussex: 'The number of great families in the County make the conversation polite, but the ruder classes of inhabitants are famous for smuggling, for which they lie exceedingly convenient'.

Smuggling! To our ears a romantic word. The men themselves may not have been in truth very romantic figures, but who has not thrilled to the story of men in small boats from France unloading their wine, spirits, tea, tobacco and lace at the dead of night and swiftly carrying the booty inland before the excisemen could catch them. Kipling, who knew Sussex well, caught some of the spirit of their life in a poem:

> If you wake at midnight, and hear a horse's feet,
> Don't go drawing back the blind, or looking in the street,
> Them that asks no questions isn't told a lie,
> Watch the wall my darling, while the Gentlemen go by!
> Five and twenty ponies Trotting through the dark,
> Brandy for the Parson,
> 'Baccy for the Clerk,
> Laces for a lady, letters for a spy,
> And watch the wall my darling while the Gentlemen go by!

All manner of men supported this trade. The lower classes may have carried out the deeds, but the upper classes consumed the goods. Without the support and connivance of rich and poor alike, the trade would have stopped. Presumably, too, it would have been the rich who, at some remove, organised the traffic.

One route ran from the *Sloop Inn* at Freshfield, on the Ouse, and crossed the Ashdown Forest via Felbridge to Copthorne, which was the central depot, so to speak. Smuggler's Cottage near to the *Duke's Head* claims a strong link with the trade. It is said to be haunted by the ghost of a murdered smuggler who was buried in the cellars. The Ancient Priors in Crawley High Street also has stories of its connection with the trade. The local residents can tell fragments of the memories of the smugglers, but little was ever put to paper. Copthorne was simply known to be a smuggling centre and, like the Mafia, its inhabitants kept its secrets.

38. The *George Inn*, 1789, from an aquatint after Rowlandson. The scene is said to be an auction of smugglers' horses.

The records of the Chief Revenue Officer who was stationed at Horsham show that peak activity was in the 1780s. He occasionally seized large quantities of tea and horses in the Crawley area. In April 1781 he took 56 bags of tea; in May 1781, 30 bags of tea; in September 1784, 24 bags of tea and 4 horses. The famous drawing by Rowlandson of the *George* at Crawley shows supposedly the auction of horses which had been taken from smugglers. It seems that Copthorne was a sort of 'no-man's land' at this time. The inhabitants were known in the district as the 'Copthorne Yellow-Bellies' from their habit of warming themselves by stretching their legs over a peat fire. The yellow smoke stained their clothing: the local phrase for this was 'drying the malt'.

Another illustration of the remoteness of the area and its general attitude to law and order can be seen in the fact that Crawley Down and Copthorne Common became well-known as prize-fighting venues. The area is close to the Sussex/Surrey/Kent borders and so if any county authorities wanted to stop a fight, which was an illegal activity, it was easy for the contestants and spectators to cross over a county boundary to safety. Thousands of people attended the fights, from the basest-born to royalty, to see two men — stripped to the waist — fight one another with bare knuckles. Each round lasted until a man was knocked down. He then had a short respite until the next round commenced. The fight ended when one of the contestants did not answer to the bell for the next round. Fights were usually very gory, and could last for hours. It was not against the rules to hold an opponent under one arm and punch him with the other. Heavy betting took place on the fights.

The public house at Crawley Down by the old level crossing has now been renamed the *Prizefighter* and records some memories of these days. To give but one example of what was seen at a prize-fight, the *Sussex Weekly Advertiser* in 1789 reported:

> On Thursday last a boxing match took place at Crawley between the noted John Smith and Ned Stanford, two professional pugilists of that place. After a severe conflict that betrayed more of a savage encounter than a scientific display of the gymnastic art, it terminated in favour of Smith, Stanford having given in whilst still standing on his legs to the no small disappointment of the knowing ones.

All in all, the eastern part of Worth parish might then have been best described as a place to avoid, at least until the roads had been made up. Its reputation has improved nowadays, as have the roads! The roads of Sussex were well known by repute, if not by experience. A writer in 1752, in a book entitled *A Journey Through Surrey and Sussex*, described: 'Sussex . . . a county . . . bad for travellers; so bad indeed as to have become proverbial; and it might justly be said that a Sussex road is an almost insuperable evil'. It is a recurring theme that the writers who lived in and wrote for London had little good to say about Sussex. The supercilious air which they introduce into their books makes Sussex seem the more attractive, which is unlikely to have been the intention of the writers!

Local people, however, also found, and recorded, difficulties. In 1776 a wealthy Horsham solicitor, John Baker, was on his way to the Lewes Quarter Sessions. He reached Crawley from Horsham easily enough, but then met problems. His diary records:

> 16th July. Came eight miles to Crawley at two o'clock. Went further end of it. Man at the *Sun Inn* by turnpike said no going to Grinstead but might get to Turners Hill, a mile or two about, but nobody would go for a shilling to show the way. Came back to the other end of Crawley, hired a boy to go behind chaise for a shilling to Rowfant. Went through grounds, and a countryman with us, through eight or ten gates, then on fine common and got before five o'clock to the [*Dorset Arms*] at Grinstead. Rode from Crawley about a mile to Rowfant very bad.

What a story this tells of the locality. Here is a man from Horsham, in midsummer, not knowing the way to East Grinstead from Crawley and unable to find it. The roads were not well-maintained, and certainly had no signposts. Why should local people put up signposts? They knew the way. If strangers wanted signs, then let them erect the signs. Road upkeep meant expense. A stranger who wished to go across country would be hard put to tell a farm track from the king's highway. He would have to rely on a local lad hanging-on behind the carriage, showing which road to take, and to stop every so often to let the lad open a farm gate across the road. It took more than a day's pay to persuade one boy to accompany the coach to Rowfant, and then walk back afterwards.

This also underlines the point that the market town of East Grinstead was not easily accessible from Crawley. Horsham was the usual 'local' market town for the Crawley district and the Horsham road was busy and, eventually, improved by a turnpike. No toll road was ever built from Crawley to East Grinstead. This does not mean that the road was already good enough, but that it was not needed. The western hinterland of East Grinstead, the eastern part of Worth parish, almost certainly used East Grinstead as a market, but the residents of the area either used the very hilly lane from Turners Hill or the network of farm tracks to Felbridge. The only road improvement to Worth parish was when the present Balcombe Road was built, and that was concerned with north-south traffic movement. Though it took place in the early 19th century, it would be appropriate to mention it here.

In 1809 an Act of Parliament was passed '. . . for the making and maintaining a road over Horley Common in the County of Surrey to a place called Black Corner and from thence to join the Brighthelmstone Turnpike at Whiteman's Green in Cuckfield in the County of Sussex'. Originally the road turned east by the present Pound Hill crossroads and then turned again southwards along Church Lane in Worth. An early toll cottage, with its deer's head plaque, still stands on the corner of the road leading down to Worth church. For a while at least, part of Worth would have become busier, but the hill leading down Church Lane from the toll cottage was much too steep for wheeled traffic. Soon the turnpike was turned away from Church Lane and an easier road was made, south from Pound Hill crossroads, to join its original route at the foot of the hill near to the entrance to Frogshole Farm. A new tollgate was built in the Balcombe Road. (Its site was near the present crematorium, on the land now used as Wiltshire's Nurseries.) A new workhouse for the parish, only demolished about twenty years ago, was built in the 1790s on the corner of the Turners Hill Road and Church Road. It was a large, three-storeyed building and served, in Worth, an extensive parish. An inventory of 1812 describes it as having 23 rooms with beds, and housing at that time 30 males and 18 females. An isolated reference to an earlier building is given in the local registers. In June and July 1739 four burials were recorded of people 'from ye work house', a surprisingly early use of the term in the area.

The 1801 census records 1,501 inhabitants, 766 male and 735 female, which was a large number for an area of such scattered settlement. For comparison, Horsham town then had 1,539 inhabitants, about the same as Worth, and East Grinstead was larger with 2,659 inhabitants. In Worth, the 1,501 people lived in 194 houses, an average of about eight persons per house.

Although landholdings were being aggregated to form estates, most of the landlords were absentee. The owners still lived in London and had not, in the 18th century, quite yet discovered a taste for actually living in the country. Though there are a few large 18th-century buildings in north Sussex, most were built in the 19th century, by which time the toll roads, and later the railway, had been built. London was not then so far away.

Crawley

Crawley had begun as a market settlement, but from the 16th century onwards we find no references to a weekly market, only to the annual fairs. It was not really a successful village by 1700. There may have been a very small weekly market, but the towns which developed were at Horsham and at East Grinstead. An attempt was made to build up Cuckfield with a new chartered market in 1670, but this was not very successful.

Worth had the feel of a quiet backwater in the 18th century, though with a vigorous life beneath the seemingly tranquil surface. Crawley, on the other hand, started slowly, but began to feel the benefit of the Brighton Road; more so once the toll road had been completed.

The state of the village in the early 18th century was revealed in a visitation of the church organised by Bishop Bower of Chichester in 1724. His commission reported that 'Crawley

39. Worth workhouse stood on the corner of the Turners Hill Road and Church Road, Worth. It was purpose-built in the 1790s, but after 40 years the poor were housed elsewhere and the building was used as labourers' cottages by the Crabbett estate. They were known as Khyber Cottages, and were demolished in the 1960s.

has four bells, but only one in order three being cracked'. Furthermore, they added that '. . . the Church [is] out of repair without and within but the repairs so great and the inhabitants so few and poor that they are not able to repair it within a few years'. (Worth church was reported as having four bells, but no mention of bells was made for Ifield church though it is known to have had at least two.) Crawley parish was, of course, only half the village. Though the villagers on the west of the High Street may have attended services at St John's, their tithes would have had to be given and financial responsibilities were to St Margaret's. Even in the later 19th century, Mark Lemon was a regular attender of St John's church but, since he resided on the west side of the High Street, when he died he was buried in St Margaret's, Ifield.

Does lack of upkeep imply lack of local wealth? The wealthy local residents did not in the later 18th century live in Crawley parish. The church might have been looked upon affectionately by the villagers, but as the century progressed, wealth was slow to accrete to the parishioners. It was the increased traffic on the Brighton Road which eventually brought greater prosperity to the shopkeepers, tradesmen and craftsmen who lived on the High Street.

Crawley's bells, however, were at last put right. The four poor bells of 1724 were recast by the famous bell-founder, Thomas Lester, who was responsible for casting almost a hundred bells in Sussex between 1738 and 1769. In 1742 he came to Crawley and set up his mobile bell-casting equipment. The result was two new bells which used the old material. The first was inscribed 'Thomas Lester of London made me, 1742' and the second, 'Francis Smith. Ch. Warden. 1742. TL fecit'. Perhaps Francis Smith organised the fund-raising for the new bells: as church warden he was in a position to do so. (The Latin inscription shows 'Thomas Lester made it'.) A new prosperity appears to have arrived. At least the cost of casting two bells was met.

If we judge Crawley village by the references to its church, we get a picture of poverty in the 17th and early 18th centuries. Yet this picture is at odds with the facts that it had some expensive houses in its High Street and had eight voters in the 1705 election. In an election for the two county Members of Parliament for Sussex on 24 May 1705, 2,914 freeholders voted. Of these only 47 lived in this area. Worth had 23 voters which confirms its wealth. Ifield had 16 voters, not far behind the Worth figure. Crawley's eight, given its small size, was a comparatively large number. Voting was confined to freeholders of property of a particular value: in most of our area this meant farms and estates. In Crawley village some of the larger commercial premises would also have had that value.

Though roads were not well regarded by travellers, and Sussex in particular had a bad name, the increase in village wealth was obviously tied up with the Brighton Road. Evidence that it was seen as important is the turnpike which was established from Reigate to Crawley. A report drawn up in 1740, however, declared that in Sussex even toll roads were not being kept in a good state of repair. Coaches often found it better to drive across fields rather than along a road! Horseback was the commonest form of travel (other than by foot) until the mid-century. There were carriers' carts for those with a little money. It was national economic need which created the impetus to improve roads throughout Britain. Crawley village benefited much from this, particularly from the mid-18th century onwards.

Behind all this lies the question of how many people dwelt in the area. For England as a whole, a slight and slow increase in the first half of the century was followed by quickening of the growth rate in the second half. Both birth rates and death rates increased, but births were in excess of deaths. Many of the burials recorded in the Crawley parish registers were of infants; child mortality was high. These included the entry on 26 April 1769: 'Robert the infant son of John King of Meastam [Merstham], who died of innoculation in the parish of Worth'. Medical improvements were not achieved without a price. On the other hand, there are entries for: '19 August 1769. Joan Tidy, widow, aged 84; 23 January 1774. John Streeter, an old man; 14 May 1774. Mary Lock, widow (very old); 15 May 1777 George Brett (an old man)'. Some people at least survived all that life threw at them and lived a long while!

National population growth was helped by, and in turn led to, more agricultural improvement. World trade and home production was increasing. This led to an increase in commerce and travel, and to a greater demand for industrial output. Though Crawley did not experience at first hand the English Industrial Revolution, its effects were obviously noticeable. The growth in wealth led to improved diet and living conditions (as can be seen in the local smuggling communities).

In the last chapter, the estimated local population in 1700 was taken to be Ifield, 350-400 inhabitants; Crawley, 120-130 inhabitants; Worth, 900-950 inhabitants. The first census, taken in 1801, reported the true population figures to be Ifield, 637 inhabitants; Crawley, 210 inhabitants; Worth, 1,501 inhabitants. Did population growth in our local parishes match the national average? It is difficult to draw any conclusion from the limited Crawley registers except to note that the increase in the number of baptisms begins after the 1720s, which is somewhat earlier than for the other two parishes.

It might be an appropriate place to discuss the pattern shown by Worth and Ifield. Worth, in the 50 years between 1710 and 1760, averaged 15.8 burials and 25.7 baptisms a year. Then the figures change markedly, so that in the 40 years from 1760 to 1800, burials

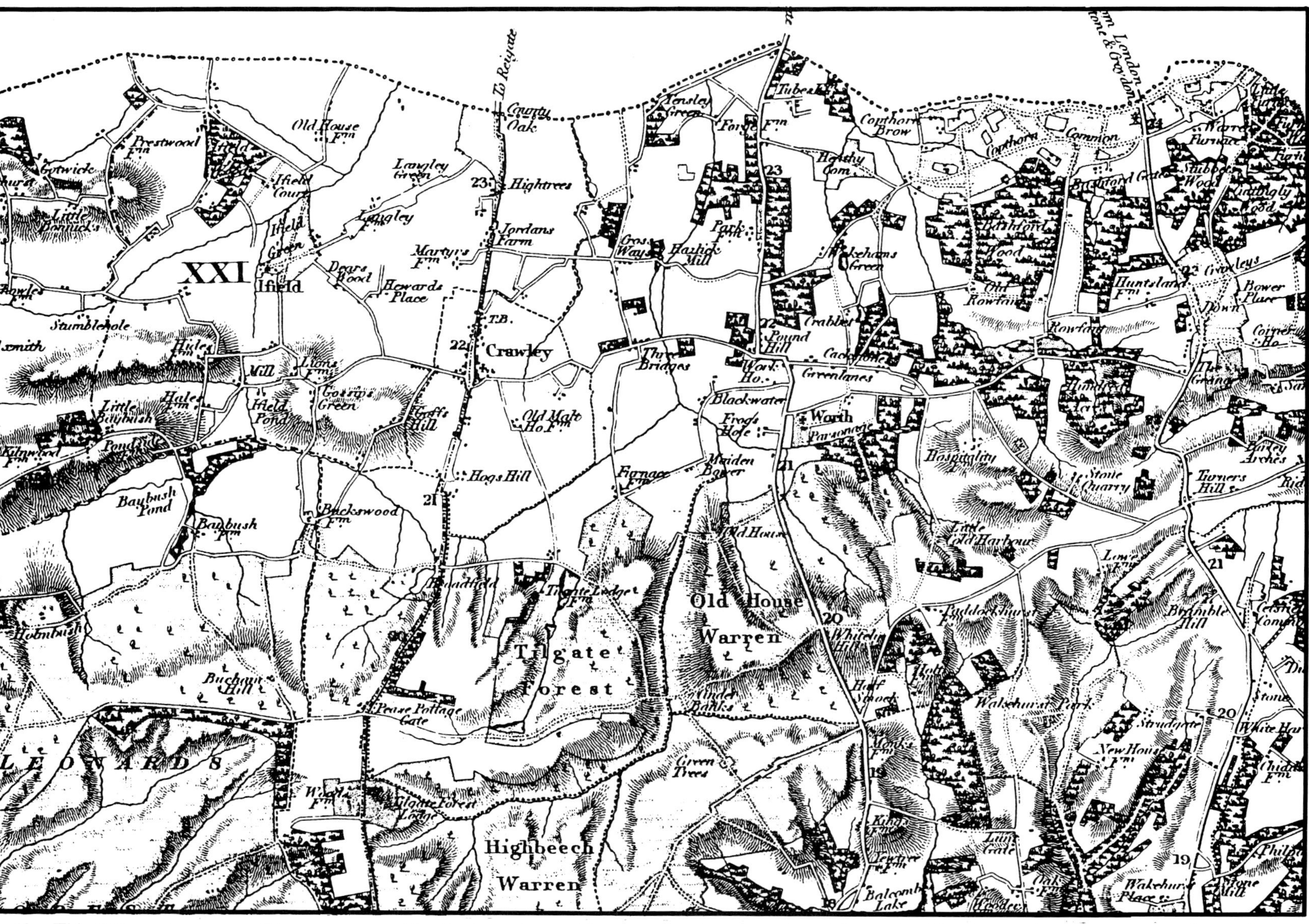

40. This 18th-century map of Sussex, surveyed by Budgen, shows villages, major farms, roads and footpaths. The figures along the main roads are the distances in miles from Brighton.

averaged 22 and baptisms 36.7 a year. Each rose by 50 per cent. The rate of population growth in Worth is likely to have increased after 1760. In Ifield, to take the first 50 years of the century and compare with the second 50 years, baptisms rose 50 per cent from 7.1 a year to 11.6, whereas the number of deaths changed very little, and just increased from 7.5 a year to 8.8. Once again the mid-century displayed a change in the number of births, though there was surprisingly little change in the number of deaths.

A number of doctors lived in Crawley, their names appearing in various documents. In the 1720s the two sons of 'William Nightengale of Crawley, Surgeon' were each apprenticed to London 'apothecaries' at a high price. In 1767, 'John Heaver of Crawley, surgeon and apothecary' was involved in land transfer. Between, and beyond, these dates we meet with the Dungate family.

John Dungate, senior, was a London surgeon in the 1730s. By 1751 his son, Charles, was practising in Crawley, and he was succeeded by his brother John, junior, in 1795. They both lived in a house called Crawley Cottage or Crawley Lodge, south of the present level crossing, which was demolished in the 1960s. When John, junior, died in 1798 at the age of 63 he was succeeded by his former assistant, Robert Smith. The Smith family of medical men lived in The Tree — Robert until his death in 1828, and then his son Thomas until his death in 1862. Thomas Smith was followed by his son-in-law, Thomas Martin, whose account of the life of Crawley doctors can be read in Crawley Library, and who spent 60 years as the local doctor. Note that the local doctors, who served Crawley, Ifield, Worth, Horley and Charlwood, lived in Crawley High Street. The village was a very attractive central place for all aspiring tradesmen and professional people who sought a good market for their services.

In 1770 there was an important new toll road, following '. . . an Act for repairing and widening the road leading from Brighthelmstone [Brighton] to the County Oak on Lovell Heath [Lowfield Heath] in the county of Sussex'. At last the London to Brighton road was turnpiked over its whole length. Of course, local inhabitants distinguished between the 'Brighton Road' (southwards) and the 'London Road' (northwards). Brighton and its sea bathing was an important part of London society's Season from the 1750s onwards, particularly after the Prince Regent began to patronise the town. He was a magnet who attracted large numbers of gentlefolk to the South Coast.

Horsham was the market town to which Crawley usually looked, and for administrative purposes was the centre for law and order too. However, Reigate was not too distant. The *Sussex Weekly Advertiser* of 3 December 1787 reported that:

> One evening, a few days since, as Mr. John Dauncey, a farmer near Crawley, was on his return home from Reigate Market, he was stopped by a single footpad, who demanded his money, and robbed him of about £10 in cash, which Mr. Dauncey delivered to him without the least resistance or hesitation. He had some banknotes about him, but the villain fortunately did not demand his pocket book which contained them.

No doubt any literate footpad would know what to do in future after having read that account! But this report shows that local farmers needed to brave an eight-mile trip to market.

The *George* must have benefited from all this. The original small building was extended northwards to include its present bar. In 1777, the landlord was named Dench. He was renowned for providing good food (not a particularly difficult achievement given the poverty of most innkeepers' fare) and his brother ran the *Talbot* at Cuckfield. By 1783, however, the innkeeper was named Anscombe and the inn's reputation had declined. John Wilkes, in his diary, records: 'To Dench's, the *Talbot*, a good inn; to Crawley, 9 miles, Anscombe's, the *George*, a bad inn. Lay there'. No doubt the innkeepers on the turnpiked Brighton Road were in the same position as the first I.T.V. regional companies: they were presented almost with a licence to print money. That trade was good is shown by the building of the new *White*

Hart opposite the *George*. The first *White Hart* was in the building now known as The Ancient Priors. This proved too small for the trade, and the new inn with extensive stabling behind was opened in 1770.

As the century drew to its close, the road became busy — and wheeled vehicles became increasingly common. Not all was sedate and well-ordered, though. The young men of the 1790s were as fascinated with speeding on the Brighton Road as their present-day counterparts, the 'Ton-Up' lads. Here is a statement published in the *Sussex Weekly Advertiser* in March 1790:

> Whereas we the undersigned, Joseph Johnson and Thomas Edes, postboys, living with Edward Anscomb of Crawley, innholder, did on the 17th day of November last (as we were driving four horses in a post-chaise on the turnpike road between Crawley and Reigate) maliciously and wilfully drive against another post-chaise going the same road, belonging to William Jenkins of Crawley, in which were the children and servants of Mr. Otto, returning from Brighthelmstone, whereby the chaise was over-turned and the persons therein providentially escaped with little hurt, and whereas Mr. Otto has commenced an action against us for the above assault, but in consideration of our having satisfied the said William Jenkins for the damage done to the chaise and horses, and thus asking pardon of the persons hurt, and promising in future never to offend in the like manner, the action is discontinued for which we offer our sincere thanks (for in all probability if it had gone on it must have ended in our ruin).

What a story hides here. Were they rival taxi-drivers quarrelling over a fare, or high-spirited lads having a race? Joseph Johnson avoided ruin, and achieved respectability. By 1815 he was the landlord of the *George*, as can be seen by his bills on display there, and he was still there in the 1840s.

In about 1797 one of the first directories was published which included details of Crawley village. This was *The Universal British Directory, Vol. II.* It described the place thus:

> It is situated on the great road from London to Brighthelmstone from whence it is distant twenty-four miles, from Horsham six, and from London thirty. The coaches pass through this village from Brighthelmstone to London, two up and two down, every day except Sunday. The letters are delivered by a cross post every Tuesday, Thursday and Saturday. It has fairs annually for Welch cattle and toys, the first the 8th May, the last the 9th September.

Then the directory gave the principal gentry listed in alphabetical order, a system which was followed for the next hundred years. They were Richard Cuddington, Nathaniel Hall, — Hutchinson, David Knox, and James Lamb. Two physicians were listed: Richard Chatfield, an 'Apothecary', and John Dungate, a 'Surgeon and Man-midwife'. Until the end of the 19th century, the way a person qualified as a doctor was by studying at university to become a physician, by taking apothecary examinations (which means treating by medicine) or by taking surgical examinations (which includes treating with the knife).

Finally, there is a list of traders:

Edward Anscomb	*George Inn*
John Ede	carpenter
— Elphick	butcher
John Grey	tailor
Nathaniel Miller	collar-maker (saddler)
Richard Smith	victualler (i.e. publican)
John Smith	victualler
— Snelling	shopkeeper
Edward Standford	shopkeeper
— Tamplin	sackmaker

Not much information, perhaps, but it serves to underline the picture of the local area which has emerged from all the other evidence. What we do not know is how many people worked at the *George* or were employed by those tradesmen. Crawley was just a lively

41. A coach and four outside the *George*. In the early 1900s an American millionaire named Vanderbilt liked to drive his coach from London to Brighton whenever he visited England, allowing the camera to record a scene reminiscent of the days of the coaching trade. Sadly, Vanderbilt was a victim of the *Titanic* disaster.

village on a busy route, but still most of its inhabitants were agriculture-based, or at least relied for much of their income on agriculture.

One last reference to the Brighton Road is in relation to the postal services. Lewes and Chichester were the chief post towns of Sussex, linked daily to London. In the 1750s postal services in Sussex deteriorated, and were therefore reorganised. East Grinstead was the postal centre for our area and was recognised as a 'post town'. In 1791, for example, there was a foot post three times a week from East Grinstead to Crawley and Ifield on Sundays, Wednesdays and Fridays. This must have involved a journey of over 20 miles on foot. Given the apparent poverty of the roads between East Grinstead and Crawley it is perhaps surprising that this was the route selected, rather than via Horsham.

Both the sender and the receiver were charged for the service — our local service was operated, as it were, under licence from the Post Office. In Crawley village there was an approved 'receiving house' where letters were accepted to await collection by the postman from East Grinstead. Additional 'receiving houses' were set up in Crawley Down and in Worth. For a while, in 1803, Uckfield took over as the 'post town' and mail for our area was transported via Uckfield (through Cuckfield). In 1805, though, East Grinstead was reappointed and the previous pattern resumed, but with posts operating six days a week. Finally, in 1810 when the London to Brighton daily mail coach began, Crawley itself was made a 'post town' as it formed an important staging post where horses were changed. James Swift, who ran the former receiving house, was appointed Crawley's first postmaster.

One of the reasons why the village population, even the well-off, may have been isolated from the better-off inhabitants of Ifield and Worth parishes is because its inhabitants were much more concerned with income from trade than from land. Wealth from land was welcomed; small traders were usually ignored by the landed. Crawley was a dynamic rather than a static settlement, but not regarded as of consequence by those in Society. It is as if its wealth was not really acceptable, and so in a period like the 17th and 18th centuries the residents had money, but little chance of entry into Society (unless they bought land and moved away from the village). Perhaps this was why the church was for many

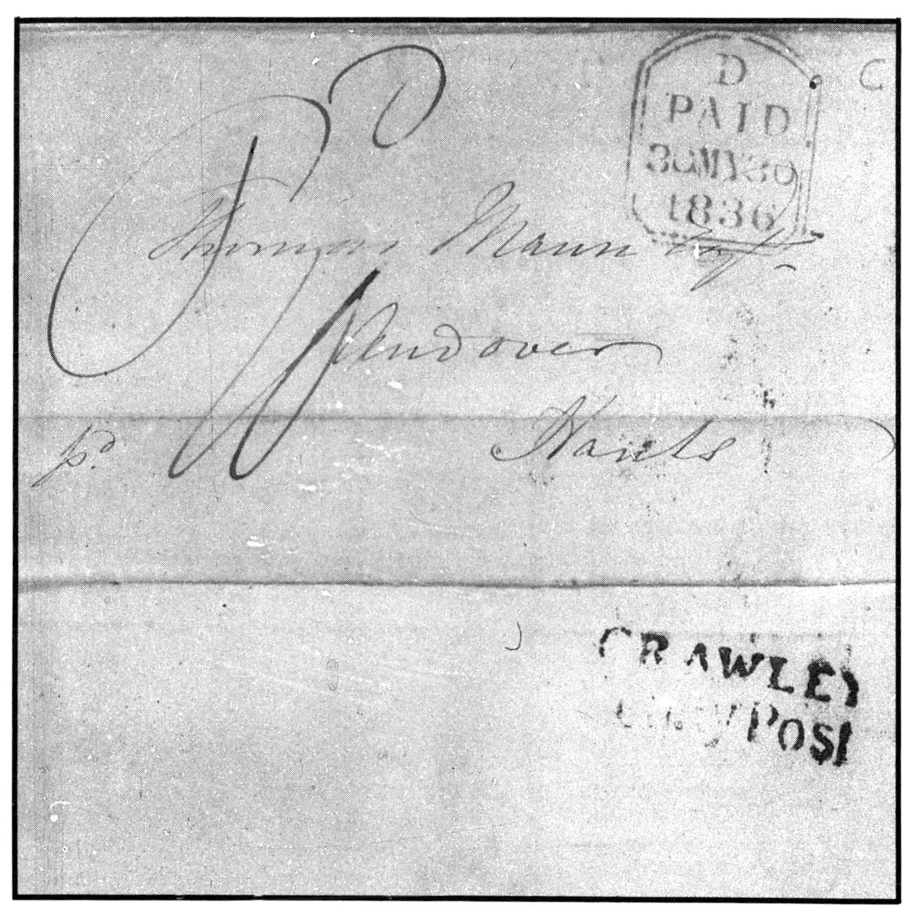

42. Each post office had its own name stamp. The postmaster also marked the letter 'Pd' (Paid) when it was handed to him and the sender had paid the postage charge. Eventually, from 1840, a system of adhesive stamps was adopted. Crawley Post Office then cancelled its letters with a postmark number '228'.

years allowed to decay? Money from trade and commerce became 'respectable' at first in London, at least, if in sufficient quantity. But Crawley had to await the end of the 18th century before money from industry and commerce became respectable.

Ifield

Simple cameo descriptions of Worth and Crawley can be given to explain the 18th century. What is the picture of Ifield at that time? We have seen it become a farming area with many good-sized farms. The main change during the century was the buying-up of much land by absentee landlords, often titled, who were content for tenant farmers to work the land. Though Worth gentry lived on their estates, on the whole the Ifield 'gentry' were living elsewhere.

In the election of 1705, 16 men of Ifield voted. By the 1734 election there were 19 voters. Most of them then supported the Rt. Hon. Henry Pelham, not surprisingly when it is realised that he was lord of the manor of Ifield, His elder brother was known as Pelham-Holles, and eventually became Duke of Newcastle. In fact, both were very active in British politics and Henry Pelham was prime minister later in the century. The link with the aristocracy forged by Denzil Holles continued.

In the election of 1774, 35 men voted. More had become eligible as freeholders which may point to a more intensive land usage in the area. Newer farm names were appearing alongside the 500-year-old names. References to 'the waste' constantly occur in Ifield's records, and it was still possible to increase the amount of land for farming use until late in the 19th century. Some of the larger units were apparently being broken up during the 17th and early 18th centuries, effectively increasing the number of voters. At that time the value of farmland close to London was rising, which also increased the number of landowners who could vote.

It may seem odd, therefore, to look ahead to the 1820 election and find that only 21 men voted in the election. Why a reduction? It might be that many potential voters did not vote, but that is unlikely. The reality is that, as the 18th century progressed, much of the land had been bought up by the wealthy. Tenant farmers did not qualify to vote. By 1836 the lord of the manor was Lord Rodney, who owned 30 per cent of the land in Ifield. This sort of ownership led to a distancing between the local occupiers and their landlords.

There are many 'land tax assessments' which detail who occupied and owned land. In the 1780 assessment, the major landowner was Lady Mary Pelham; another was James Clitherow (who had inherited one third of the Gale estate). One of the largest occupiers was Daniel Knight, a farmer, who was also one of the two local tax collectors. The landowners themselves had to assess and collect taxes from themselves — a peculiar form of torture no doubt! Daniel Knight's farm was owned by Lady Pelham: Doctor Dungate's property, Tree House, was rented from Mr. Clitherow.

That there was wealth in the parish is made evident by the work carried out in St Margaret's, Ifield, in 1760. A large gallery was built, in which musicians were housed to accompany the singing, and high box-pews were installed in the church. These, however, were second-hand and came from St Margaret's, Westminster. Did the Westminster church look to help a church with a similar dedication, or did one of the local gentry use his London connections to obtain the pews?

Just as the land at Worth was becoming attractive as an investment, so it was in Ifield. In 1771 there was an Act of Parliament which provided '. . . for repairing and widening the road . . . from the turnpike road between Cuckfield and Crawley . . . to Horsham'. Road improvements were part of the general aid to developing the 'waste' or common land left in the area. Considering that Ifield was already a settlement at the time of the Conquest, it might seem surprising that much unused land still remained there in the 18th and 19th centuries. Yet the lord of the manor was still allowing squatters to take over small plots of land alongside the highway, and build houses there. Some of these became shops. In the

18th century we also have references to shop premises; in 1729, for example, the late Thomas Felrey, blacksmith, left both 'household goods and shop goods'.

However, since Ifield was still the major farming area of the locality, some idea of what it meant to be a farmer towards the end of the 18th century can be gathered from a long letter written by the curate of Newdigate church to a gentleman in London in 1794. This village is a few miles north of Ifield but contains much the same type of farmland. The clergyman's letter paints a picture of a hard life on the clay soils.

> The mode of husbandry has varied but little . . . for time immemorial . . . The nature of the land is for the most part a poor clay . . . Many expensive experiments have been tried by speculative farmers to improve the present system — none of which have produced the desired effect . . . Mr. Hesslen is now endeavouring at the heavy expense of three pounds per acre to land-drain his farm . . . The farmers here sow but two sorts of grain for sale, wheat and oats, but you may occasionally find barley, peas or beans for home consumption . . . The southern part of the parish, adjoining Rusper, is particularly poor, not producing on average more than three sacks of wheat or five of oats per acre . . . The distance tenants are obliged to go for manure, the difficulty in getting the harvest home in wet summers, the badness of the roads to market for more than half the year, the great and alarming rise of parochial dues (especially for poor relief), together with the dearness of land, render it the last place in the world I should choose to farm in . . . The landlords, from seldom seeing their estates, keep their cottages in very bad repair . . . It is not without great difficulty and the crowding together of several families in a house that the parishioners can find a shelter either from the summer heat or winter cold. Population has greatly increased but building has not kept pace with it . . . owing to the wetness of the ground there are but few sheep in the parish.

This tells its own story. Farmers just about made a living. The lack of clear distinction between tenant farmers and servants may have been a reason for the strong Nonconformist strain in Ifield, just as the poverty of the labourers in local areas may have led to the founding of a Baptist church in Handcross in 1775. Nonconformity was often a reaction against the Established Church and its support of the stratification of society, and not necessarily only by the labouring poor.

There are, in the county record offices and in the Public Record Office, a number of probate inventories. They are itemised lists of the contents of a house made, for probate reasons, when a person died. These are being transcribed at present and are extremely useful in showing the sort of possessions a farmer, craftsman or tradesman had. They relate both to personal home possessions as well as to items relating to a person's trade. From them we can see that, on the whole, our local population did not amass much personal wealth. Most of the value of a person's estate was in household goods, stock and small quantities of cash. The picture drawn by the vicar of Newdigate was equally valid for the Crawley area fifty years earlier.

General Comments

The 18th century witnessed changes in agriculture; a rapid increase of overseas trade; new inventions and the beginning of steam power were about to revolutionise the industrial pattern of this country; wars were fought in Europe with the Dutch and with France. Across the Atlantic the American colonies became independent; elsewhere, especially in the Far East, British possessions grew. No doubt these were of passing interest to the local population, but for the majority of parishioners life was a hard grind to make a living, and though some of the growing population moved away, and overseas, it was the old and traditional forest, farm and workshop employments which occupied the attention of the local inhabitants.

Perhaps the harsh nature of life was reflected in the increased burden of poor relief in the district. As already described, a new enlarged workhouse was built in Worth in the 1790s. A smaller, earlier one had been built in 1747 on the west side of Ifield Green (it is now

43. Standing on the London Road, half a mile north of the village, this building was used as a workhouse until the 19th century. It is now known as Fir Tree Cottage.

called Tweed Cottage). In Crawley a workhouse was set up in a late 17th-century house (now called Fir Tree Cottage) on the London Road near the present Tushmore roundabout. Little new building took place, but there were many extensions or improvements to farmhouses in the district and virtually every building in the High Street was altered (or improved) between 1750 and 1850. The only good example of Georgian brickwork is to be seen in what until recently was Bastable's Fish Shop at 34 Crawley High Street (which a hundred years ago was a public house called the *Star*).

National events, however, were to leave their long-term mark on the town. An old person who lived through the 18th century would have noticed a very substantial increase in through traffic on the Brighton Road, and the change in use of some local buildings. On the other hand, the work done by the people would have changed little during the century, neither would equipment nor methods. The scenery would not have altered much, though the demand for horses by travellers would have changed the use of many fields along the Brighton Road around Crawley to grazing land. The pace of life was starting to increase, however; it became faster and faster in the 19th century.

Chapter 10

Victorian Prosperity

The stage coach and the prosperous village of Crawley

It might be thought that enough had been said about the Brighton Road to make further comment superfluous, yet this would be to ignore the vital shaping effect it had on the area. The rapid development of Brighton in the late 18th century led to a spurt in the growth of Crawley. Just as a modern motorway service station sucks in a haphazard collection of travellers who seek 'food and shelter and running repairs' for themselves and their transport, so Crawley occupied the same position with regard to 18th-century traffic. Stables, saddlers and smiths were as necessary as inns.

In 1756, there was one stage coach a day from London to Brighton, which cost 16s. (80p) and went via East Grinstead and Lewes. It took a whole day for the journey. By 1790 there were five coaches and six goods wagons which left London each day for the south coast, and which travelled via Crawley. The journey time was between eight and nine hours, and the fare was 18s. In 1815 about thirty coaches a day were using the Brighton Road, as well as a far greater number of private vehicles. The intense competition pushed the average speed up, and companies were advertising a six-hour journey. At its peak in the mid-1830s there were over 20 fare-carrying coaches passing daily through the district in each direction, and the journey time had been reduced to five hours for the most rapid coaches.

Each coach owner had his own named coach and a fixed departure point from London. In 1830, for example, W. Cripps and Co. had two coaches, one named 'The Alert' and the other 'The Emerald'. They departed from the *Yorkshire Stingo* in Paddington at 8 a.m. and 9 a.m. with four passengers inside and 11 outside. The coaches arrived in East Street, Brighton, after a six-hour journey. For the first coach, the journey was via Sutton, Reigate, Crawley, Handcross and Hickstead. The later coach went via Croydon, Purley and Redhill to Crawley, and thence by the same route. George Shillibeer had a coach named 'The Diligence' which left Oxford Street at 10.30 a.m. This used the road via Sutton, Reigate, Horley, Pound Hill, Cuckfield and Hickstead. For the majority of coaches Crawley High Street was the stopping point, although a quarter of the services used the Balcombe Road and stopped at the *King's Head* in Pound Hill. The Horley to Balcombe turnpike, opened in 1809, helped to relieve some of the congestion on the main route through Crawley.

Fierce competition during 1828 drove down the price of the single journey from 21s. to 7s. Not that this was all advantage to the customers. The coaches were driven furiously, drivers were renowned for being reckless or drunk or both, and coaches tended to be overcrowded. Horses only lasted for three or four years on the coach routes before being worked to death. Everybody thought that the inns were overcharging, as they had a monopoly, and the passengers' comfort was a low priority. Some attempts were made to introduce a steam-powered coach: Sir Charles Dance travelled in one from London to Brighton in 1833 at a rate which varied between 10 and 12 m.p.h. The steam coaches, however, were very heavy and met united opposition from both the horse-drawn traffic and the road-owners. The use of steam power for road transport was abandoned, but when special iron tracks were laid we start a new story.

Not only the regular coaches used the roads: they were far outnumbered by private coaches and chaises. It was chaotic at times in Crawley High Street as foot travellers, slow goods wagons, sedate private chaises and fast passenger coaches all tried to pass along in

44. The level crossing, Crawley High Street. A peaceful scene taken in the 1890s, showing the road before the intrusion of the motor-car. The horse-drawn wagon would, to modern eyes, have been more at home in a cowboy film.

both directions. A local joke among the children was 'Which is the longest street in the world?'. The answer was 'Crawley High Street. It has the *Sun* at one end and the *Half Moon* at the other!'.

In *The History of Sussex* by Horsfield, published in 1835, the local villages are dealt with somewhat summarily. Crawley village '. . . is pleasantly situated on the Brighton Road. It consists of one wide street, on the north of which stands a remarkably ancient elm tree . . .'. Ifield village '. . . standing on the south-west of Ifield Green, is in the centre of the parish . . .'. Finally, Worth village '. . . consisting of a few straggling houses is about two miles from Crawley . . . The Inn, formerly the *Kings Arms* at Pound Hill is now converted into a private house, the seat of Mr. Laing. A new inn, called the *Norfolk Arms*, built of Worth Stone, stands by the side of the London Road'. It is curious that at the height of the coach trade one inn should have been closed and a new one built, several miles to the south and in the forest. Did the local landowners object to the coach passengers, or was the inn too small, or was its position — halfway up a steep climb — too inconvenient?

Reference to the Crawley Elm brings us to a well-known landmark of the time. Standing outside the Tree House (hence its name) was what Horsfield called '. . . an exceeding fine and venerable elm'. He quotes another author, Strutt, who wrote about trees in Britain.

> It is well-known to all who are in the habit of travelling that way, and arrests the eye of the stranger at once by its tall straight stem which ascends to the height of 70 feet, and by the fantastic ruggedness

> of its widely spreading roots. Its trunk is perforated to its very top, measuring 61 feet in circumference at the ground, and 35 feet round the inside at two feet from its base.

This tree must have been several hundred years old at that date and, standing outside the manor house, was likely to have been a well-known meeting-place. By 1830 it was hollowed and in its decline, but at its peak is estimated to have been about 130 ft. (40 m.) high. Storms before that date had reduced its stature, and another severe storm in 1883 tore away another section. The final remnant of the elm was cleared away when the New Town arrived: it had taken a long time to die. Many tales are told of how the hollowed inside was used for meetings, to billet soldiers or to house travellers overnight. Its entrance was bricked over and a door inserted. Though now gone, it was remembered with affection by generations of Crawley residents and by travellers.

Some building in the High Street took place during this period. The market stalls which had become shops were expanded, so much so, in fact, that the original wide street became two narrow routeways with open gaps between the central houses, known as Upper, Middle and Lower Squares. During the 18th century some of the timber houses in the High Street had been given brick outer shells which gave extra weatherproofing and a more modern, up-to-date appearance. The trend was continued into the 19th century until only one or two houses retained their old appearance.

More houses were turned into shops, though a survey of 1836 reports only three of the houses as actually being 'shops'. Most early shops developed in the front downstairs rooms of houses, or as a stall in the front garden. Later, the front gardens were built upon, which leaves us today with a, usually, single-storey extension outside an earlier house, as can be seen in the shops facing the roundabout at the end of Haslett Avenue. There used to be one delightful Georgian house, with a bay window, just below the *George*, which was well-known in this century as Camfields the tailors. This building was demolished when the New Town was built.

Other building was taking place either by extending the High Street, or in West Green. There is a row of houses along the south edge of West Green, facing the church, dating from the early 1800s. The records of the Manor of Ifield 'General Court Baron' continue to record the growth of the neighbourhood throughout the 19th century. For example, on 11 June 1827:

> William Lidbetter of the parish of Ifield hath inclosed a small Parcel of Land lying on the waste situate on the South Side of the Road leading from the Town of Crawley to the Village of Ifield adjoining the farm called Goffshill and opposite the farm called Ewhurst Place containing about eighteen Rods and built a cottage thereon . . .

Again, on 3 May 1833, we learn that:

> Thomas Brown . . . hath made an encroachment upon the waste of the said Manor . . . and erected and built a Wheelwrights Shop and a Shop used by a Shoemaker . . . and a Cottage with a Butchers Shop and a Stable attached and a Bullock pound and a small yard behind . . . on the West Side of the Ifield Green nearly opposite the Old Plough Public House.

Four years later, another meeting of the court recognised that James Bristow, farmer and miller, had taken over some waste ground on Ifield Green and erected a windmill there. Population growth had encouraged him to increase the cornmilling capacity of the district supplementing that provided by Ifield watermill, which was itself rebuilt in 1817. This may suggest that many of the farmers were growing wheat in Ifield, even though the land is not really suited to it. It was a response, no doubt, to market demand. In Britain as a whole there was an increase in wheat consumption in the early years of the century, and farming had benefited by improved drainage made possible by the production of cheap mass-produced clay pipes, and more iron or steel for implements, including ploughs, harrows and rollers. James Bristow later, in 1844, built a blacksmith's shop on the edge of the Green.

It is possible to trace the population growth of the area quite clearly as a result of the institution of an official national census, taken at 10-year intervals, in 1801. The table opposite shows the population of Ifield, Crawley and Worth — and four neighbouring parishes — during the early 19th century, and the housing stock during the same period.

45. A late 19th-century view of the shops in Crawley High Street now facing Haslett Avenue. These shops had all been built on front gardens. Vine Cottage, the home of Mark Lemon, is the building on the right. Note that each shop needed blinds to prevent its displays fading.

These figures are interesting pointers to the area's general prosperity during the first 30 years of the century. The population of the parish of Worth was always larger than that of Crawley and Ifield combined. In these 30 years the population of Worth grew by 23 per cent, that of Ifield (remember, that includes half of Crawley village) by 44 per cent, and of Crawley by 88 per cent. Obviously it was urban development which became most important. The previously quoted entry in the Ifield manorial court had expressed local perceptions by using the descriptions 'the *Town* of Crawley' but 'the *Village* of Ifield'.

Census Returns for Seven Local Parishes

Parish	Population				Occupied Housing Stock			
	1801	1811	1821	1831	1801	1811	1821	1831
Worth	1,501	1,539	1,725	1,859	194	288	264	303
Crawley	210	234	334	394	26	41	51	66
Ifield	637	654	758	916	73	94	111	146
Total	2,348	2,427	2,817	3,169	293	423	426	515
Burstow	606	601	715	736	103	103	106	139
Horley	871	942	1,063	1,164	140	148	176	166
Charlwood	860	959	1,134	1,176	136	158	156	159
Rusper	399	450	487	531	67	72	69	86
Total	2,736	2,952	3,399	3,607	446	481	507	550

At the same time, the housing stock increased at an even faster rate, by 56 per cent in Worth, 100 per cent in Ifield and 154 per cent in Crawley. Overcrowding was lessened. From the census we find that in 1801 there were 2.0 families per house on average in Crawley, compared to 1.1 per house in Ifield and Worth. The average number of people per house in the three parishes combined fell from 8.0 in 1801 to 6.2 in 1831. This all points to the fact that money was being invested in the housing stock of the locality at a faster rate than the population was growing.

Comparison can next be made with the four adjoining, but more rural, parishes. Their population for the 30-year period grew by about 32 per cent (the combined growth for our three parishes was 35 per cent), but their housing stock only rose by 23 per cent, compared with the growth in our three parishes of 76 per cent. Conditions in Charlwood clearly deteriorated, and only in Burstow did the average house occupancy fall. In these four parishes the landowners either lacked the money or the inclination to improve housing conditions.

One last piece of information from the census returns: not surprisingly, of the seven parishes Crawley had the lowest percentage of population engaged in agriculture, and the highest engaged in trade. In fact, it was the only parish with more families earning a living from trade than from agriculture. It is likely, given the population statistics, that the actual village of Crawley doubled in population over the 30 years. Much of that increase would be accounted for by inward migration. Large numbers of young men and women having been drawn in to satisfy the labour market, the number of marriages then rose. In Britain at this time much internal migration was short distance. The young servants resident in Crawley were likely to have been mostly locals.

Elsewhere in the area we see an early example of the changes to be encountered in the 19th century. The Hon. Thomas Erskine, a son of a famous lawyer and eventual Lord Chancellor, bought a large estate in the detached part of Crawley parish and in Lower Beeding, near to Pease Pottage. He built there, in the early 1800s, a large mansion which he named Buchan Hill after his father, the Earl of Buchan. The house (now Cottesmore School), garden and the estate required an army of servants to keep it up. There were, in 1801, only two modest mansions in the area — Crabbett Park and Rowfant House — but during the ensuing century mansions loomed large in the local economy.

A military-inspired census looked at the number of livestock in the locality in 1801, as part of the planning concerned with the Napoleonic Wars. It gives a snapshot of the differences in farming pattern between the eastern and the western parts of the Crawley area.

Parish	No. of Cattle	No. of Sheep	No. of Pigs	No. of Draft Horses	No. of Draft Oxen
Worth	492	1,045	300	110	30
Ifield	235	200	185	102	10
Crawley	31	18	53	25	0

Worth still had a mainly pastoral economy, and in particular had a large number of sheep. Yet both Ifield and Worth had approximately the same number of draft horses, which reflects the importance of arable farming to the Ifield farmers. Crawley probably had a different use for its draft horses, not necessarily connected with agricultural work; in fact, in comparative terms, Crawley for its size had the most horses. It had the Brighton Road.

It is also apparent that the method of taxation, still being land-based, favoured the urbanised areas. For example, the populations of Charlwood, of Horley and of Crawley/Ifield combined were broadly equal in size in 1815, that is about a thousand persons. Yet the rate assessment for that year was £5,079 for Charlwood, £6,421 for Horley, but only £2,991 for Crawley/Ifield. This is unlikely to have reflected the true distribution of wealth and income in the district.

After Waterloo, when Europe resumed a peaceful existence (for a while at least), there was a very depressed period for agriculture. Farm prices fell. Rural parishes felt this keenly, and the amount given in the Wealden region for poor relief rose sharply. Demands for a rise in agricultural wages and to cease the use of labour-saving farm machinery were widespread in southern England. No wonder that a steam coach was unwelcome! The agricultural changes of the previous century and the subsequent war boom had left a rural society where the main link between farmers and labourers was wages. Equally, the link between farmers and landowners was also cash, in the form of rent, though a more remote connection.

Inevitably, there was much discontent. The labourers could face their employers and demand more pay: the farmers and small shopkeepers found it more difficult to see their landlords and ask for a rent reduction. Instead, they complained about the church tithes and the Poor Rate, which were additional expenses. There was rioting and breaking of agricultural machinery by agricultural workers throughout Sussex in 1830, carried out in the name of a mythical Captain Swing. On 18 November there was a noisy meeting in the parish church at Horsham where hundreds of farmworkers forced the assembled householders and gentry to agree a basic daily rate of pay of 2s. 6d. (12½p). They were supported in this by the farmers who in turn called for lower tithes and rates. The church and churchyard were damaged. A local man reported the next day 'Today the mob is gone to Shipley and Rusper'. From this time onwards there was an increasing gulf between town and country. The differing experiences of the tenant farmers and owner-farmers on the one hand, and the village professional men, craftsmen and shopkeepers on the other, led to a separation of interests.

Crawley village became even more socially distinct from its agricultural hinterland at this time. Whereas until the 19th century agricultural workers were also part-time manufacturers, from then onwards we meet clear distinctions developing between, for example, farmers and butchers, agricultural workers and cloth workers, Crawley folk and the neighbouring countrymen. There were many self-employed in the village, who could not rely on wages and poor relief supplements in the same way as farm workers could. Shopkeepers, carters, innkeepers, craftsmen, these were the people who formed a Friendly Society, with its early form of savings plan and sickness pay, in Crawley in 1827.

In 1834, the Poor Law Amendment Act abolished individual parish workhouses and created Unions of Parishes instead, supervised by Boards of Guardians. Ifield and Crawley parishes were part of the Horsham Union. At first, to save money, it was decided to concentrate the poor in particular buildings. In October 1835 it was agreed that the able-bodied would be lodged in Horsham workhouse, the aged and infirm would be sent to Shipley, female children would go to West Grinstead, male children to Ifield. Consequently, families were split up if they needed relief.

It was soon found that Ifield and West Grinstead workhouses were too small and inconvenient for the numbers seeking relief, so the plan was changed; all children went to Shipley and the aged and infirm were sent to Warnham. Unfortunately Shipley, too, became overcrowded. Many children died because epidemics spread easily in the cramped conditions. Fear of more agricultural uprisings led to the construction of a large new building at Horsham to hold all the poor in one workhouse. It is now part of the Forest Hospital in the Crawley Road in Horsham.

Meanwhile, the East Grinstead Union (containing Worth parish) met with similar problems: the Guardians there were faced with a riot when over 50 labourers armed with stout sticks assembled from Ardingly and Worth parishes and threatened them over their administration of Poor Relief. It was not possible to please everyone; reducing the amount paid in social relief may delight the tax and ratepayers, but causes much distress for the poor when their benefits are reduced, particularly when there are many poor.

There were distractions to the hard life of the times. Prize-fighting continued at Copthorne Common (or Crawley Common as it was sometimes called) and at Crawley Down, and the locals could enjoy the free entertainment. Prize-fighters were equivalent to the pop-stars of today — as had been Dick Turpin and Jack Sheppard, the highwaymen. In December 1810 there was a famous fight when Tom Cribb, the British champion, beat Tom Molyneux, an American negro. John Keats' friends attempted to distract him in 1819 when his brother died by persuading him to go to a fight at Crawley Down. William Cobbett enjoyed prize-fighting: he lived in the area from time to time and wrote his famous book *Rural Rides* whilst staying at Worth Hall farmhouse. Seemingly lawlessness was approved of by the masses; no wonder that smuggling and prize-fighting went hand in hand. Fights continued locally until the early 1820s. The magistrates in Kent, Surrey and Sussex were supposedly less opposed to pugilism than those in other counties surrounding London. Later, when Sir Arthur Conan Doyle wrote a book, *Rodney Stone*, about prize-fighting, it was set partly in Crawley and Copthorne. However, his artistic licence changed the geography of Sussex, as readers of the book have discovered.

For less bloodthirsty sportsmen, cricket was available. Ifield Cricket Club was formed, it is believed, in about 1804. Unfortunately, most of the club records were lost in a fire, but there are isolated references to local matches. In the early 1800s there was a match at Lovel (Lowfield) Heath which was remembered because one player, Morley, of the Sussex XI was in for two hours and only scored one run! Cricket was a sport which, with Gentlemen and Players, united all social classes in one team. In time most country houses in the district had a team. Usually they were captained by one of the family from the house, and most players were estate workers and servants. For some talented but lower-class players, a servant's post was doubtless the equivalent of today's American University sports' scholarship.

The other pastimes — upper-class this time — which could be indulged in were hunting and shooting. Only landowners were permitted, under a law passed in 1389, to hunt with dogs, or even to keep ferrets. By 1603 this had become interpreted as lords of manors and wealthy freeholders or leaseholders. From 1671, gamekeepers could be appointed to take game, and a law of 1710 reiterated that lords of manors or their gamekeepers could hunt game (for example, hares, partridge, pheasants, grouse) but no-one else. In part this may explain why, in documents, a farm will from time to time be called a 'manor'. It was not in the legal sense a manor as was understood by the term in medieval England. The name 'manor' was applied to enable a farmer or estate owner to grant himself powers of hunting and then to appoint one of his friends as 'gamekeeper' to share the pleasure. There is a long list of 'Gamekeeper Deputations' which gives the names of those appointed locally between the 1780s and 1840 (it appears in the S.R.S. Vol. 51). Some are clearly friends (for example,

Thos. Dennett, Esq., of Ifield appointed John Henry Dungate, Gent., surgeon) and some really are gamekeepers (for example, Francis Blunt of Worth appointed Rowland Connap, his servant).

Finally, mention should be made of the Crawley and Horsham Hunt. This was founded by Mr. Lee Steere in about 1832, when he was still a young undergraduate. There is a recorded succession of masters, and the hounds have been kennelled at Warninglid,

46. A meeting of the Crawley and Horsham Hunt outside the *Plough* at Ifield. The present public house was built on the site of the stables, next to the old building, in about 1900.

Staplefield and West Grinstead. The hunt still meets, though rarely in the Crawley area; nowadays it meets more often in Worth Forest and St Leonard's Forest and their surrounding farmland to the south and west of Crawley.

One strange event during these years publicised the Crawley area for strictly non-sporting reasons. There was a doctor in Lewes who was also a keen amateur geologist, named Dr. Gideon Mantell. He and his wife often went looking at geological sites, particularly searching for fossils. In 1822 his wife found some fossilised teeth in Tilgate

Forest, near to Crawley. Mantell recognised that they came from a very large, extinct animal, and continued to search. He was told that the teeth resembled closely those of an iguana.

This was a time when the theory of the existence of long-extinct reptiles was gaining acceptance — long before Darwin wrote about the evolution of life forms and so offended many Christians. Mantell called the creature an Iguanadon, one of three fossil reptiles which were grouped together eventually in 1841 and named 'Dinosaurs'. He probably did not dream that the fossils could be from creatures which had died over 65 million years ago, but the scientific study of palaeontology began in Tilgate.

Mention has previously been made of the local post service delivering to Crawley from East Grinstead in 1791. When the Royal Mail coach service from London to Brighton was set up in 1810, Crawley itself became a post town. The Royal Mail coach, though not quite as fast as some scheduled coaches, always had priority on the road. Toll-gates had to be opened in advance, hence the post-horn to warn toll-gate keepers. Horses had to be changed at the post-town and the man who had already been working as a receiver of letters, James Swift, was appointed the first postmaster. Until 1829 the recipient of a letter had to pay a penny before being allowed the delivery, but from that date the sender only paid.

When James Swift resigned in 1838 his nephew William Mitchell (a tailor) was appointed postmaster, and he it was who first sold the new Penny Postage stamps to the village in 1840. The first postage stamp cancellations were a Maltese Cross. Later, each post office was given a number and the postmarks were oval, partly shaded and contained that number. Crawley post office used '228' as its cancellation. The office (since demolished) was on the north side of the *White Hart*, where there is now a passageway to Crossways. This is a good example of a family keeping a job to itself: William Mitchell retired in 1876 to be succeeded by his son Charles Mitchell, who worked as postmaster — and moved to the new post office in Robinson Road — until he retired in 1908. Three generations of the same family were postmasters for a hundred years!

The final word can be left to the *Pigot Directory* of 1832. Of Crawley it states:

> . . . it derives its sole importance from its great thoroughfare situation, and the inns afford every facility to the traveller . . . The town possesses nothing attractive but its neighbourhood is ornamented by a number of tasteful and elegant villas, upon parts of Tilgate forest, adjoining the Cuckfield Road.

The Railway — and the transformation of the forest areas

During the early 1800s canal building was still taking place all over Britain. Fear of attack by the French ships had led to the construction of the Royal Military Canal. There was much talk, during the French wars, of constructing a canal to connect the Chatham dockyard with the Portsmouth dockyard. Plans were drawn up and lodged in Parliament for a canal which would follow the Medway up to Turners Hill, then cross the Worth and St Leonard's Forests, to join the Arun south of Horsham. The engineering would have been difficult, and there were worries about the water supply at its highest point, near to Crawley. Eventually the wars ceased and the plan was dropped, though the Wey and Arun Canal was built.

The Surrey Iron Railway, from Wandsworth to Croydon, was opened in 1803. Two years later it was extended over the North Downs to stone quarries at Merstham. This horse-drawn railway was originally conceived as a canal using the River Wandle. During the French wars there were proposals to extend it to Portsmouth, and other proposals followed at intervals, including one to extend it as far as Brighton. Nothing came of all this, however, and so Crawley had to wait a few more years.

When, in the 1830s, steam railways were seen to be viable, it was obviously only a matter of time before one would be built from Brighton to London. The first bill to be brought

47. The new Post Office building in the 1890s. A small cul-de-sac leading from the High Street by the railway line was renamed Post Office Road when this red-brick building was erected, facing the British School.

before parliament was in 1836. Five separate schemes were presented and very large sums of money spent by the proponents of each scheme. The least-expensive presentation cost £16,500 and the dearest cost £72,000. Only one scheme was to be accepted.

Why was parliament involved? There were two main reasons. First, a joint stock company was needed to raise the share capital required, and this needed parliamentary approval. Second, the route approved was effectively a compulsory purchase order on the land, though much negotiation was subsequently required to agree the price to be paid. The successful scheme was that presented by the London, Brighton and South Coast Railway (L.B.S.C.R.) though part of its route required shared facilities, such as Redhill station, with the London, South-East and Chatham Railway (L.S.E.C.R.).

The objections to the scheme were of three main types. There were the farmers who did not want a noisy, dirty engine upsetting their farm animals. (Later the farmers discovered the benefits which the railways brought to their land.) Then there were the landowners and estate owners who wished for their mansions to remain in rural peace. Finally there were the town and village dwellers who feared closer contact with London, and in particular the roadside businesses and transport operators that feared a loss of income. These latter did have cause to worry.

Five years of planning and action followed. It is still a marvel to consider the tremendous civil engineering feats performed by men who used only spades and barrows to bore tunnels, construct bridges, dig cuttings and build embankments so that the railway could be as flat as possible.

On 12 July 1841 the first L.B.S.C.R. train ran from Croydon to Haywards Heath. A

48. Three Bridges Station and engine sheds.

station was built at Three Bridges, elevated upon an embankment, and at first it was called East Crawley station. The task of crossing, or rather tunnelling beneath, the Downs took a little longer to complete. Finally, on 21 September 1841 the first train containing passengers for London left Brighton at 6.45 a.m. The first to leave London departed at 9.45 a.m. on the same day and comprised 13 carriages. The passengers included the company directors and their friends, and they arrived at Brighton at 12.15 p.m.

There are still some older people in the Crawley area who, as children, were given eye-witness accounts of the first train, by older relatives who were themselves children at the time. All the stations on the line were decked with flags. Three years later, on Easter Monday 1844, the first excursion train ran to Brighton. When it left London Bridge at 9 a.m. it consisted of 45 carriages drawn by four engines. Both at New Cross and at Croydon stations, six more carriages and one more engine were added. The entire collection arrived at Brighton at 1.30 p.m. The normal journey time, however, was 90 minutes for the two first-class trains a day, two hours for the four first-and second-class trains and two-and-a-half hours for the two all-class trains. A writer in the *Illustrated London News* later in 1844 made the point that he was not one of those who regretted the good old coaching days and the roadside inns: '. . . now the chances are, we are comfortably housed in Brighton before, under the *ancien regime*, our vehicle would have clattered up to the *Greyhound* at Croydon'.

Although they did not do so immediately, it did not take the public long to realise that the railways were faster, more comfortable, safer, cleaner and ultimately cheaper than the stagecoach. Soon the plans to connect Horsham with the Brighton line were made: their townsfolk must have felt snubbed in that East Crawley had a station whereas Horsham did not. There was a proposal to branch off at Horley and run a line via Lowfield Heath, north of Ifield and down through Faygate. Eventually, however, Three Bridges became the junction and the present line was opened in February 1848. Crawley village itself benefited and got a station where the railway crossed the High Street at the southern edge of the village. This meant providing a level crossing, which is as inconvenient now as it must have been 140 years ago, and further ones were needed on the Horsham Road and on Goffs Lane in West Green. A fourth level crossing was at Ifield.

Finally, the line to East Grinstead was constructed. This opened on 9 July 1855. The owner of the Rowfant estate negotiated for a station to be provided close to Rowfant House, and for the right to stop a fast train at Three Bridges to connect with the branch line if the family wished to travel to and from London. Another station was provided at Grange Road to serve the Copthorne and Crawley Down area, though because of a dispute with the owner of The Grange this did not open until 1860.

The busy junction at Three Bridges transformed the small hamlet, which straggled along Crawley Lane near a crossroads at Hazelwick Mill pond. New Street was built, and North Road, to provide cottages for the railway workers. A public house was erected by the station, from which travellers could hire a pony and chaise to reach parts of Worth. This was the foundation for a taxi and garage business. Three Bridges station had large sidings and a railway shed. Engines started and finished their shifts at Three Bridges; the railwaymen needed to live very close to the station to get to and from work at unsocial hours. There was talk of building a locomotive works there, but Brighton was selected instead. Later, in the early 1900s, a carriage works was set up at Lancing. Had either been located at Three Bridges, and this was a strong possibility in each case, the area would have developed quite differently.

Obviously, the impact of the railway on the district was considerable. If nothing else, the level crossing at the end of Crawley High Street caused a traffic delay when one of the half a dozen trains a day passed through. Until the Crawley by pass was opened, the main Brighton Road crossed the railway here. During the 1930s there could be queues over a mile long of stationary traffic, coaches and cars, trying to get through Crawley on a Bank Holiday. For the tradespeople in Crawley the effect must have been marked. Even though the road still produced some traffic, the volume of passing trade faded. But in its place came more local trade. The railway enabled cheap building materials, including softwoods, slates and coal, to be brought in. West Green in particular, but Crawley in general, expanded around the station. The area turned in on itself and generated its own growth.

The railway had been laid at the southern edge of the village of Crawley. Thereafter, building was close to the railway. Leopold Road, Albany Road, Princess Road and Victoria Road have names which were often given in England at this time. (In 1881 Queen Victoria's son, Prince Leopold, was created duke of Albany.) Spencers Road was named after Spenser Smith who owned the shop on the corner of the High Street and the Ifield Road. Houses sprang up along the Brighton Road, and East Park and Springfield Road were begun. Not only were new houses built along the Three Bridges Road but also in Church Lane, Worth. Others were erected around Ifield Green, and up the hill from Ifield Halt. They displayed the new fashion for slate roofs, and cheap bricks from the east Midlands, breaking away from the traditional Sussex bricks and tiles.

Local and cross-country traffic continued to use the road — and still does. Gideon Mantell kept a diary and in 1843 he recorded some of his journeys. One day he travelled from Winchester to London by train in three hours. On the next he started off to return to his Lewes home in his coach. Leaving London at 11.30 a.m. he records '. . . went to Crawley, arrived at four and dined. This little town is quite desolate from the Brighton railroad. With difficulty obtained a beefsteak for our dinner'. Eventually he reached Cuckfield at 7.30 p.m. and stayed '. . . a thoroughly wet and stormy night . . .'.

The coach trade gave the initial impetus to Crawley's growth. Once it had vanished the village at first lost income, but then picked up again. From about 1850 it resumed expansion, though not because of the passing traffic. One explanation is that the quick rail access to London brought more London-based folk to the area. A good example is seen in the burst of country house building.

To the west was Holmbush and the Broadwood family. Buchan Park had become a large residence housing a judge; Tilgate Forest Lodge was the home of Sugden, the Lord Chancellor of Ireland. The Joliffes, and later the Nix family, transformed Tilgate House itself, the building being designed by an eminent Victorian country house architect. Paddockhurst was a grand mansion built by Robert Whitehead, who invented the torpedo. Later, the house was sold to Sir Weetman Pearson who became the first Lord Cowdray. Both Crabbett Park with the Blunt family, and Rowfant House with the Locker-Lampsons (a fusion of the cultured Lockers with the American-born Sir Curtis Lampson, a rich businessman) had houses with a longer history, as we have seen. Broadfield House was built in 1830 and Worth Park House was purchased by Sir Joseph Montefiore, a wealthy London banker, in about 1850. The original house was destroyed by fire in 1853, but a larger mansion was built to replace it, completed in about 1860.

The Worth Park mansion and estate illustrate in many ways the typical lifestyle of the rich in the locality. The house contained 10 reception rooms and 10 bedrooms for the family and guests. The stable quadrangle, still in existence by Milton Mount flats, had accommodation for 18 carriages. The lodge gate — now a dentist's — can be seen at the junction of Worth Park Avenue and Worth Road; Worth Park Avenue with its line of trees was the drive to the house. The lodge was only a few hundred yards from Three Bridges station. The whole estate comprised over 2,000 acres (including 15 farms let to tenant farmers), and more than 20 gardeners were employed in the grounds. Tilgate House also had a very long drive built across its estate to a lodge gate (now a bank), also only a few hundred yards from Three Bridges station.

The wealthy and famous from many walks of life — industry, commerce, society, the arts, politics — visited these houses. The one with the most romantic story was that occupied by Wilfred Scawen Blunt (a great-great-great-grandson of Leonard Gale) who married Lady Anne (a granddaughter of Lord Byron). Wilfred inherited the estate at Crabbett Park and the couple moved in during the spring of 1873. He was a poet, a sculptor, a man who supported many political causes, an intrepid traveller. He and his wife travelled widely in the Middle East to look for and buy pure-bred Arab horses. The Crabbett Arabian stud became world famous and until the 1970s it was a common sight to see Arab horses grazing in the fields alongside the Turners Hill Road and by Frogshole Farm. His life, and his poetry, can be enjoyed all the more by readers who know the Worth countryside which Blunt loved.

One final example of the character of the neighbourhood can be shown in the number of names worthy of listing in each parish. The 1855 directory shows:

49. In the 1920s a girls' boarding school, Milton Mount College, occupied Worth Park Mansion. The site is now that of a block of flats, which has enabled the council to retain the formal gardens. The balustraded staircase still remains.

CRAWLEY:	Gentry, 6	Traders, 47	(inc. Farmer, 1)
IFIELD :	Gentry, 5	Traders, 27	(inc. Farmers, 17)
WORTH :	Gentry, 22	Traders, 75	(inc. Farmers, 22)

Worth, the largest area, had by far the majority of the local gentry. It also contained the largest area of population growth, hence the number of traders. But Ifield was still proportionally the strongest farming community.

Ifield had its old farms, and larger houses for successful tradespeople. The wealthy folk who moved into the parish seem to have invested money in the farms and improved the buildings, the land, the stock and even the labourers' cottages. It is as if Ifield retained its agricultural image. No doubt the rich could enjoy the 'tax loss' element of spending money on a farm to avoid paying income tax on it.

Crawley developed its urban society mainly through the efforts of one man — Mark Lemon. He had been born in 1809, became a writer and in 1841 was appointed first editor of *Punch*. In 1858 he moved to Crawley and bought Vine Cottage in the High Street, a former farmhouse just north of the level crossing: the building is still visible behind the shop-fronts facing the end of Haslett Avenue. Crawley was very convenient for him, an easy rail journey to London Bridge and so to Fleet Street. He was an energetic, gregarious man, and became the centre of local society. During his years in Crawley he helped to found a cricket club, a rifle club, army volunteers, and a fire brigade.

He helped to organise relief for the poor, especially at Christmas, when money raised at winter concerts was used to give soup during cold weather, and gifts of beef, bread, flour and coal on New Year's Day. When Edward, Prince of Wales, married Princess Alexandra in 1863, he helped to organise the celebration with a dinner of roast beef and plum-pudding for 50 poor people at each of three inns (the *George*, the *White Hart*, the *Station Hotel*), a band concert in the Squares, field sports behind the *White Hart*, fireworks in the evening and a dance at the *George*. Mark Lemon was a large man; when he attended Crawley church, instead of his parish church at Ifield, he had to sit in the gallery where there was the only pew large enough to hold him. When he died in 1870, all the village shops closed and hundreds attended his funeral procession to St Margaret's church.

His family also set up a shop in their High Street house, and subsequently built premises on the front garden (*see* Ill. 45). Some measure of the increase in retail outlets can be shown in that while the 1845 *Kelly's Guide* lists 32 shopkeepers in Crawley, the 1855 version lists 39, and the 1882 *Trade Guide* 49; since the 1797 directory only listed 10 tradespeople, the growth is clear. Whereas in 1797 much of the village street comprised houses occupied by labourers and farmers, by 1882 there was a large, local shopping centre in the High Street. A gas works was built in about 1855, the gas-holder being on the corner of the London Road and Kilnmead. Crawley and Ifield parish councils got together to arrange gas lighting for the High Street. To underline this attempt at unity, it can be added that the Crawley and Ifield Co-operative Society was founded in 1868.

50. Mark Lemon, first editor of *Punch*, which he produced for thirty years. For most of that time he lived in Crawley. He died in his 61st year on 23 May 1870.

The large country estates provided much employment for the areas around the village, as well as custom for the shopkeepers. Another source of employment was the building industry. Both small builders, who were willing to put up houses on the number of building sites being sold off piecemeal, and the two large building companies needed men. The industry was labour intensive. Richard Cook was established in West Street, and his order books reveal the variety of work he carried out. He built houses, but was also involved in such diverse jobs as the wall around Ifield churchyard (1886), alterations to the school at Handcross (1887), the stables for the new Gatwick racecourse (1890), the *Gate Inn* at Ifield (1890) and St Peter's church, West Green (1892).

The largest firm, however, was James Longley's. He bought a small brickworks at Malthouse Farm, just by the railway station in Crawley, and in 1881 moved to the East Park site from Turners Hill, where he had started work. The family home, The Beeches, was built on the site of the old brickworks for James Longley, who died, aged 79, in 1915. His grandson, Sir Norman Longley, still lives there. This company built many houses (for example, most of Malthouse Road) but were especially noted for churches and for railway work for the L.B.S.C.R. There are few of this company's stations which Longley's did not either build or extend. By 1898 the company employed over 700 men, and was confident enough to tender for very large contracts. It built, for example, Graylingwell Hospital at Chichester and Christ's Hospital at Horsham.

The problem about working on a Longley's site last century was that the workplace was likely to be a long way from Crawley, and many would live away from home during the week. A good example of the hard nature of this work can be seen in the contract to build the King Edward VII Sanatorium at Midhurst in 1903. The site was a five-mile walk from Midhurst Station, and the workmen had to start work at 6 a.m. each day.

The local paper in 1867 carried a report by a writer who had known the 'delightful little town' in its coaching days, and recalled that after the railways had come '. . . Crawley subsided into a dull, quiet and almost deserted village'. But he had now revisited the place and found a change.

> We learn that the price of land has greatly advanced, and that considerable quantities have been sold or let for building and houses are already springing up. A field adjoining the Station has, within the last few days, been laid out in plots for building, a great part of which was at once disposed of . . . We are gratified at observing that the houses already erected . . . on the Brighton Road, are built in a style, both substantial and ornamental, reflecting credit alike on the proprietors, the architects and the locality.

That our area remained prosperous can also be shown by the work done to the three parish churches. The local paper, in May 1878, reported a speech by the rector of Crawley: 'For some time past the congregations in Crawley church, at evening service, have been so large, many people being unable to obtain seats, that it has been evident that an enlargement of the church is a necessity'. He wanted to create space for an extra 200 seats by building a large north aisle and removing the old gallery, and to improve the lighting, ventilation and general convenience of the building. The cost was estimated at £1,600. In July 1882 another speech was reported: 'Speaking of the Church restoration work he must say that there was not one of those stones which go to make up that building they would willingly have destroyed . . . [but] they must make their church, when altered, convenient and adaptable to modern conditions'. On the whole, despite some opposition, the work was carried out with taste.

Worth church was altered in 1871, and 'repairs' made to the west and the north walls, the chancel and the south transept. In this case the building work led to a chorus of complaints from architects, historians and archaeological societies. During the building work some Saxon features were uncovered; some were destroyed and some were inserted. There were many letters published at the time which forcefully supported one of two points of view. On one hand, '. . . the dangerous conditions of the walls has been more and more exhibited . . . we cannot but rejoice that the evil has been detected in time . . . without destroying the old walls'. The massive buttresses which had over the centuries been added around the building, in particular supporting the chancel, were removed. On the other hand there are statements like: '. . . it is an outrage that the chancel is vanished clean away . . . the desecration of the place . . . the mischief done . . . the disfigurement by a recent restoration. . .'. The present bell-tower was also built at that time.

Ifield church was also altered three times during this period. The roof was repaired in 1847, and a new vestry was built. (Oak for this came from the famous County Oak landmark that was taken down at the time.) A bell turret was put over the porch. In the 1870s heating was installed. Finally, in 1883 the present tower was built, the old gallery removed and new pews installed.

It seems that in each parish the church repairs took a different form, reflecting the character of the neighbourhood. The farming parish paid up quietly, improved conditions for the worshippers and proceeded without fuss or controversy. The urban parish went ahead with publicity and pride, and increased its capacity. The gentrified parish spent the most,

51. Before organs were universal, church music was often led by a small choir accompanied by a few woodwind or string instruments. Ifield church had a choir loft, now demolished.

and engendered the largest chorus of disapproval from other strong-minded rich, cultured and important persons.

There were new denominations among the churches. A Strict Baptist chapel was built in 1858 at the far end of what is now Robinson Road. The Catholic Church returned to the area in 1859 after a break of 300 years. The Congregational church was also built in Robinson Road and the Baptist church in Station Road: these came in the 1870s and 1880s. An Evangelical church was started for Three Bridges in 1875.

The final church development towards the end of the century completed the circle. In the Church of England itself there were two contrary movements, known sometimes as High Church and Low Church. Crawley church was quite definitely Low Church. The Revd. John Barratt Leonard, who became rector of St John's in 1867, was a strong but unorthodox parson. He was a good advertisement for what was elsewhere called 'muscular Christianity'. Sometimes he walked to Brighton, then along the Downs, before walking home. During the week he dressed in grey tweeds and only wore his clerical collar on Sundays. For 22 years he was rector; he it was who carved much of the ornamental woodwork in the new chancel.

For those living on the west side of the High Street, the parish church, St Margaret's at Ifield, was remote. In a move mirroring that which had happened 700 years earlier, a chapel attached to the parish church and dedicated to St Mary Magdalene was built in Alpha Road in West Green. Some parishioners wanted a High Church chapel, but the diocese of

52. St Francis of Assisi church, the original Catholic church, built in the second half of the 19th century. It was capable of holding a large congregation.

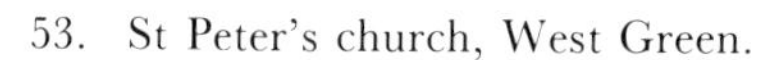

53. St Peter's church, West Green.

Chichester would not spend the money to build one. Consequently a church was built by private subscription, dedicated to St Peter, and offered to the church authorities. They accepted it and in 1892 the church was established; 10 years later a new ecclesiastical parish of West Crawley was carved out of the eastern part of Ifield parish. The former chapel became the church hall and has now been demolished.

As a counter-balance to the growth of the Churches, other aspects of life were also changing. Perhaps the real long-term effect of the railway was to take some of the local emphasis away from the Brighton Road and place it on the hinterland of the railway. The former rather desolate areas of Worth started to open up. The road from Crawley to East Grinstead got busier, and the rather vague area of Copthorne was, as a result, given a definite village setting.

Parcels of Copthorne Common were built upon as many small enclosures took place, the first settlers putting down roots near to the *Abergavenny Arms*. Then, in 1855, much of the common, in particular the Surrey portion, was enclosed leaving the present pattern of fragmented pieces of common land still remaining. A school and a church were built at Copthorne Bank. The church of St John the Evangelist was opened in 1877 and replaced an earlier temporary chapel.

The railway to East Grinstead provided a station at Grange Road in Crawley Down. The growth of this settlement began early in the 19th century with one or two pleasant houses. The demand for bricks led to a brickworks being set up near to the present *Prizefighters* public house, originally named the *Royal Oak*. As the population grew, a church, All Saints, was erected. The railway subsequently attracted a number of wealthy businessmen to the area, who built houses such as Tiltwood and Down Park. The multiplier effect was thereafter seen at both Copthorne and Crawley Down.

In the 1861 census there is reference, in the Sussex volume, to developments in Worth. It states:

> Crawley Down, Tilgate Forest, Old House Warren, Pound Hill, Rickman's Green, Copthorne, Wakeman's Green and Turners Hill are in Worth. The increase in population in this parish is attributed partly to the extension of railway communication, and partly to some woodlands having been cleared and brought into a state of cultivation, causing a slight increase of agricultural labourers.

So the censuses for Worth show:

1831	1851	1871	1881
1,859 people	2,475 people	3,209 people	3,571 people

In the Sussex volume, the 1881 figure is broken down into: Worth, St Nicholas parish — 1,615 persons; Copthorne, St John the Evangelist parish (from 1871) — 620 persons; Crawley Down, All Saints Parish (from 1826) — 1,336 persons. In 1831 there were 303 houses in all of Worth. By 1881 the number was 674, distributed thus: Worth, 308; Copthorne, 115; and Crawley Down, 251. At long last, the expanse of Worth parish had been more intensively settled. In fact, an 1858 Sussex gazetteer (Melville and Co.) listed all the 10 public houses in Worth parish. The list was dominated by those only recently built:

Plough	Three Bridges	*Abergavenny Arms*	Copthorne
Fox	Three Bridges	*Dukes Head*	Copthorne
Kings Head	Pound Hill	*Norfolk Arms*	Worth
Blue Anchor	Pound Hill	*Red Lion*	Turners Hill
Prince Albert	Copthorne	*Crown*	Turners Hill

The public house adjacent to Grange Road station in Crawley Down was built after 1860. In the same gazetteer, Ifield had only the *Plough* listed; Crawley High Street had the *George*, *White Hart* and *Station Inn* (the old *Sun* was just a beer shop).

Worth parish was, in truth, at last at the same position that Ifield parish had been over 800 years earlier. This time, however, the colonists who were creating homes out of the forest land had more money to spend, hence the public houses.

It could be said that Worth parish had more than its fair share of places in which to drink. But to give another view of this we can look at a Temperance Society advertisement in the Horsham newspaper of January 1877: 'Behold the town of Horsham, 60 Public Houses and beer shops, 3 breweries, 4 Refreshment Rooms, 3 Wine-dealing Grocers, 4 Spirit Dealers, i.e. 74 Drink Shops for 10,000 inhabitants.' Horsham had proportionally double the drinking places that Worth had!

54. The *Fox*, Three Bridges, now demolished, stood opposite the present station entrance. The original entrance was under the bridge and up a slope to the right. Two cottages, hidden in this photograph, stood between the *Fox* and the railway.

One way to catalogue the local changes is to see what the many trade directories say. Take house building as an example. A rapid population growth creates demand for housing. Two men can be cited as examples of how the area coped with it. In Crawley in 1832 we have 'Henry Ockenden — Carpenter; William Gates — Bricklayer'. In 1845 they are shown as 'Ockenden — Carpenter and Builder; Gates — Bricklayer'. By 1852 the titles have been upgraded to 'Ockenden — Builder; Gates — Stonemason', and finally by 1855 both are described as 'Builder'. Their status had been elevated as builders became men of substance in the community.

In a book published in Crawley in 1866 there were a number of advertisements which show that the building industry was by then well established. Men offering their services included: S. Gates, Architect; W. Rudge, Auctioneer and Valuer; Robert Gates and Richard Cook, Slaters and Bricklayers; Richard Gates, Paper Hanging; C. Bisshopp, Water Closets; C. Bisshopp, junior, Gas Fitter; J. Stacey, Furniture Warehouse. The 1852 directory for Worth only lists four craftsmen: one stonemason at Crawley Down and three carpenters at Turners Hill, Crawley Down and Three Bridges. By 1874 four men were listed as builders, and they were themselves employing craftsmen. James Longley set up in business originally at Turners Hill. Worth was the growth area, and at first had more builders. When the larger firms developed, however, Crawley became the place to situate the business.

Cycles and motor cars: the Brighton Road revives

St Michael's, Lowfield Heath, was built in 1868 to serve the little community which had grown at the crossroads, together with Tinsley Green and Hookwood. The old Lowfield Heath had been enclosed as a result of an 1846 enclosure award. All the fields on the old Common had straight edges where the land had been apportioned rather than the less even field shapes which had developed over the centuries in the surrounding countryside. There was also an enclosure award made in 1857 for Ifield, but this was for a different purpose and had the effect of narrowing all the very wide roadways by giving much of the grass verges to the farmers whose fields bordered the road.

Lowfield Heath was, of course, in Surrey until recently. Its growth underlines the fact that despite the competition of the railways, road transport did not totally decline. The vast amount of railway business, both of goods and of passengers, gave a boost to all local roads which had to distribute the goods and people to and from the railway stations. Through traffic might be less, but local traffic flourished. Developments in road transport encouraged longer journeys again and increased the number of local journeys.

In 1869 three men rode from London to Brighton in 16 hours on 'boneshaker' bicycles, so-called because their wheels were made entirely of metal. It was reported in *The Times* as 'An Extraordinary Velocipede Feat'. Two months later another man cut the time to seven hours. The public were made aware of the uses of the bicycle, or rather its potential uses, and design improved.

Early cycles were driven directly from pedal to wheel hub, rather like a young child's tricycle today. One turn of a pedal meant one turn of a wheel. Thus, the larger the wheel diameter, the further one could travel for one pedal turn. Bicycles were built with enormous front wheels — the better able to give speed and distance — and the rear wheels small for lightness. They could reach 20 m.p.h. and numbers rapidly increased in the 1870s and 1880s. (They were not called 'penny-farthings' until about 1890.) The size of a front wheel was dictated by the rider's inside leg measurement; normal size was a 54 in. diameter.

By the mid-1870s over 30 firms were making bicycles and they cost about £12 each. For a simple local working man, earning about 6d.(2.5p) per hour, this sum would represent about two months' pay, perhaps equivalent to £1,200 today! Cycling was for the well-off, not the common people, until prices started to fall. In fact, the prices of bicycles kept steady for many years whilst rates of pay slowly increased.

The Cyclists' Touring Club (C.T.C.) was formed in 1883 and increasingly cycles were seen in Crawley, in groups or on organised outings. It must have been a memorable sight in the early 1880s when the London Bicycle Club organised a ride from Croydon to Crawley. Over 250 made the trip, and were given a meal at the *George* — imagine Crawley High Street with all the Penny-farthings lying on the grass verges! Imagine too the fun which ensued when all the cyclists, having wined and dined well, came outside to attempt to find, to reclaim and to remount their own machines!

Both the Bay Tree Coffee House, now the George Buttery, and the Northgate Restaurant

55. The Bay Tree Coffee House. The Shaw family, which owned the business, developed it into a garage, next door to the *George Hotel*.

(subsequently the site of Brewer's wallpaper and paint shop in the London Road, now a solicitor's) catered for cyclists for 50 years and more. Eventually two further refinements came. Chain-driven safety cycles, with two smaller wheels, were developed from 1884 and pneumatic tyres were introduced in 1888.

The point about bicycles in Crawley's story is that they reawakened the through traffic in the village. Though farm labourers could not afford cycles until the 1920s onwards, once people with money to spend started to pass through the district again, the road trade revived.

The census returns reveal how the total population grew in step with national growth.

For England and Wales the 1801 population was nine million, it had doubled to 18 million by 1851, and doubled again to 36 million by 1911. The combined Ifield, Crawley and Worth parishes had a population of 2,348 in 1801, 4,034 in 1851 and 8,764 by 1911. However, the growth locally was uneven. The small Crawley parish hardly altered after 1851 whereas Crawley village expanded mostly in Ifield, and to a lesser extent in Worth parish. In fact, Ifield parish expanded almost sevenfold between 1801 and 1911 and most of this was accounted for by the expansion of the village of Crawley.

	1851	1881	1901
Ifield	1,112	2,043	3,383
Crawley	447	451	441
Worth	2,475	3,571	4,297

The village of Crawley had one great problem — how to get water in and sewage out. As the area expanded, so its demand for water and sanitation grew. Until almost 1900, water still came from its old wells, with or without pumps, and most of these were still close to the cesspits. The rapid recycling effect led to many wells being condemned as unfit. Local government was, quite frankly, chaotic. The village of Crawley stretched into three parishes in the late 19th century. Worth had been put into the East Grinstead Union for poor relief and sanitation purposes and Ifield was part of the Horsham Union. Crawley was originally with the East Grinstead Union since Worth and Crawley had been together in Buttinghill Hundred for centuries. When the two Boards of Guardians for East Grinstead and Horsham refused to co-operate, a real problem developed.

The *Weekly Horsham Advertiser* from 1874 onwards chronicles the lack of progress in creating an acceptable drainage scheme for the village. Dr. Martin wrote in June 1874 an account of what had happened so far. A committee of 'townsfolk' had been set up to carry out a drainage scheme, but a new Sanitary Act had given the Boards of Guardians the role, so the local committee had been dissolved. Nothing had been done by either Horsham or East Grinstead and, as a doctor, he thought the town was in a bad state. Eventually, in 1880, Crawley was transferred from the East Grinstead Union to the Horsham Union and so, at long last, it seemed a scheme could be agreed.

Yet in April 1884, the local newspaper reported that the '. . . Crawley and Ifield Vigilance Committee [had conducted a] successful opposition to the drainage scheme proposed by the Guardians of the Horsham Union'. They wanted a better scheme. The Vigilance Committee were an early pressure group: in February 1884 they were complaining about the overflow of water and soil from Richard Cook's brickyard at the New Town, Ifield. A few years later the drains were at last laid and no doubt the health of the villagers improved.

In 1888 the two county councils for Sussex were set up. Crawley and Ifield parishes were at that time situated in West Sussex, and the West Sussex Record Office contains many of Crawley's old records. However, Worth was in East Sussex and many Crawley records from the past are kept in the East Sussex Record Office. This causes difficulty to the historian, given the distance between Crawley, Lewes and Chichester. When the 1974 boundary changes were made. East Grinstead and Worth were moved to West Sussex. This will probably make it a little easier for future historians.

The first water company was founded in 1897 when six local influential men (including Dr. Martin, Charles Longley and Moses Nightengale) purchased land at the end of a cul-de-sac called Goffs Park Road. After boring down almost 950 ft. (300 m.) water was reached, and so mains water could be supplied to those in Crawley and Three Bridges who wanted it.

For anyone wishing to find out what life was like in the last 25 years of the century, it is a straightforward and fascinating, though tiring, task to read through the local newspapers which are kept on microfilm at Horsham Library. Here are some random 'snapshots' of interest:

> November 1874. Crawley Bonfire Society was set up, meeting in the White Hart monthly, to collect money for the annual village bonfire night. They collected money for fireworks, arranged torches for a procession at 7 p.m., hired the local brass band, built and lit a fire on the Green outside what is now the entrance to The Broadwalk. The Fire Brigade stood by.
>
> May 1878. The Crawley and District Friendly Society met to celebrate its 51st anniversary. 'The members met at the White Hart Inn, and headed by the Fire Brigade Band proceeded through the town to the Church.'
>
> September 1878. A Harvest Thanksgiving was held at Hogs Hill Farm. '. . . farm workers and employees from their establishments in Lambeth attended.'
>
> December 1878. The twentieth A.G.M. of the gas company was held. 'The electric light was discussed but no one seemed intimidated.'
>
> December 1878. The newspaper editorial was scathing about '. . . the possible depression in trade (which) arises simply from . . . the present Trades Unions'.
>
> January 1882. A labourer pleaded guilty at Horsham Court '. . . to being an incorrigible rogue' and was sentenced to 12 months' hard labour.
>
> January 1882. The Horsham Police Division comprised one superintendent, one sergeant, and 13 constables, one of whom was stationed at Ifield.
>
> January 1882. The A.G.M. of the Ifield and Crawley Cricket Club was held. 'It was decided that challenges be sent to Ockley, Slinfold, Leatherhead, Handcross and Three Bridges.'
>
> March 1883. The 14th A.G.M. of the Horsham and Crawley Permanent Building Society was held.

All the various facets of contemporary life can be gleaned from these newspapers. The large number of public houses and the strong temperance movement; the village bands supporting any local organisation or charity; sports matches and concerts; reports of crimes and religious homilies.

The 1895 parish guide to Crawley lists a large number of societies, sports clubs, slate clubs for savings and loan schemes, local banks and public institutions. An air of vibrant activity pervades the village. In part it explains the use made of the post office. It was open each day from 7 a.m. to 9 p.m., though on Sunday only from 8 a.m. to 10 a.m. Letter boxes were emptied four times a day and there were three deliveries a day. To give an example, a post card could be posted in the morning at Three Bridges to say that the writer would be calling on a relative in Ifield that afternoon, and know that on arrival he would be expected! The postman's day was obviously very long.

The greatest changes in Ifield parish were, as we have seen, actually happening in Crawley village. The Victorian house-building boom, much of which occurred after Richard Cook began building locally in 1861, led to the provision of many shops and public houses to serve the locality. The other part of life — the spiritual — was shown in the provision of many churches.

But it was with the road that this section opened, and will close. From the 1870s onwards, many people from London started to visit the countryside at weekends. They came by pony and trap, by bicycle, by railway or on foot. A stream of guides was published for the traveller; each gave a brief description of the area and a judgement on its suitability for a visit. Harper's book *The Brighton Road* was published in 1892, and is friendly towards Crawley:

> The somewhat steep ascent by the highway from London to Crawley village, and the extreme length of its long street, together with the quaint cottages and their homely front gardens, gives the place so pleasing an air of rusticity . . . The large and long patches of grass that take up so considerable a selvedge of Crawley Street, seem to speak with eloquence of those dead days of coaching necessity . . . Then the *George*, an inn where cyclists now do mostly congregate, was a

56. Celebrations for Queen Victoria's Diamond Jubilee in 1897 included a pageant. Here some of the participants are assembled in the grounds of Hazeldene.

> scene of continuous bustling. Now there is little in this place to stir the pulses or make the heart leap.

Many might still echo that last sentiment today!

Two years later Augustus Hare wrote a guide to Sussex. His description of Worth, as was common, concentrated upon the church, '. . . prettily situated on a woody knoll approached by an ancient lych-gate'. He liked the Saxon building though not its restoration. '. . . But all that vulgar tiles, revolting glass and coarse woodwork can do to spoil a church has been liberally bestowed.'

Then, in 1896, Black's *Guide to Sussex* commented on the area. Three Bridges '. . . has not much to say for itself'. Worth: '. . . this fine neighbourhood is naturally much invaded by private grounds and cottages of gentility'. Crawley was described in terms of its

> . . . very 'railwayish' *Railway Hotel* and . . . two cosy looking inns, the *George* and the *Sun*, that have made the common mistake of calling themselves hotels . . . This place is one of those peaceful,

> roomy English villages tempting one to settle in it for life; and a fringe of red-brick villas and 'freehold plots for sale' shows that the temptation has not always been resisted.

Ifield was ignored; indeed it was rarely mentioned in such works, being off the main road system and having little to interest the cultured, inquisitive traveller, it appears.

Meanwhile, in the High Street cars were appearing, hampered rather than encouraged by the legislation of the day. Cars cost several hundred pounds to buy, so only the very rich could afford them. The boom which cyclists had started changed as the motor car came through Crawley. The author, Jerome K. Jerome, described early motoring. 'It was rarely that one reached one's destination. As a matter of fact, only the incurable optimist ever tried to . . . Generally one returned in hired coach.' In his autobiography he recalled one famous occasion.

> In a morning in 1896 a line of weird-shaped vehicles, the like of which London had never seen before, stood drawn up in Northumberland Avenue outside the *Hotel Metropole*. They were the new horseless carriages, called automobiles . . . The law, insisting that every mechanically propelled vehicle should be preceded by a man carrying a red-flag, had expired the day before, and at nine o'clock we started for Brighton . . . By the time we reached Crawley, half our number had fallen out for repairs and alterations.

The idea was for 25 cars to arrive in triumph at Brighton between 12 and one o'clock, to be greeted by the Mayor. In fact the first reached Brighton at half-past three, and others straggled in. Jerome was the last, but he got there. This event is still celebrated each year in November. Because of the tenacity of early motorists, Crawley's place in motoring lore became fixed.

Schooling developments in the 19th century

One final important change needs to be investigated, because it was the most important and far-reaching change to be witnessed during the whole of the century. It affected everybody. This was the introduction of an education system to the country.

From time to time, references are found to small schools in the area. Occasionally the word will be a grand name to describe the house of a child-minder who may have known less than her young charges, though in our area the schools do seem to have imparted some rudimentary knowledge of reading and writing. The Church was often involved in schooling; there was a school at Charlwood run by the Revd. Mr. Bristow in the 1630s.

In 1835 there was a national enquiry into education provision. Crawley, it was stated, had no school in the parish but the children of the poor attended a charity school at Ifield. (It is puzzling that the 1836 tithe map shows the building now occupied by Bartley & Ward, which stands in Crawley churchyard, described as '. . . a house and school house . . .' occupied by Thomas Flutter.)

Ifield had three 'daily schools', in all of which the children were instructed at the expense of their parents. The first had 25 boys, the second had 37 girls, and the third, opened in 1829, had 34 boys and girls. Then there was a 'boarding school' (opened in 1831) in which two boys and 10 girls were being educated. Where these schools were is unknown. Finally, there was the 'one-Day and Sunday School' (sponsored by St Margaret's) containing 90 boys and 42 girls, which was partly funded by voluntary subscriptions and partly from the pupils. If one assumes that the day schools served local people then Ifield and Crawley parishes, which contained about fourteen hundred people, provided some form of education for 228 children (16.3 per cent). This must have been a goodly proportion of the children.

In Worth there were four 'daily' schools. One was endowed with £8 per year to pay a salary for a teacher (money left by Timothy Shelley) and contained 60 boys and girls. The other three held 20, 18 and 23 boys and girls. The last two had commenced in 1826 and 1833. For all these schools the parents paid fees. There were two Church-sponsored Sunday schools; one, opened in 1826 by the Revd. Dr. Bethune held 127 children, and the other, in the east of the parish founded in 1825, held 65 children. This gave 313 places for pupils in a parish of about two thousand inhabitants (15.7 per cent).

The interesting point that emerges from these rather dry figures is that the notion we now hold that children in the 1830s received little if any education in the rural areas is not substantiated. The education may have been sketchy but it seems that the majority of children would have had some form of instruction. Of the 11 schools mentioned, seven had been opened in the previous 10 years. There is a tradition of local schooling, therefore, reaching back at least 200 years, and a burgeoning of provision which took place in the 1820s and 1830s. The latter fact is strange since, although the urban area was thriving, the agricultural areas were doing less well during that period. Once again, Crawley is shown to be somewhat out of step with the general trend. We know that there was an increase in national awareness of the importance of education at this time, and our area was well advanced in acting on it. This attitude was sustained throughout the century.

In the early 19th century two men, independently of one another, devised a system of schooling whereby teachers taught older pupils, called monitors or tutors, who in turn taught the younger pupils. Joseph Lancaster was a Quaker; Andrew Bell was an Anglican. The system offered the chance of teaching large numbers at comparatively low cost, and was therefore a good idea! In 1811, the Church of England formed the National Society for Promoting the Education of the Poor in the Principles of the Established Church. Schools set up under the aegis of this society became known as 'National Schools' for short. In 1814, the Nonconformist bodies who had already founded the British and Foreign School Society formed the Institution for Promoting the Education of the Labouring and Manufacturing Classes of Society of Every Religious Persuasion. Their schools became known as 'British Schools'.

In 1825, a National School was opened in the Ifield Road. This was under the care of the Revd. Mr. Lewin, Rector of Ifield, and built as a result of public subscription. The school at first accepted pupils of all denominations. Indeed, Sarah Robinson (who was a Quaker and whose husband farmed the Manor Farm on the London Road) was a co-founder and fund raiser. The school is now used by Southern Counties garage, on the corner of Spencer's Road. In 1852 a new rector was appointed to Ifield Church: he wanted the National School to fulfil its sectarian function so all Nonconformist children were turned away.

Sarah Robinson once again set about raising money, and this time a British School was built. It opened in temporary accommodation until a new building was completed and opened in October 1854 at a cost of £510. The building was in a road now called Robinson Road. (The original building was eventually replaced in 1916, and is now used by Crawley College.) The British School was fully interdenominational. By 1852, therefore, the people in the local area had a choice of two good schools in Crawley village to which their children could be sent. The pupils paid a small sum if they could afford it, and there was a constant struggle to keep the schools solvent.

Soon there was a large number of National Schools in Britain as a result of the energy of the Church of England ministers and their parishioners. Locally we had Charlwood School in 1840, Copthorne in 1842 (built on land donated by the Blunts), and Worth (Pound Hill) in 1852.

In Ifield village a Sunday school was set up in 1843, as can be seen from the foundation stone set in the wall of the old school buildings near St Margaret's church. Eventually, in 1872, another National School was created there, for the western portion of the parish. The local paper reports: 'It was much needed in that locality, although it resulted in a considerable number of children being withdrawn from the Crawley National and other schools'.

57. The British School, Robinson Road. These, the original building and schoolmaster's house, were replaced during the First World War.

Most people are aware that not long after the 1870 Education Act attendance at school was made compulsory for all children. Throughout Britain school boards were set up locally, with power to levy rates, if there was insufficient provision of places for the local child population. Worth, Crawley and Ifield never had a school board. The local population had already provided enough school places, and with a mixture of government grants (from 1860) and local fund-raising they carried on. After 1890 fees could no longer be charged, which put an extra burden on the managers of our local schools, but they still persisted until the 1902 Education Act gave responsibility for the maintenance of the local schools to West Sussex County Council.

Horsham, on the other hand, had a school board. For many years Collyer's provided an education for a few local pupils, mostly children of middle-class parents. A school board raised the money to build school places for all Horsham children. This was not universally applauded. The editorial comment of the Horsham newspaper of April 1875 said: 'What on earth are we coming to? Five palaces are to be built in the town for 350 — perhaps not pauper — children, but the result must be to pauperise all above the rank of paupers'. Education for all, without charge, has never been fully appreciated.

There were also private schools in the Crawley district. In 1875 there was the North House Academy in the London Road, Northgate, and a newspaper reported 'Master R. Hardwicke, a pupil of Mr. J. Rowse at North House, has succeeded in passing the examination of the Royal College of Preceptors'. The 1895 Guide refers to the Young Ladies' School in New Street, Three Bridges, and an infants' school in New Town. Also Mrs. Montefiore had set up a girls' school in the Balcombe Road (adjacent to the old Pound Hill Telephone Exchange). Local children had good opportunities.

As a counterpoint, it might be salutary to give some extracts from local school logs. If sickness intruded, children may be a danger to others by attending school. In the winter of 1870 there are many references to boys '. . . suffering with a bad throat'. On 20 March 1871 Dr. Smith called '. . . to enquire respecting the drainage . . . on account of the diptheria which has been stirring so long in the parish'. Some children died. Later, in May,'. . . Heard that Scarlet Fever is stirring at Hazelwick Mill', and further cases were reported in Three Bridges. In September the girls' school banned the Three Bridges children for a month, and '. . . sent William Potter home as his sister is only just recovering from an attack of Scarlet Fever'. Similar comments were made at Crawley, where the British School was reported closed from time to time because of outbreaks of chicken pox, measles and whooping cough.

The other major reasons for absence related to (i) the farming calendar, (ii) the activities of the gentry, and (iii) local events. Any excuse seems to have been good enough for taking a day off from Worth school, for example:

(i)	3 April 1865	8 boys away gardening
	5 June 1865	Not very full school on account of hay harvest beginning
	13 June 1865	Several boys away gathering wild strawberries
(ii)	27 June 1865	Cricket match at Crabbett Park — scarcely any boys present
	2 October 1865	four or five boys away beating for pheasant shooting
	5 February 1866	14 boys late, they having been with the fox hounds
	25 January 1887	11 boys late, they having been stag hunting
(iii)	8 May 1865	Crawley Fair, attendance worse than I have known for weeks
	16 May 1865	A holiday on Wednesday — Pound Hill Club Feast
	8 June 1865	Rector visited — said two boys required next week to assist the organ tuner
	14 September 1865	Stool-ball match at Three Bridges
	13 November 1899	(Crawley) No school this afternoon. Motor car procession London to Brighton.

The last entry shows that the trip undertaken originally by Jerome K. Jerome in 1896 has been enlivening — and interrupting — local life ever since.

Chapter 11

Into the Twentieth Century

The Edwardian Age and the Great War

In the years leading up to the First World War, Crawley was a quiet prosperous area in north Sussex. Though the new parish called 'West Crawley' was created, centred on St Peter's church, the civil administration still remained vested in the original Crawley and Ifield parishes. The area showed a continuing population growth, eight per cent between 1901 and 1911, though this was slowing down after the 19th-century population explosion.

	1901	**1911**
Crawley Parish	441	426
Ifield Parish	3,383	3,995
Worth Parish	4,297	4,343
Total:	8,121	8,764

It was generally assumed that the 3,995 in Ifield were roughly split into 2,000 for those living in the Crawley village area and 2,000 for those in rural Ifield.

At this time, about ten per cent of the employed population of Britain was working in 'personal service'; there were few families of the lower middle-class and upwards which did not have at least a maid, if not a cook. The plethora of large houses in the area needed a constant supply of young men and women to work in them and in their grounds. The days of the large house were numbered, however, and once the Great War started, the decline became pronounced. Local society was still multi-layered: railway workers, agricultural workers, tradesmen, foresters, prosperous business owners, professional men and the gentry. This structure became blurred as a result of the Great War, when a generation of young men was decimated.

Much local unity could be attributed to various leisure pursuits which sometimes crossed the borders of social groupings. Two local brass and silver bands appealed to a variety of types of people, as did an Orchestral and Harmonic Society. There were two choral societies, a Women's Institute in each village, sports organisations, Boy Scouts, fireworks day, fair days, Christmas and other festivities, and a local cottage hospital. There are photographs and postcards which constantly amaze by the number of times that apparently the whole population, everyone wearing a hat, turned out to support a local event in the early 1900s. The various churches were very active and supported many clubs, though with the exception of the Catholic church these tended to perpetuate social divisions. The strong sense of King and Country which became manifest during the Great War had already been shown by the villagers' passion for planting trees in the High Street to mark royal events.

The first was an oak planted in 1887 at Queen Victoria's Golden Jubilee. A copper beech was planted in 1893 on the marriage of the Duke of York (who later became George V), and another oak in 1897 for Queen Victoria's Diamond Jubilee. The coronation of King Edward VII in 1902 was marked with an oak, a horse chestnut, a beech and an American elm. Later in the 20th century more trees were planted to celebrate coronations and a silver jubilee. (It is a pity that these and later trees are not properly identified by a plaque, though many plaques have been placed and removed over the years.)

In 1909, the Robinson family sold the house next door to the British School for £557. It was to become a cottage hospital, and its support was something for which the whole community readily united. The money received from the sale was given to the school to set

58. Crawley played host to the South of England Amateur Band Concert on about five occasions. When this happened, as here in 1907, the High Street was noisy and crowded for hours. Note the shop occupied by F. Rich. He was unlucky enough to patent an inflatable car tyre at almost the same time as Dunlop.

up a trust fund. The school itself was rebuilt a few years later and the present buildings were erected. Because of the war, no public ceremony was held to mark its opening on 1 May 1916.

One example of the class divide, however, can be pointed to. There were celebrations in 1897 for Queen Victoria's Diamond Jubilee. The Conservatives, the gentry, the National School children and the Church of England had a fête at The Elms, in the Horsham Road. The Liberals, the tradespeople, the British School children and the Nonconformists had a fête in the cricket field near the *White Hart*. It was not overtly arranged as such: it just happened.

Photographs taken at a parade to raise money for the cottage hospital show a stronger local unity. Bands playing and marching along were followed by lines of people representing local organisations, also marching behind their own banners, which proclaimed titles such as 'Workman's Provident Society', 'Young Women's Christian Association', 'Temperance Association'.

Crawley High Street was a natural focus for local events. We tend to forget nowadays that shopkeepers and office managers used to live, so to speak, above the shop or behind it. At this time shops and offices were also homes, and local residents were aware of life continuing there in the evenings, even when the shops were shut and the blinds closed. Until 1914 there were still some small gardens, and a large number of trees, all along the High Street. In the morning the residents would sweep and wash down the pavement in

59. Fancy dress at the fête at Buckswood Lodge in aid of Crawley Cottage Hospital, on the occasion of Princess Alexandra of Teck's visit.

front of their premises. It was all in very marked contrast to the present scruffy appearance of our town centre, which dies once the shops have closed at 6 p.m.

As the British population grew, so did the inevitable ribbon development along the main roads. Fortunately, some fine large houses continued to be built southwards along the Brighton Road, but fewer were built to the north, along the London Road.

House-building proceeded steadily. When the New Town Corporation surveyed the proposed neighbourhoods in the Crawley New Town area in 1947, they noted the houses built between 1880 and 1914 which still remained. There were 36 in Ifield, mainly detached and standing on large plots along Ifield Road and Rusper Road. The Langley Green and Gossops Green areas only contained a few farm cottages built in this period. From this we can confirm that up to 1914 there had been little development — except for the moderately wealthy — in the rural area of Ifield parish. The area we now call Southgate had had 60 houses built. There were both small-and medium-sized ones in Malthouse Road, East Park, Springfield Road and West Street, and large detached houses in Goffs Park Road. West Green was an area of continuing development as we have already shown, and the Northgate neighbourhood contained a small row of houses known as Albert Cottages, opposite the

Sun. Otherwise, there was a deal of infilling around the village area, though sometimes buildings were demolished — as when a row of cottages was removed to permit a good entry at last to Crawley church. For hundreds of years the main entrance to the church was by the small footpath which still runs from the High Street. The church could not, in fact, be seen from the High Street. The area of Worth parish nearest to Crawley can be divided into the railway-inspired housing development at Three Bridges and a few farm cottages built in Pound Hill.

The 1907 Pike's local directory gives much information regarding the occupations of the local householders. The addresses confirm how Three Bridges was intensely railway-orientated. In Station Hill, now demolished, stood a small row of cottages which were occupied only by railwaymen and their families. But the main aggregation was in Hazelwick Road (33 railwaymen), with others in New Street, Mill Road, Crabbett Road and the High Street. Sixteen drivers are listed, six guards, four firemen, seven signalmen, seven porters, and 17 assorted other grades. Only one railway employee was listed in Pound Hill and Worth, and he lived close to the station in Crawley Lane. Add the station master to this list and it is clear that about sixty railway employees — not counting their sons — lived within a few hundred yards of Three Bridges station.

Meanwhile, in Crawley village, the major change in the High Street during this period was doubtless the creation of 'garages'. It is fascinating to trace the way local businesses adapted to the motor car. Just south of the level crossing, at 16 Brighton Road, was

60. A late 19th-century view of Crawley High Street, taken from the level crossing. There were still some trees in the High Street, marking the line of the former front gardens.

Nightingale's cycle shop. A young employee, named Gadsdon, decided to work for himself and, early in the 1900s, he purchased one of the houses facing the shop at 5 Brighton Road. He built new premises on the front garden to provide somewhere to sell motor accessories and cans of petrol, and to conduct repairs to motor vehicles. Gadsdon's, Nightingale's and Lindfield's (93 High Street) all described themselves as 'Motor and Cycle Engineers' in 1916.

61. Central Garage, High Street. Before planning laws it was simple to turn a house into a garage, and erect whatever signs the owner wished.

Next to the *George* was the Bay Tree Coffee House run by the Shaw family, and popular with cyclists. One of the sons became interested in motor engines, built a motorcycle, and so began Shaw's Garage. In 1916 this was described as Shaw and Sons, motor builders. A few doors away, a medieval house was used for the Central Garage by Mr. Fisher. The publican of the *Sun* opened a garage attached to his premises. Similarly, the livery stables and horse-drawn cabs by the *Fox* at Three Bridges station became, so to speak, mechanised and developed into a separate garage and a taxi business. These were the precursors of what eventually caused more changes to the British environment and settlement pattern than anything else since the coming of the railways — the motor industry.

In the Crawley area, most local garages developed from cycle shops. Many early motor vehicles were, in truth, bicycles or tricycles with a small engine attached. Though motor cars caused a stir when they appeared in the locality, there were probably many more motorcycles around than motor cars. They were cheaper to buy and easier to build and maintain. Though the horse was still the major motive power source it was rapidly superseded. In 1916 Willett's local directory recorded that there were as many local men claiming to be 'chauffeurs' as there were men claiming to be 'coachmen' or 'carters'. One final reference to the infancy of the local motor car is shown in the listing of Mr. W. Jacob of 4 St Peter's Road as 'Motor Scout'. He was well-known as the first A.A. man to patrol our Brighton Road.

Another facet of motorisation is recorded with the comment, again in 1916, that the '. . . Omnibus leaves Crawley for Handcross on Weekdays at 9.15 a.m. and 7.40 p.m. and on Saturday at 2.45 p.m.'. For the inhabitants of those villages which were some distance from the railway station it was a marvellous aid to be able to get a bus into Crawley and back; for villagers unable to afford motor transport or a pony and trap, having to walk to the local town and back had been, for centuries, rather a daunting and time-consuming operation.

It is said that the First World War started on horses' legs and ended on motorised wheels. This process of change, accelerated by the war, is clearly seen locally. Still other, newer, activities in the area were to have long-term effects on the nature of local life.

First, Pike's 1907 directory noted that the new post office (in Post Office Road, now Robinson Road) was open and that '. . . the Telephone Exchange and Telegrams were available from 8 a.m. to 8 p.m.'. Some of the entries now included telephone numbers with their addresses, for example:

> Wood, Son and Gardner, 11, Brighton Road [auctioneer]
> Telephone Number: Crawley 2
> Ockenden and Son, 27-31, Ifield Road [builder] ('Established 1828')
> Telephone Number: Crawley 5
> Sproston and Co., 34, High Street [fishmonger]
> Telephone Number: Crawley 28

By 1916 Willett's directory shows that there were over 100 subscribers to the telephone, and that there was also an exchange at Pound Hill.

There were obvious early benefits to the tradespeople, who could use a telephone to give orders for supplies. As the private subscribers increased, so traders could take orders for immediate delivery. Many local tradespeople advertised their willingness to deliver goods in the locality. Ifield Laundry, at 10 Leopold Road, sent vans as far afield as Horsham, Newdigate, Turners Hill and Cuckfield; Hibbs the baker delivered daily over an area stretching from Lowfield Heath in the north to Slaugham in the south.

It is a strange coincidence that two of the pioneers of the telephone and telegraph service lived in Worth. Sir Curtis Lampson was behind the laying of the first submarine telegraph cable across the Atlantic, and he lived in Rowfant House. J. E. Kingsbury was the first agent of the Western Electric Telephone Company, which introduced the telephone to the City of London. He died at the age of 91 in 1940 at Snow Hill, Crawley Down.

Second, another new venture was the arrival of electricity in the area. The 1907 directory informed that some places in Horsham had the electric light. The well-off could install their own generating systems in their houses. It was in 1909 that the first steam-powered generator was built in Crawley, able to supply customers with power cables. In May 1910 the house called Deerswood in Ifield was to be auctioned. The sales prospectus stated that 'Electric Light could be supplied by the Crawley Company'. The local cinema would also have needed a power supply.

The 1917 directory carries an advertisement for the Sussex Electricity Supply Company. In Cross Keys, a small lane leading off the High Street, was listed the Electric Light Generating Station, with a resident engineer. The local company representative was Mr. Edward Prior, based at 56a High Street. He offered, additionally: '. . . complete installations for Country Houses, including a generating set, storage battery, wiring and everything necessary for switching on the light'. Many of the High Street premises were by then connected to the power supply. The builders, Bartley and Ward, were describing themselves as, among other things, 'Electric Light and Gas Fitters'. A photographer, Percy Swan-Taylor, of the Rembrandt Studio in the Brighton Road, was advertising 'The Latest for Electric Light for Portraiture'. So by 1916 we had in Crawley a piped water supply, a sewage system, gas, electricity and the telephone. Not for everyone, however.

This was a time of change. The front garden of the house next door to Gadsdon's garage was built upon for Crawley's first cinema. Opened in 1912, it is not really surprising that it was called the Imperial Cinema, given the strong belief in King (and Empire) already described. At 37 High Street the shop of Cook, Chart and Co. in 1917 sold pianos, gramophones and records. Even Miller and Sons, the established saddler's business, was having to move with the times. It is a reflection of the changing emphasis of the age that three-quarters of its advertisement was concerned with other things than saddlery. The shop was described as a 'Sports and Athletic Outfitters, Bags and Portmanteaux, Cricket, Football and Golf Requisites kept in stock. Agents for various sports goods and Eley's Cartridges. All kinds of Motor-cleaning requisites'. Sport was becoming popular, particularly when Saturday afternoons became generally free from the need to work. In addition to cricket and football, a lawn tennis and bowling club was set up (on a site now occupied by C&A Modes), and a golf course laid out on Copthorne Common. Perhaps the changes to Miller's shop can be taken to sum up the High Street businesses, responding to changing demands yet retaining links with their original functions.

The one thing which is, strangely, hardly mentioned in the 1916 directory is the Great War. Until that year all recruitment to the armed forces was voluntary rather than by conscription. It is surprising how many men were still listed in the directory. No shortages are reported; the advertisements show prosperity. It is a fact that newspapers kept the truth of trench warfare away from readers for as long as possible. Perhaps the villagers only had a dim realisation of what was really happening across the Channel.

It was mainly the lower-paid workers of the country who rushed to join the county infantry regiments, such as the Royal Sussex Regiment. These suffered severe casualties. The local war memorials show the result. Only the back page of the 1916 directory refers to the hostilities. It shows a soldier, his arm in a sling, being greeted by two young children. In the background is a smiling group, waving a Union Jack. The caption reads 'Our Daddy's Come Home'. All very cheering, but hardly realistic.

It is possible that the war itself did not have immediate effects in the area. Though some shortages occurred, an agricultural area can always get food and the traders can always make profits. Employment was high. The death of servicemen, however, would mean that the realities of war were never entirely forgotten. There had been a strong territorial unit in Crawley, and the men were attending their summer camp when war broke out in 1914. During the war years, many troops were stationed in the district, particularly in a camp in Tilgate Forest near to Pease Pottage. Once Lord Kitchener reviewed troops locally. Many of the local men served in the Middle East, and some were buried in Jerusalem.

That the men were missed is obvious. More women were employed locally, even in traditional male jobs on farms and in the forest. More female shop assistants appeared, and a few women left the village to nurse or to work in munitions factories. From 1916 there were fears of Zeppelin attacks, and a blackout was ordered at night. Some moved to the area from London, and the old comfortable village life was eroded. A writer in 1912 had written, in describing Crawley:

> It has not the sense of quiet dignified repose that adorns so many of our smaller Sussex towns. Railway trains shriek through its very centre east to west, and north to south their track is crossed by a ceaseless stream of flying motors that dash along the London-Brighton Road, and leave the air thick with clouds of dust and vibrating with discordant hoots.

The world was changing indeed.

62. This house in the Brighton Road was decorated with hundreds of red, white and blue coloured glass bowls and Chinese lanterns, all lit by candles, in celebration of peace in 1919.

The Twenties and Thirties

Though it was not fully realised at the time, the halcyon days of the immediate pre-war years marked the peak of the country-house lifestyle. After 1919 it was never recaptured. Country-house owners tried at first to live as if the war had not happened, but unsuccessfully. Income tax and death duties hit hard; investments and farms were not very profitable in the 1920s. The wage bills for house staff and estate staff rose, so the number of servants declined. The very large house was a white elephant to those of fixed or declining incomes, and some houses experienced a change of function.

Take, for example, Worth Park. Joseph Meyer Montefiore had purchased the estate, and for his son, Sir Francis Montefiore, Worth Park was his country seat. Sir Francis was a local J.P. and a Deputy Lord Lieutenant for Sussex; he was very much a local benefactor. The hall in Hazelwick Road, Three Bridges, was given to the villagers by the family. It must have been rather surprising when on 16 September 1915 the 2,055 acre estate was put up for auction following the death of the widow of Joseph Montefiore. The estate was described

63. Crawley's first scout troop at camp. Note that the bandmaster and the rector played their part as well as the scoutmaster.

by Knight, Frank and Rutley as a 'Residential, Manorial, Sporting and Agricultural Domain', and included local farms, the *George Hotel*, Crawley cricket ground and Crawley fire station. This reminds us that much land was occupied by tenants on leases.

Some years earlier a boarding school had been established on a hill near Milton, Gravesend, for the daughters of Congregational church ministers; not surprisingly, it was named Milton Mount College. During the Great War it was evacuated to Cirencester. The school managers looked for suitable larger premises than those vacated at Gravesend and decided to buy Worth Park Mansion (*see* Ill. 49). For the buildings and 80 acres of land they paid 30,000 guineas (a guinea was worth £1.05). The girls arrived on 21 October 1920, and the official opening ceremony was performed by Dame Margaret Lloyd-George on 23 June 1921.

Here was an early example of a pattern closely followed by the owners of many other large mansions. It is clear that institutional use, or use by a large public body, is now the main way such buildings can remain. Over the subsequent years a similar fate befell many other local buildings. Rowfant House became a country club; Buchan Park became Cottesmore School; Paddockhurst became Worth Abbey School; both Crabbett Park and Tilgate Mansion at first became flats; other large houses have become hotels or, as at Brantridge Park, time-share apartments; Goffs Park became council offices. Broadfield has been a country club, New Town Commission headquarters, Crawley council offices and now houses Radio Mercury.

Sir Francis Montefiore moved into a smaller, more comfortable house near Milton Mount called 'Farmleigh', which until quite recently stood at the top of Grattons Drive. The Locker Lampsons moved into a smaller house on the Rowfant Estate in similar circumstances, as did Baroness Wentworth at Crabbett Park. Only at Standen House, near East Grinstead, has the National Trust maintained a local Victorian house in much of its original condition, but this building was far smaller. It is interesting that Philip Webb, a friend of William Morris, was the architect of Standen. When Webb retired he did not have much money; his friend William Blunt gave him the use of a house on his Crabbett Park Estate. This was Caxtons, still standing on the Turners Hill Road in Worth.

Obviously the declining importance of the mansion was one phenomenon which much affected local employment. It was accompanied by the break-up of the large estates, and their sale documents (of which there are copies in Crawley Library) make interesting reading. The Worth Park estate comprised mainly 10 farms, and other properties included houses in New Street and North Road in Three Bridges, Northgate School and the Tree House in Crawley.

The next break-up of an estate occurred on 20 September 1916, when much of the Crabbett Park estate was auctioned at the *George Hotel* by order of the Hon. Mrs. Blunt Lytton. It comprised 1,635 acres in Worth, Ifield and Charlwood. Farms sold included most of those in Three Bridges and Pound Hill, and other properties included Hayheath, on the Turners Hill Road, and the Ancient Priors in Crawley. The 129 acres of Hazelwick Farm and water mill fetched £3,000 and the 229 acres of Woolborough Farm fetched £3,800. Hayheath was withdrawn at £4,000.

The change between pre-war and wartime attitudes towards large houses can be shown by these and by two other examples. In 1910 Deerswood in Ifield had been advertised as being close to the hunts (Crawley and Horsham Foxhounds and Warnham Staghounds), shooting (local partridges) and golf (Ashdown Forest). The next year, Ifield Court and its estate was described as 'Residential and Sporting' and included Hyde Cottage nearby which

64. Buchan Hill. A house built in a Jacobean style in 1882, as a centrepiece to a 1,000-acre estate on the border of Ifield parish, adjacent to Bewbush. It is now a boys' boarding school, and partly surrounded by a golf course.

was an '. . . old-fashioned cottage, capable by expenditure of a little money of conversion into a house for a gentleman's occupation'. Eight potential building plots were included.

When Worth Park was sold, the sporting aspect was played down and much more emphasis was placed on building sites in Copthorne, and land fronting the Three Bridges Road was described as 'Ripe for development'. The Crabbett Estate went all out to push potential building sites. Where farmland abutted the main road — as along the Three Bridges Road and in Tinsley Lane — small plots were fenced off and offered for building. Only at the remote Heathy Ground Farm by Rickmans Green (poor farmland, woods and a lake) was 'Wild Fowl Shooting' put forward as an inducement to buy, with its 'Mallard, Teal, Pochard and Snipe'.

The break-up of these estates greatly increased the amount of land available for house-building. As these sales documents show, many of the village and town properties were on short leases, not owned by the occupiers. It is surprising, perhaps, that though the family of doctors had lived in The Tree for over 120 years, it was rented all that time. From the 1920s onwards new building was usually for sale freehold, and this was quite a change in the area. Many new housing estates were proposed, both before and after the break-up of these large landholdings. One of the earliest was a St John's Estate, projected just after the turn of the century, for land which eventually was used by the tennis club and as the War Memorial Gardens.

In the 1920s and 1930s a succession of small developments took place. Most of it was speculative; the larger firms were not involved, but the smaller ones, such as Stoners, Jenners or Bartley and Ward, would develop a small plot of land with whatever capital they had available. The housing was almost totally to be owner-occupied, the new vogue. Who were the purchasers?

First, there were those who retired and sought a place in the country, and those better-off railway workers who had saved enough to put down a deposit, for whom a small bungalow costing from £350 to £500 was ideal. This is clearly seen in the Northgate area. Second, there were the richer middle-classes who sought detached houses within reach of London. Typical of housing bought by the latter was the Ifield Estate development. In the late 1920s the estate offered houses near the golf club (opened in 1927) along the Rusper Road. 'We intend to develop this Estate on novel yet sane lines; every house is to stand in its own grounds with ample room for a tennis court, orchard, flower garden, garage.' Various designs were available, ranging from a three reception/three bedroom 'Bijou Country House' from £1,350, to the largest three reception/four bedroom plus maid's parlour, for £2,500.

In the early 1930s the Crowell Estate, publicised by Ronald Ayling, was offering houses and bungalows along Tushmore Lane. At the same time, a glossy publication was issued by C. F. Taylor and Co. of 2 The Square, Crawley High Street, which gave a glowing description of the town and its surroundings. Crawley was, apparently, rich with historical associations. 'The Ancient Prior's House . . . built in the reign of King Stephen . . . visitors included Queen Elizabeth, Anne Boleyn, highwaymen and smugglers'! The town was healthy, '. . . invigorating air direct from the South Downs . . .', and housing was very attractive: '. . . artistic and commodious residences'. The hyperbole of advertising claims is not a modern device!

The *West Sussex County Times* of 1 March 1919 carried a long report about a lecture on housing and town planning which had been given at Horsham by Mr. C. D. Purdom, Secretary of the Garden Cities and Town Planning Association. 'The Chairman said that in years gone by, private enterprise had supplied the housing requirements. Now there was a shortage of working-class houses, and the urban council was taking steps to acquire a site.' This marked the beginning of council housing. The Horsham Rural District Council asked parish councils to let the R.D.C. know what council-built houses were required. At the end of March 1921 it was reported that Ifield required 20 and Crawley four. These were subsequently built.

Land for new building continued to become available. On 27 July 1926 the northern portion of the Rowfant Estate, comprising 660 acres, was sold. Just over half of Buchan Park, 1,550 acres, was sold in 1928, and the rest in 1937. The last release of land in the 1930s took place on Thursday 7 September 1939. It is strange how the largest estates were sold in September in wartime! This was the Tilgate Estate, comprising 2,185 acres and auctioned at the Montefiore Hall. Apart from the mansion itself there were a large number of local farms and land in Three Bridges village. Also included was the Three Bridges cricket ground, described as suitable for cricket — or as an ideal building estate. A speculative builder bought it. He cut down many old oak trees along the Three Bridges Road as a prelude to building, but in the meantime allowed the cricket club to continue to use the ground. This it did until an unfortunate error by an official led the owners to withdraw the offer to the club. Luckily it was able to continue to play as a nomadic club until the coming of the New Town put the land back to use once more as a cricket ground. Finally, in 1943 the complete Ifield Estate of 1,268 acres was auctioned, comprising farms as well as many of the large houses which had been constructed along the Rusper Road from the church to the golf club.

The New Town research reports reveal what was built in the inter-war years. Little had been erected in rural Ifield. Only 38 houses were built there and Gossops Green just had a few commuter houses built by Dower Walk. Langley Green had had some building along Langley Lane. In Southgate there was development within walking distance of the station. The major activity had occurred in Northgate, where 229 houses were erected in the fields opposite the *Sun*, around Tushmore Lane, Green Lane and Cobbles Crescent. In Northgate Road especially there was the sort of development which we normally think of as typical 1930s housing. In West Green over 100 homes, including council houses built by Horsham R.D.C., had been built along and near the Ifield Road.

Three Bridges was the other major growth area: 221 houses had been built in the 1920s and 1930s. These had spread along North Road, Tinsley Lane and the Three Bridges Road. The first St Richard's church was built south of the High Street. Fifty-two council houses had been built by Cuckfield R.D.C. in West Street, now West Way. As Worth parish was in East Sussex, that authority had built a primary school in North Road, which opened on 24 October 1938. The school log-book recorded the attendance of 119 children, cared for by the headmistress (Mrs. Inkstep) and two teachers. On Pound Hill there was a new estate of 102 houses along St Mary's Drive and the closes off it, and another 92 along Worth Road and Worth Park Avenue. They formed part of a large scheme which was halted by the outbreak of war in 1939, leaving 20 acres of land cleared but derelict for a time.

The 'suburbanisation' of Crawley was an important change. The 900 or so houses built during the inter-war period had brought very many new residents into the area. These were not necessarily aware of Crawley's roots and had a different attitude towards the rural area, its employment and its amenities. The new inhabitants had in many cases left the London area deliberately to live in a smaller, more rural settlement. It is not surprising that they were the most vociferous opponents of the proposed New Town in the 1940s, with its threat of moving Londoners 'en masse' to the country.

As houses were built, and the population expanded, two other changes can be seen which also had a long term impact on the area. One was the growth in the number of commuters, who travelled towards London each day from Ifield Halt, Crawley, Three Bridges and Grange Road (Crawley Down) stations. The main-line service to London was electrified in 1932; the branch line to East Grinstead continued to use steam trains until it was closed. Commuters are still an important section of the local population — people who do not

65. The buildings marking the edge of the old settlement of Crawley can clearly be seen in this aerial view except to the south, at the bottom of the picture, where houses had been built south of the railway line.

earn their living in Crawley and have their own attitudes towards local industry and the development of the town.

The other was the development at Gatwick. In 1891, the former steeplechase racecourse at Waddon, near Croydon, was closed and a new site was found at Gatwick beside the main-line railway. The railway company provided a railway station, with sidings for horse boxes, and the racecourse opened in 1891. It was a well-equipped course, popular, and held both steeplechase and flat races. In fact, during the Great War the Grand National was held there instead of at Aintree; Lester Piggott's grandfather won the 1918 race at Gatwick. The original Gatwick station was at approximately the same place as the present station.

Later, also at Waddon, a local aerodrome was expanded in 1920 to form Croydon aerodrome, which became London's main airport. Most aircraft followed the track of the railways before crossing the Channel en route to Paris and beyond. As aviation expanded, so did the demand for landing grounds. Land at Hunts Green Farm alongside Tinsley Green Lane was used as an airfield in the late 1920s and first licensed as an approved aerodrome in August 1930. The land was immediately adjacent to the racecourse, and so was known as Gatwick Aerodrome. The Surrey Aero Club was started almost immediately. A company, Home Counties Aircraft Services Ltd., issued a booklet: 'Learn to Fly at Gatwick: Thorough Tuition: Moderate Fees: No Risks'. Lessons cost £4 an hour, and you could buy a Blackburn Bluebird aircraft for £595. The old Hunts Green farmhouse was the first clubhouse for the Aero Club.

Because of shortage of money, Gatwick remained a small airfield with scant facilities for some time. The Redwing Aircraft Company bought the aerodrome in 1932 and operated a flying school from there. Some of the racecourse users found the airfield convenient, particularly on race days, but not exclusively so. A few small companies were based at Gatwick, including Spartan Air Lines, which operated internal scheduled flights.

In 1933 the aerodrome changed hands yet again. Because the railways feared loss of traffic to the aeroplane, a number of early airlines were owned or part controlled by railway

66. Gatwick Aerodrome. A view taken in about 1935, when the old farmhouse was still the main clubhouse. When the new 'Beehive' was built a few years later, it was sited just off to the right.

companies. They tried to co-ordinate rail and air routes. Croydon never linked with the Southern Railway's main line, but a joint venture did take place at Gatwick between the Southern Railway, Imperial Airways and the Gatwick airport owners. In September 1935 a new station was opened just south of the racecourse station, and called Tinsley Green. After pressure from the airport owners, its name was changed to Gatwick Airport Station in June 1936. Until a few years ago, the remains of the platforms of this station could still be seen north of the road bridge at Tinsley Green.

The major building works which took place at the airport involved the construction of a large circular terminal building, surmounted by the control tower, linked by a 130-yard tunnel to the railway station. Passengers could alight from the train and walk under cover all the way to the aircraft. At the time this was a radical design, which gained world-wide acclaim. The white building was soon nicknamed 'The Beehive', and it can still be seen today, 50 years later. Because of the good rail link Gatwick and Croydon were equidistant in journey time from central London. The newly-formed British Airways was pleased to operate many of its services from Gatwick, to destinations such as Paris, Amsterdam, Malmo, Copenhagen and Hamburg.

Once again the fortunes of the airport fluctuated. Two fatal air crashes in 1936 put doubt into people's minds as to the safety of the aerodrome; both involved night flying, even then a contentious local issue. A little before midnight on 15 September a night mail aircraft crashed nearby at Rowley Farm, just after take-off. In the early hours of 19 November another plane crashed in Tilgate Forest, four miles south of Gatwick, on its approach to land. Doubts about the airport's safety, fears about its proneness to fogs, a heavy clay soil which was frequently waterlogged, and the introduction of heavier aircraft combined to undermine the airport's reputation. The railway, trying to protect its interests, banned competing airlines from using Gatwick and threatened travel agents who would not co-operate. This may have helped British Airways, but did not help the airport. Though some improvements were attempted, the Mole and its tributaries crossed the area and a period of heavy rain left the passenger tunnel flooded and heavy aircraft unable to use the grass strip. Faster aircraft needed a longer approach and landing areas, and British Airways moved all its operations back to Croydon in 1937.

The airport reverted to private aircraft use and was aided when the Royal Air Force offered a contract for the setting up of an Elementary and Reserve Flying Training School using Tiger Moths and Hawker Harts. Apart from flying use, other companies set up operations, in particular Airwork and Southern Aircraft, concerned with repairs and maintenance of aircraft. The owners of Gatwick — Airport Limited — were trying hard to keep afloat, or rather to keep dry.

In 1939 the racecourse continued to run its May, June, July and October meetings, including the Worth Stakes and the Gatwick Handicap, but the airport was in difficulties for most of the year. This was probably to the advantage of the racecourse; the racing people always claimed that the large low-flying aircraft interfered with both racing and the training of racehorses. The war, however, in 1939 changed the fortunes of the airport yet again.

Much of the story of the inter-war period had involved the growth of motor-traffic and the proliferation of house-building. As early as 1921 the local paper for 29 October published the result of a traffic census taken over the August bank holiday. (At that time the bank holiday was held on the first weekend of August.) On Sunday 31 July and Monday 1 August the census showed that between 9 a.m. and 9 p.m. the following traffic passed through Crawley High Street:

	Sunday	**Monday**
Bicycles	2,204	3,295
Motor-cycles	1,002	1,097
Cars	1,261	1,410
Omnibuses/Charabancs	492	756
Horse-drawn	45	77

This shows just how congested the High Street was becoming. The parish council was getting complaints about the '. . . filthy condition of the Square, caused by rubbish . . . being thrown on the highway by passengers in motor and other vehicles'.

When the *Albany Hotel* (which occupied a site approximately where the present cinema stands, and was originally *Terry's Temperance Hotel*) was sold in July 1921, it was claimed that there was '. . . huge demand arising, with the last decade's rapid increase in road travelling'. If Crawley residents imagined that the traffic was busy then, they could not have envisaged the enormous increase in motor vehicles which continued throughout the 1920s and 1930s. It was inevitable that a bypass should be built, and this was one of the early ones, which was completed just before the outbreak of the Second World War. The traffic problem was the main reason why the High Street fairs were not held after 1922. It was very inconvenient to close the main road twice a year. The Punch Bowl became a 'Tea Shoppe' and even more garages sprang into being. Bus routes developed, Southdown and the East Sussex Traction Company (later part of London Transport) operated services. A bus garage was built in the London Road in 1929.

The entries in *Kelly's Directory* for 1938 show how the village of Crawley had indeed become an urban area. There were nine motor engineers, and both a car-hire company and a 'petrol station' were listed; there were 11 cafés, restaurants and tearooms; there was enough work for four solicitors; a large new cinema, the 'Embassy', was being operated by Shipman and King. And in 1939 a new parade of shops was started next to the *George*, though never quite completed to the original design. Into this parade moved Boots the Chemist, Woolworths and the Labour Exchange. The place was large enough at last to attract the multiples.

In Ifield and Worth there were some changes in the farming pattern as nurseries and market gardens were opened to cater for the growing consumer demand from London and locally. In Langley Lane there was a well-known herb farm called Sepril Lodge. Even the farming community became more urban orientated.

Two events in the later 1930s show another facet of urban life. The friars of the Capuchin Friars Minor had come to the district in 1859 to serve the Catholic community, and their church had been built on land given to them by Francis Scawen Blunt. In 1933 the Sisters of *Nôtre Dame de Namur* opened a convent in Pound Hill, also on former Crabbett Park land, and a school developed from there. Forty years later they realised a large sum of money for their order by selling much of the land for housing development. In the late 1930s the St Francis of Assisi School was opened in the Three Bridges Road.

To conclude this section, three entries from the Three Bridges School log-book can be used as an illustration of the past, present and future as shown at the time.

> 11 November 1938. Armistice Day was remembered this morning . . . Members of the staff and two of the older children read extracts from poems etc. while the Head Teacher gave an address. The two minutes' silence was observed.

Even after twenty years, the Great War was still remembered and its memory marked in schools.

> 19 April 1939. Mr. O. F. Brown, Air Raid Precautions Organiser, called this morning and discussed measures to be taken in case of War. He recommended Trench shelters.

It is interesting to note how early war preparations were being made.

> 13 July 1939. This afternoon about 70 of the older children paid a visit to Gatwick Airport, and were conducted around each type of plane, except the bombers.

These would have been Whitley bombers. The school children were privileged to have a preview of what forty years later was to dominate the local labour market.

The Second World War — and after

When the Second World War started in September 1939, people did not really know what to do. Much of everyday life altered immediately: organised sport ceased, a blackout of lighting at night operated, the population was fitted with gas masks, air-raid warnings were tested, shelters built, rationing introduced, conscription brought in — then nothing

67. Silver Jubilee celebrations in Lower Square in 1935.

happened. In Northgate, the Dyers' almshouses were nearing completion. Building work was stopped, but after a few weeks, when the expected bombing and gassing had not materialised, the builders, Longley's, decided to carry on and complete the buildings. This was the period of the 'Phoney War', and although life was greatly changed war was not felt in quite the way everyone had expected.

Of course, the war did affect the locality in many ways. Men were called-up into the armed forces and women once again were expected to take over many traditional male jobs. The number of local residents who were killed in action, however, was far fewer than those lost in the First World War. Employees of local firms which were involved in making weapons and munitions were exempt from call-up.

All local farms were encouraged to increase production and much marginal land was brought into use. Spare land was turned into allotments and for a few years local agriculture once again was a dominant industry. This was felt especially in Ifield and Worth. All shops experienced difficulty in getting stock. Food and clothing were rationed, and petrol was only available for those car-users who were given petrol coupons. Many local cars had to be laid-up for the duration of the war and the roads, though busy with military traffic, were much quieter.

Crawley was far enough away from London to be considered 'safe', and two London schools were evacuated to the area. Three Bridges School closed for the summer vacation as usual on 3 August, but the children of Ravenstone School, Balham, were moved to the locality and billeted on the local residents. Three Bridges School did not reopen until

11 September, when it operated two shifts — one school occupied the premises from 9 a.m. to 1 p.m., and the other from 1 p.m. to 5 p.m. Including private evacuees, the school roll was 165 local children and 141 London children and these numbers slowly rose. Later the Montefiore Institute was taken over during the daytime to hold some classes. Meanwhile, in Crawley, the Parkside Boys' School of Clapham had arrived with 150 boys, and they operated a similar sharing scheme until the Congregational church premises opposite the school in Robinson Road were also used. Within a year, however, most evacuees had returned to London, as happened all over Britain. Only 45 of the Parkside children remained in Three Bridges after one year.

Not only were children moved to the area. Many London businesses sought accommodation in large houses outside London, and the military requisitioned properties it required. Tilgate mansion was occupied by the Canadian army for some years; the new bypass became a kind of military car-park. Some 'holiday/weekend homes' were also requisitioned for bombed-out families from London.

Railway workers spent long hours at work during the war, moving military and civil passengers as well as supplies, despite the frequent bombing of the tracks. Route-planners and track-gangs all worked overtime to keep the railways running; Redhill station was the central junction for the whole of the Dunkirk invasion. It seems that, on the whole, the Brighton line outside London escaped comparatively lightly during the German bombing raids, considering how large the sidings and locomotive sheds were just south-west of Three Bridges station.

Gatwick Airport was requisitioned by the R.A.F. in September 1939 and aircraft maintenance continued. Croydon airport closed to civil aviation and plans were again made to turn Gatwick into London's south-of-the-river airport for passenger aircraft. B.O.A.C. staff, customs and immigration were all prepared to operate from Gatwick, when Germany finally over-ran the whole of the mainland of Europe and most civil routes were lost. Consequently the R.A.F. took over the airport completely.

A bomber wing was stationed at Gatwick; later, Defiant night-fighters, army squadrons and, eventually, Fighter Command operated from there. Though some fighters were based at Gatwick the aerodrome was mostly used for repair and refitting work, and as a general airfield for a wide variety of aircraft. Dozens of different types landed at Gatwick, from a Tiger Moth to a Gloster Meteor, from a Wellington bomber to a Liberator. Wire mesh runways were laid and the racecourse buildings were taken over for personnel and to expand the landing area. Despite its busy activity Gatwick always had a temporary air about it — prefabricated and reused buildings rather than permanent ones.

The Crawley area, being between the coast and London, had aircraft flying overhead throughout the war. In the circumstances, the fifty or so high explosive and the two thousand incendiary bombs which fell on the area may be considered a light load, particularly as most fell on open country. The school logs contain recurring references to bombing. From September to December 1940, during the Battle of Britain, air raid warnings were regular, and at all schools the children often spent much of the day in shelters. It is ironic that much of the bombing of London took place after most of the evacuated children had returned home.

The two serious bombings of Crawley took place later in the war. At 8.30 a.m. on 4 February 1943 a line of bombs fell on the town centre. Two bombs hit and badly damaged the rear portion of the National School in West Green. Luckily, it was just before the children were due to arrive, and although a cleaner was present she escaped injury. Another fell on the Westminster Bank building in the High Street, near to the level crossing, and four more opposite at the new Post Office building and the adjacent shop. Others fell in Station Road. Two people were killed.

The second attack was by two V1 flying bombs (or 'doodle-bugs', as they were commonly known) which happened on 10 July 1944. One landed near to the railway line at the junction of West Street with Oak Road, resulting in seven deaths and 44 injured — 15 houses were destroyed. The other fell in the street at Malthouse Road but luckily did not explode. Residents were evacuated until a bomb disposal squad could make it safe. There is a large map in Crawley library, drawn up by the electricity board and the civil defence units, of the location of all bombs which fell and all aircraft which crashed in the area.

The bombings were recorded in the local press, but although photographs and details of casualties were reported, the newspapers kept actual locations unnamed. For example, although the February 1943 bombing of Crawley formed the whole of the front page of the East Grinstead newspaper, the report says 'A well-known town in the south-east of England was bombed . . .'. Local people were supposed to guess where the location was — and the photographs made that not difficult! East Grinstead itself had the most serious casualties in north Sussex when a number of bombs fell on the town centre late in the afternoon of Friday 9 July 1943. The Whitehall cinema and many shops were destroyed and 108 people were killed, necessitating a mass funeral. The rural nature of much of the local area, however, minimised the effects of bombing even though individual houses and farms suffered damage in Ifield, Three Bridges, Crawley Down, Copthorne and Turners Hill.

Though the war had its undoubted impact on Crawley, decisions which had more far-reaching effects on Crawley's future were being made in Westminster during the early 1940s. Town and country planning had been introduced in a very limited form to Britain in 1909 and its scope was extended in a 1932 Act. As a result, local authorities were given some planning functions. For example, the Dorking and Horley R.D.C. had had to approve the plans put forward to develop Gatwick Airport in the 1930s. The ministry inspector at the time commented that the local council was not supportive of the plans since it could see no benefit to the area in allowing Gatwick to be developed. The council may have feared that, if Gatwick were allowed to grow, neighbouring landowners and residents could have claimed compensation from the local authority. Interest locally in planning issues was beginning and, in particular, the then members of the local W.E.A. class became active in organised discussion.

The Crawley W.E.A. group was started in 1932, and its local Tutor Organiser, Roy Armstrong, no doubt had an impact on the way in which the class developed. Though never a large group of people, and professedly non-political, it exerted quite an influence on local opinion during the next 15 years. Funds were always in short supply. The minutes record in April 1935 that '. . . suggestions for Whist Drives, Dances and Socials were made but thought rather impractical owing to the large amount always held in Crawley'.

On 15 August 1935 the group organised a day exhibition in the Congregational Hall on the subject of 'Town Planning' which was well attended, and Roy Armstrong gave a talk on 'Housing' in the evening. Over the next 10 years this was a recurring theme. A class in 'Local Government and Town Planning' was held in 1936/7. In 1943 a discussion was held on 'The future of Crawley as a model town' and during the 1943/4 session a class was held to discuss 'Town and Country Planning'. Various ideas were expressed by class members; it was generally agreed that there should be no more auction sales of land.

During the course the tutor had suggested that the class should write a paper and draw up plans for Crawley as they would like to improve it. This was done and a public meeting was held in 1944 to discuss the plans: it was well attended and many influential local people were there, including most of the parish council. (One specific result of this was that a letter was sent to Cuckfield R.D.C. from the W.E.A. asking that 'The Hawth' be scheduled as a public open space.) Later, in 1945, the Square and Smith's Corner came onto the market. The W.E.A. wrote to West Sussex County Council asking it to purchase the property

'. . . for the future improvement of Crawley'; this was done. In November 1945, another debate was arranged: 'That the local government of Crawley, Ifield and parts of the parish of Worth should be under one authority'. There was a large and interested audience. Gen. Sir Desmond Anderson of Ifield and Mr. Gladstone Moore of Three Bridges proposed the motion: Mr. Gilson of Worth School opposed it. At the end of the evening only one person voted against the motion. Subsequently a county council planner from Chichester came to talk to the group.

Meanwhile, in Ifield, wartime camaraderie and social activities had led to the setting up of an Ifield Assocation. Meetings were held in January and March 1945, resulting in the creation of the association '. . . to foster a sense of community through the service of the social and cultural needs of Ifield'.

One of the by-products of this growing civic awareness was that a Crawley and District Community Association was proposed during 1945/6. Messrs. Norman Longley, Ernest Stanford, R. M. Crowe and A. J. Weston took the initiative to call a meeting in November 1945. Eighty representatives of local organisations attended and the Community Association was born in April 1946. The importance of local initiative following individual popular active interest and public education had always been stressed as an essential precursor of organised local planning and progress.

Nationally there had been a succession of committees reporting on a number of inter-related matters of planning; the fact of the war played little part in this movement. The Barlow Commission report (1940) had urged the containment of existing urban areas, and the decentralisation of population and industry from old city centres. It recommended garden cities and satellite towns around great cities. It also recommended that planning should be dealt with in unified units. The Scott Committee (1941) wanted new towns to be sited so as not to encroach on top-quality agricultural land. The Uthwatt Committee (1942) pointed out that land may have to be compulsorily purchased; that the personal wishes and interests of landowners may have to give way to the public good of the community.

These principles were to be well aired after the war. The Abercrombie Plan (1944), seeking to improve over-crowded housing conditions and the concentration of industry which co-existed in London, wanted to move one-and-a-half million people from London. Ten satellite towns were recommended for half a million of those people, each town to be 20-25 miles from central London. When the Labour Party took power in the 1945 election, Lewis Silkin became Minister of Town and Country Planning. As a result the New Towns Act 1946 was passed by parliament.

No thought of a New Town for Crawley, however, was in anyone's mind in 1946. The men in the Forces were slowly demobilised and returned to their homes. Rationing and shortages continued for some time. Building materials were in short supply, and to obtain them one needed a licence. Houses which had suffered neglect and damage since 1939 were not easily repaired. A willing householder was severely restricted as to the amount of timber and bricks he could get. When the New Town research group surveyed the existing housing in 1949 it made a point that a great number of existing houses were sub-standard. In Pound Hill only six-and-a-half per cent of houses needed extensive repairs or were unfit for habitation. In Three Bridges, on the other hand, 22 per cent did. Cuckfield R.D.C. built houses in the Pearson Road/Worth Road area; Horsham R.D.C. built others along the Ifield Road. Some of the first post-war private housing was in the small closes along St Mary's Drive in Pound Hill.

There were a number of builders and timber merchants, hardly surprising given the amount of construction work that had occurred in the previous 30 years, and some engineering companies which had been busy on military precision engineering work during the war and beyond. They were all hampered by the shortage of stock. There were still local laundries, and the agricultural district supported a blacksmith. The decline of the farm horse had been delayed by the war but was hastened in the immediate post-war years. There was also a seed-cleaning mill by Three Bridges station.

Gatwick was changing slowly. The R.A.F. was still interested in giving work to the aircraft maintenance firms, but in the immediate post-war period a number of small charter companies, using ex-R.A.F. aircraft, were based at Gatwick. Cargo transport was needed at a time when Britain was being exhorted to export as much as possible. Passenger travel was much less important, especially as there were still restrictions on foreign travel. In particular, currency regulations permitted so little money to be taken out of the country that foreign holidays were impractical even for the well-off. The Minister of Civil Aviation used Gatwick as a testing centre for would-be pilots. The airport however, though conveniently placed, was inconveniently provided with services and still badly drained: it remained small and its continued use was precarious.

Local newspaper advertisements of the time were concerned much with the same matters as they had been for the previous 10 years. Rationing continued; waste paper was needed to make ceiling board for the building industry; the Minister of Agriculture constantly gave advice to farmers; the Victoria Wine Company wanted all empty bottles to be returned for reuse. For those who wanted a meal out the Jordans Country Club offered lunches for 3s. 6d. (17½p) and dinners for 5s. (25p); the *Felbridge Place Hotel* offered dinner dances. Hardly any cars were for sale; the 'Situations Vacant' still mainly offered women work as cooks and domestics.

Yet despite the austerity, Sir Malcolm Campbell, who had many times captured the world's land speed record in his cars, was now looking to take the world's water speed record. His motor boat, Bluebird II, was kept in a workshop at Tilgate (where he owned much property) and was regularly floated in Tilgate Lake.

When, in May 1946, a small hall and prefabricated classrooms were opened at Three Bridges School, the headmistress wrote in the log-book that this was the first time since July 1939 that the school had been all together on one site. The post-war period was spent attempting to clear up or obliterate the effects of the war.

Chapter 12

The New Town — Maturity

The origins of Crawley New Town: the first skirmishes

In October 1945 a committee was set up, with Lord Reith as Chairman, to consider all matters relating to the establishment of New Towns. They were intended to be '. . . self-contained and balanced communities for work and living'. Virtually everyone consulted agreed that a government agency should develop the towns, and the New Town Act was introduced into parliament in April 1946 and passed by July. It received royal assent on 1 August 1946. Originally 20 new towns were envisaged. Eight of these were built to disperse people and employment from London, and Stevenage was the first to be designated, in November 1946.

The Greater London Plan had suggested that two towns be established to the south of London; one at Crowhurst, south of Oxted, and the other at Holmwood, south of Dorking. At the same time the south-east regional office of the Ministry of Town and Country Planning was suggesting that there was a need to urbanise the Ifield-Crawley-Three Bridges area in view of the unco-ordinated and hotch-potch development which had taken place after the break-up of the great estates. The two county councils concerned had already agreed that the area's population should be allowed to grow to between twenty and forty thousand.

In retrospect, it was only to be expected that Crawley would be selected as the site for a New Town. The agricultural land was not particularly good, road and railway links were excellent, Gatwick was not to be developed, and although water and sewage schemes were needed these were feasible. At a meeting of the Horsham Rural District Council in May 1946 the councillors were nevertheless surprised by a letter from Lewis Silkin, the Minister of Town and Country Planning, explaining that Crawley had been recommended to him as an area to be designated a New Town. The letter was simply a confidential notification of what was happening.

Local councillors and officers from the various planning authorities were next invited to a meeting with the minister on 10 July 1946. These were Surrey, East Sussex and West Sussex County Councils and Dorking and Horley, Cuckfield and Horsham District Councils. The parish councils were ignored, not being planning authorities. Thus, Ernest Stanford and Norman Longley were the only two local residents who attended the meeting, being Horsham R.D.C. councillors. The Minister explained that the meeting was a formal consultation with the local authorities concerned; he also told the group that he had just told the House of Commons that he intended to designate Crawley as a New Town. Not one of the councillors objected to or criticised the decision.

Most of the local population seem to have looked favourably upon the proposal. Some of the older residents did not like the idea of losing the 'village' atmosphere in which they had been brought up, though in reality this was already past and could not be recovered. In addition those who had already left the London area to buy property in Crawley were likely to object to the prospect of thousands of Londoners being moved into rented accommodation in the area. One can have some sympathy with those who, having sought a 'rural' location (or rather one which was comparatively rural in relation to Greater London), now faced the prospect of a town being erected around them. The local Property Owners' Association was worried about the possible decline in value of its members' properties. Had they been able to foresee what happened, they might have been more enthusiastic.

The active members of the local W.E.A. group obviously supported the proposal, and arranged a public meeting in the Congregational church hall on 25 July, with Norman Longley in the chair. Ernest Stanford, who was vice-chairman of Horsham R.D.C., spoke about the proposals and explained why he was in favour. As the W.E.A. chairman subsequently reported '. . . all points of view were put forward, being the first meeting of its kind'. There were more meetings, and the opposition grew vociferous. Many local parish councillors felt insulted at not being consulted by the minister. The Property Owners' Association collected money from its members to plead their case at a public inquiry.

The local Conservative M.P. was strongly against the proposal, though in the event the Conservative Party never lost the constituency seat. On 11 December 1946 the Duke of Norfolk addressed the Young Farmers' Clubs in Crawley. The local paper reported his speech, and the Duke had obviously gauged the mood of his audience.

> You know better than I do the possible calamity which is about to befall Crawley and the Three Bridges area. All that I can say is that I give every possible sympathy to those people who love rural England and to those people who find themselves in similar circumstances as do the people of this locality.

But at least he went on to say that they had a golden opportunity to try to bring the people who lived in the towns and the country closer together. Mr. Stanford proposed the vote of thanks to the Duke. 'Some people say that the town and the country will never mix. The war, I think, proved that to be materially wrong.'

Because of objections, the public inquiry at the Montefiore Hall lasted three days from 4 November 1946. Unfortunately, this was the start of a protracted legal battle by the committed few who did not want a New Town. They did delay it, but the only real beneficiaries were the legal profession who earned good fees from the case. It must also be noted, however, that some of the New Town Corporation employees privately conceded later that the delay gave them more time to prepare a good plan for the town, and that on balance it was not too much of a setback.

The main objections, perhaps understandably, were from those who feared that their homes would be taken away from them, and at a low price. Other objections were from 'experts' who confidently stated that, among other things: (i) it would be impossible to provide an adequate water supply — said a consultant engineer; (ii) the railway would require hundreds of bridges — said a town planner; (iii) people would not work in Crawley and live in Crawley — said a town planner; (iv) the *George*, the Ancient Priors, the Punchbowl would all be destroyed — said a consulting surveyor; (v) the railway would have to be completely reconstructed — said a consultant surveyor. In view of subsequent events, many of those who gave evidence at the time at great expense may have been embarrassed later to be reminded of what they argued.

The inspector made his report, and on 9 January 1947 the minister confirmed the order designating Crawley as a New Town. It was challenged in the High Court, and an appeal against the decision was dismissed on 30 July 1947. It was next challenged in the Court of Appeal and on 12 December 1947 the Master of the Rolls dismissed this appeal. Fortunately for all, except perhaps the lawyers, no further appeal was lodged. With great relief the work could proceed.

The minister had set up an advisory committee for the proposed New Town in October 1946. Ernest Stanford was the only local resident, though another member — Caroline Haslett — had been brought up in Three Bridges and had attended the Robinson Road School. This advisory committee became the Crawley Development Corporation (C.D.C.) in February 1947. What were its duties and powers?

Once the outline of the area was designated the C.D.C. could acquire whatever land it required by compulsory purchase; it could provide houses, factories and public buildings; it could arrange for roads, lighting, water supply, gas, electricity, sewerage and main drainage to be provided; it could employ whatever administrative and specialist staff it required; it could employ a direct labour force or use outside contractors; it could borrow money at the market rate from the government, to be repaid over 60 years; it could determine all rents, and subsidise housing if it wished. Local government was not, however, part of its duties. The town was to become a separate county district. When the population of the New Town reached 30,000 in 1956 Crawley Urban District Council was created. Later, in 1974, it became the Crawley Borough Council.

Despite much activity at the planning level, little tangible work was performed for a year or two. The protracted High Court cases created uncertainty until December 1947, and the post-war economic crises caused delays — almost, at one point, abandonment. New Towns were not given any priority in obtaining either building materials or a labour force. At least, however, the planners had time to draw up plans to provide a sound infrastructure of water supply, sewerage, roads and services.

Another uncertainty at the time was that the first chairman, Sir Wilfred Lindsell, had appointed Thomas Sharp as consultant to prepare an outline plan by 1 March 1947, with a preliminary plan by the end of the year. Lindsell was not dynamic enough for the minister, Lewis Silkin, and within a few months he had replaced him with Sir Thomas Bennett. The first annual report of the C.D.C., for the year ending 31 March 1948, gave a summary of the progress made since 1946. Mr. Sharp had submitted his plan on 1 March 1947, but, 'In delivering his provisional outline plan and the results of his early research, Mr. Sharp intimated that he did not wish to continue as Consultant to the Corporation'. The reason behind this extraordinary decision was no doubt a personality clash, never completely explained. In the event, Anthony Minoprio was appointed as planning consultant instead, on 5 June 1947, and he also produced a provisional plan. Others were appointed consultants for sewerage and drainage, water supplies, land policy, and forestry. All this added to the delay in starting, but in view of the appeals going through the courts it was not a serious delay.

This first annual report also gave details of the work in progress on a number of fronts. The target population of 50,000 was to be reached in 15 years, i.e. by 1963. The C.D.C. proposed to provide, in order: sewers, factories and residential neighbourhoods. The housing would proceed: (i) Crawley North, (ii) Crawley South, (iii) Three Bridges. As a start, a contract to provide roads and site works for 34 houses for key workers in West Green had been awarded to H. J. Paris of Hove at a tender price of £7,397. Land was being purchased, including Broadfield Hotel and Country Club to be used for the C.D.C. offices and land by Rolls Farm in the north for a sewage works.

The second annual report, to March 1949, laid down some guiding principles. The design of the town was to be with '. . . a ring and radial pattern of roads, with residential neighbourhoods grouped in a double ring round the town centre, and a single industrial area at the north'. Nine neighbourhoods were planned, and the order in which it was proposed that they were to be started was West Green, Northgate, Three Bridges, Pound Hill, Southgate, Tilgate, Langley Green, Ifield Green and Gossops Green. Two neighbourhoods were to be in course of construction at any one time, thus giving choice to prospective residents.

One other principle was that the town was to comprise a balanced community. Though the C.D.C. would deny that they were in any way engaged in social engineering, the concept of workers and managers living together was discussed. Consequently it was decided that 80 per cent of the houses would be 'Manual Standard', that 15 per cent would be 'Intermediate Types', costing between £2,000 and £2,500, and that 5 per cent would be detached, costing between £3,000 and £5,000. Each neighbourhood would have its proportion

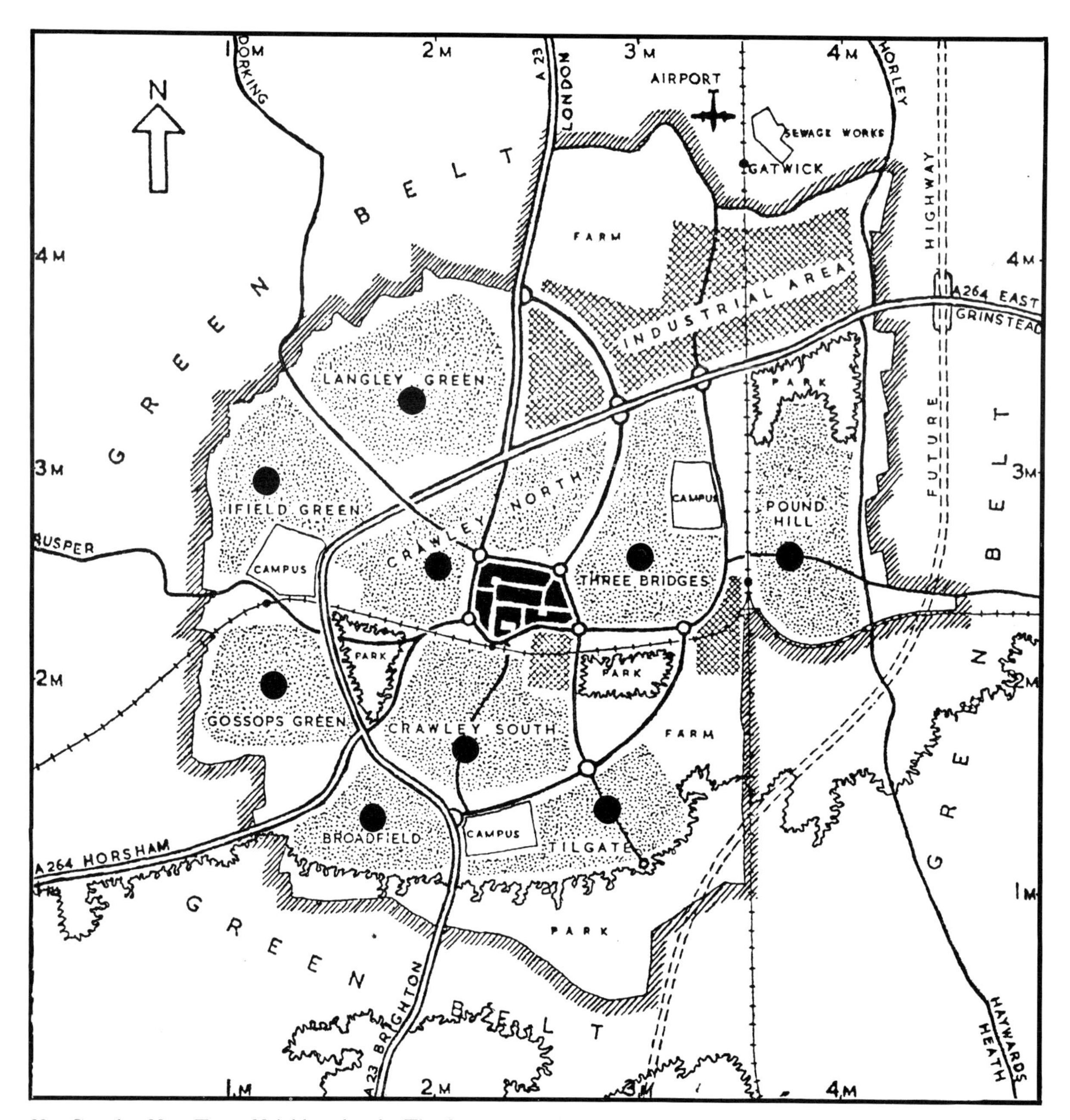

68. Crawley New Town Neighbourhoods. The first proposed neighbourhood structure of the New Town. Note that the present M23 was anticipated this early.

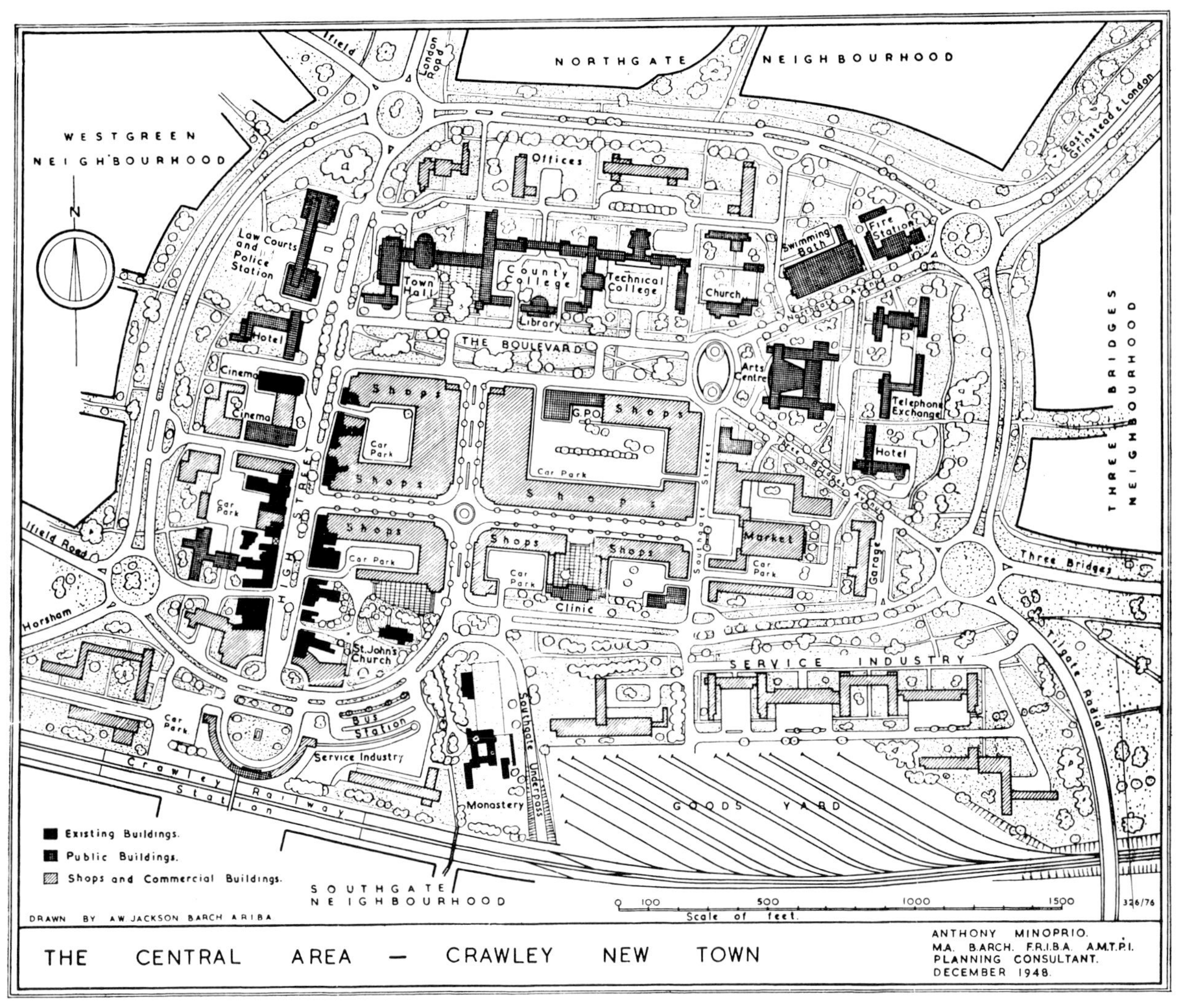

69. Crawley New Town centre: the original proposal by Anthony Minoprio. It is interesting to compare this visionary 'Garden City' plan with what was in fact built.

of each type of housing. In 1949 the contract for the first 34 houses in West Green was awarded to Hoad and Taylor at a cost of £45,220.

By 1950 these were occupied; 155 other houses were in course of construction at West Green; 162 were being started at Northgate. A factory for W. C. Youngman was being built by Longley's; factories for A.P.V. and for Vitamins Ltd. were at the design stage; standard factory blocks were under way. The New Town had really started.

Over the next 25 years and beyond, the bare facts given in the annual reports show the achievement of the Corporation and its successor, the Commission. Sir Thomas Bennett was seen as inflexible, dogmatic and highly successful. He pursued the goal of turning Minoprio's dream into reality, and in 15 years reached the goal. Unfortunately, by that time the goal posts had been moved. The New Town obviously loomed large in people's conversation — speculation, fact and rumour were well intermixed — but there were other topics of conversation also.

In 1943 John Haigh, a pleasantly spoken and charming 34-year-old gentleman, had come to work in Crawley. He lodged with a local family, joined local activities — particularly musical events — and was well received. He hired a small workshop in a yard in Leopold Road in West Green. Later he moved back to London, but still retained his links with Crawley. It was a tremendous shock when he was arrested in London at the end of February 1949, and charged at Horsham Magistrate's Court with having murdered a woman at Crawley. He had shot and killed her in the Leopold Road workshop. The case was particularly notorious because he had dissolved the body in an acid bath in the workshop, and whilst the body was dissolving he had calmly had tea at the Ancient Priors and later dinner at the *George*. Police found the acid, rubber gloves, a revolver and ammunition on the premises, and enough evidence to show that a body had been disposed of, though not completely.

After a trial at Lewes he was hanged on 10 August 1949. At the time the case was of far greater interest to the local people than the construction work at West Green, the compulsory purchase orders on the local shops and land, or the air display at Gatwick. Many knew Haigh; he had always set out to impress and charm people. The case is still remembered as 'The Acid Bath Murder'. It was the sort of publicity the town could well have done without.

The airport was not to the forefront of local affairs, though in ministry offices in London it was central to many discussions. The fact that the C.D.C. kept on reporting that there were no plans to develop Gatwick seems to indicate that they did not really believe it. In November 1948 the airport owners were warned that the aerodrome was likely to be derequisitioned in September 1949. This caused them great concern. If it happened, then the Ministry of Civil Aviation would remove telecommunications, wireless and customs facilities, and the land taken from the racecourse would have to be returned.

The Daily Express organised air pageants at Gatwick in July 1948 and again in July 1949. They were hugely successful and over 70,000 people attended. Behind-the-scenes opinion, however, was still in favour of Stansted as London's second airport. The chance happening which altered all this was the appointment of Peter Masefield to run British European Airways. He was pro-Gatwick, and in October 1949 the derequisitioning of the airport was deferred and the C.D.C. were told of proposed changes. Despite opposition from the neighbouring local authorities, the cabinet early in 1950 agreed that Gatwick ought to be the alternative to Heathrow. More B.E.A. flights were switched, and B.E.A. helicopters were based at the Beehive from 1951 for many years. Thus, when the Government decision to develop Gatwick was finally announced in July 1952, it was no longer a surprise. The local people were by then aware.

Perhaps the event which, in most people's minds, finally brought home the inescapable realisation that the world had changed was when Princess Elizabeth came to open the industrial estate on the site of Manor Farm on 25 January 1950. She named the estate 'Manor Royal'. There was no turning back.

The story of the New Town takes over the historical narrative of local life from 1950 onwards. In 1951, however, there was a final, almost defiant, look back over Crawley's history. To celebrate the Festival of Britain, local bodies throughout Britain arranged events to mark Britain's heritage. In Crawley, the community association with its usual drive set to and organised an 'Historic Crawley' exhibition in the Congregational Hall from 18 to 23 June 1951. An appeal was made for items of local interest, and collecting points for exhibits were set up in Ifield, Crawley and Three Bridges.

When the exhibition opened, there were more than 1,000 exhibits. There were various displays, such as 'Where they lived', 'Where they worked', 'How they celebrated'. Many photographs were produced, and a number of objects aroused interest. These included old church hand-bells, clothing, Elizabethan church plate, a 17th-century Quaker marriage certificate and a 17th-century trade token. It is obvious from reading the contemporary accounts that there was intense interest in the area's history among its residents — some of whom could trace their ancestry in the North Sussex area for hundreds of years.

In addition, a series of public lectures was held on eight successive Friday evenings. 'These talks will . . . provide as complete a picture as possible of the history of the locality, its people, their houses, and their way of living, recalling some local personalities.' The talks were on such topics as general history, the railway, iron working, the Franciscans and literary connections. A strong feeling of community comes over in these accounts: despite the divergent paths of development taken by Ifield, Crawley, Three Bridges and Worth, there was a sense of 'place' and the community association displayed it in action.

The 1950s and 1960s: establishing the New Town community

When the New Town was designated, there were about ten thousand people living in the area. Within the C.D.C. boundaries it had taken almost 1,000 years to reach a population figure of about two thousand inhabitants in 1801, and a further century to reach just over

70. Princess Elizabeth, accompanied by the Lord Lieutenant of the county, the Duke of Norfolk, arriving in the High Street to meet local people, in 1950.

5,000 in 1901. This growth was mostly the result of what is known as 'natural' increase, that is, an excess of births over deaths, though part of the population had always been transient and it was nothing new to have people moving into and out of the area.

After 1901, house building and the development of Crawley up to 1951 had changed this trend, because to the natural increase was added the large inward migration of people from outside the area. It was from the new inhabitants, the migrants, that most opposition to the New Town had come, though many newcomers had shown an eagerness to integrate with the old-established population, and were among the strongest New Town proponents. Those who were in positions of authority must have worried whether their positions would be attacked: the cosy nature of local society was about to be shattered. To an extent their fears were well grounded. On every front — political, social, commercial, economic, cultural — the New Towners were eventually to take over from the original population. It was a situation reminiscent of 1,500 years earlier when the Saxons came to a Celtic Sussex.

Anyone who had been born and bred in London, and lived through the 1940s there, would have experienced over-crowding, poor facilities, widespread bomb damage, and often insanitary conditions. When such people moved to Crawley it was like a move to the Garden of Eden. They found houses where everyone had a garden, gas, electricity, an indoor lavatory and a bathroom. The air smelled so fresh and sweet that visitors from 'The Smoke' commented on it. The new residents were interested in the present and the future. They were used to a pace of life unknown to the original inhabitants. Although many of the latter tried to integrate with the New Towners, it was not easy.

Consider the difficulties. The new neighbourhoods themselves were not integrated with the original housing stock. Langley Green, Northgate and Three Bridges were built on farmland. The New Towners worked for firms which they had already worked for in London, and even though a few local people did take up work in the industrial estate, they were a minority. The men brought their workmates with them, and in these groups their wives mixed. Factories set up their own social clubs: new neighbourhoods had their own community centre in which New Towners' activities developed. Only in shops and public houses did old and new meet, and the neighbourhoods were soon given their own local shops and pubs.

Many of the New Towners were homesick. Each weekend saw a large exodus of residents to 'back home' in London. The Sunday evening taxi-service did well at Three Bridges Station from people returning to their Crawley homes. There was also some understandable jealousy among the older residents who saw 'luxurious' homes being given to strangers and denied to locals. This is not to ignore the links which were made and the integration which did come, but writers and sociologists who examine the community spirit in the New Town tend to ignore one fact. The New Towners became unified, but the old residents had to agree (either willingly or by default) to become absorbed: absorbed and lost.

Nowadays, a chance remark by an acquaintance may lead to the query 'Are you Old Crawley?'. An affirmative reply will leave the questioner gazing in wonder at this relic of days gone by, before the New Town came. Old Crawley people still keep in touch with one another, know what has happened to schoolfriends, watch closely old landmarks. Three Bridges primary school celebrated its Golden Jubilee in October 1988. Many of the former pupils who came reminisced about the pre-war, wartime and post-war days. They knew what had happened to their schoolfriends. There is a strong network, but it no longer exerts influence on the locality.

The politicians, the central and local government employees, the managers, the staff of multiple shops, most voluntary organisations — all these groups are dominated by those whose families moved into Crawley. There is, in the late 1980s, a large body of 55-60-year-olds in the town. This is one of the largest age-groups. They are still Londoners. Their

71. & 72. A first view of the New Town. These two pictures show a group of A.P.V. workers and their families visiting West Green in September 1950 to look at the new houses available for them to choose from before moving to Crawley.

children may have been born and bred in Crawley, but not the Crawley of pre-1950. The family stories of pre-1950 relate to elsewhere. Those who are born in the 1980s in Crawley may be unaware, however, that there ever was a difference between family backgrounds.

* * *

At first in the 1950s people had to get used to living on a building site. Land, especially farmland, was compulsorily purchased as required and compensation offered in accordance with procedures laid down by parliament. Most landowners objected to the amounts offered. Land was bought as farmland and then redesignated as building land. The profits, if any, accrued to the development corporation rather than to the landowners. This was a central tenet to the socialist view of land. The corporation was not popular among landowners. Farmer Lee managed to be evicted from a succession of local farms, and achieved wide fame — or notoriety — from the publicity.

The neighbourhoods were developed as planned though the order varied slightly from the original scheme: West Green, Northgate, Three Bridges, Langley Green, Pound Hill, Ifield (no longer to be called Ifield Green), Southgate, Tilgate. The master plan showed a town of 50,000 people using 4,000 acres of the 6,000 acres in the designated area. Almost immediately the minister asked for a target of 60,000 instead.

73. Shops at West Green, the first neighbourhood shopping centre, newly opened in the early 1950s.

By March 1951, Youngman's factory (from Wandsworth) had begun production and A.P.V. (of Wandsworth, White City and Slough) had started to build their own factory, as had F. H. Bourner (of Croydon). Later in that year, Vitamins Ltd. (of Hammersmith) and

Young Randall and Co. (of Croydon) started construction work. In the meantime six standard units had been occupied, including one by Johnson and Bloy still sited in Manor Royal. To deal with the larger school rolls, prefabricated buildings were hastily erected on the school site in Northgate and the bombed National School site in West Green. Because the New Town straddled two county council areas, East Sussex County Council was planning to build the Hazelwick Campus, though less enthusiastically.

On 1 April 1953 virtually all the New Town area was moved under West Sussex County Council control. Crawley Parish Council applied for urban district council status (and independence of Horsham Rural District) and this was finally agreed in May 1956. In 1954 the town centre was finally started and The Broadwalk, a pedestrian shopping way, was opened by the minister (Duncan Sandys) on 10 December 1954. Queens Square was started next, and in 1956 the college site was developed.

That year saw the diversion of the A23 road across Lowfield Heath in order that the new airport could be started. The old airport station was closed and a new station — integrated into the airport complex — was to be opened on the site of the former racecourse station. Gatwick was closed to all aircraft except helicopters from April 1956 to 30 May 1958 when a Transair Viscount landed. Its official opening was almost its real opening — a most unusual occurrence — when the Queen and Prince Philip arrived in a Heron of the Queen's Flight on 9 June 1958. Many local people watched this on their new black and white television sets. A good number of aircraft charter companies, which started and closed in quick succession at the time, used Gatwick. The significant step-up was when in 1960 the Hunting-Clan Air Transport Company merged with Airwork Ltd., a company with 30 years' experience of working at Gatwick. The new company was named British United Airways (B.U.A.) and Freddy Laker was soon appointed its General Manager. Gatwick became synonymous with B.U.A.

How, then, did the town coalesce? That it did is obvious. In fact, in the 1970s no local person would refer to the place as being a New Town. The name was dropped — after 20 years; despite continued expansion, what was *new* about it? The newcomers had dug in roots and taken over. It might be useful to examine the ways this community spirit had developed. A visiting American professor spent some time in the town in the 1970s seeking to establish just that. Those who had been involved in the community in the early days were invited to give their thoughts and opinions, and the pattern which emerged was interesting.

When shopkeepers applied to rent premises, they were interviewed and those selected were the ones who showed that they were prepared to enter the life of the community. As the New Town developed, a gap grew between the High Street/town centre shops and the neighbourhood shops. Local shops were meeting places for housewives and helped to foster local awareness: this was assisted by the provision of neighbourhood 'pubs' and churches. Also, and right from the start this was viewed as most important, the local Community Hut was erected.

The community centres were given, sometimes reluctantly, to the Crawley and District Community Association to administer. This organisation had supported the New Town from its inception. The association was one of the few old Crawley organisations to continue to flourish, and many of its original members worked in harmony with the new residents to create a community feeling. Perversely, the success of the local community centres helped to push the New Towners into a dominant position. The Community Centre Committee was a cornerstone of the association's management structure, so it claimed, and was of fundamental importance to community life.

Another important influence was the Trade Union movement. Both A.P.V. and Edwards came to Crawley already unionised; the Amalgamated Engineering Union (A.E.U.) was very strong and their shop stewards became an organising committee urging all other new factory staff to unionise. They were highly successful — until the 1960s there was strong

74. The town centre. Taken in the mid-1950s, this shows the shopping centre taking shape adjacent to the old High Street.

support for the unions and they played a leading role in the local Labour Party. Once the parish council had a Labour majority, this influence was carried through to the U.D.C. and subsequently to the borough. The town has remained Labour-controlled ever since, except for a couple of years, 1969-70. Even an undoubted affluence and an almost zero unemployment rate has not changed this political leaning.

In that the newcomers were predominantly factory workers, the shop floor became the place where issues common to all were raised and discussed. Teething troubles within the new community were likely to be channelled via shop stewards to the Trades Council and so to open debate. The private housing, however, which was also a part of the planned growth, attracted a different kind of resident. Pound Hill in particular developed as part of London's commuter zone and Three Bridges Station was its focus.

A Crawley Industrial Group developed to give managerial input into the arena of public issues — it was concerned with ensuring a constant labour supply and was active in pressing for more housing. Since most senior managers lived outside the town, however, their role in local affairs was limited.

Community spirit is often stronger in adversity, or when pursuing a cause. The New Towners, though grateful to the C.D.C., nevertheless from time to time had disputes with it. There was a rent strike in 1955 as a protest against rent increases. The services to be provided by the local authorities (e.g. schools, recreational facilities) or by other governmental bodies (e.g. a hospital) were not always provided in the correct sequence. For example, school places in the first areas lagged behind house building; later Gossops Green School was opened with only one pupil. Community huts were achieved, it seemed, only as a result of continual agitation for them.

Unfortunately, having 'permissive legislation' means that bodies can spend money on facilities as they wish. In many matters both the C.D.C. and the W.S.C.C. were permitted to make community provision. Each expected the other to do it. It is commonly accepted that the master plan's weakness was an absence of social service provision. And even when the master plan provided a hospital site, the health authority said that they could not afford to build it.

The community association acted as a non-political focus. There were common links between it and the local consumers' group which conducted surveys into such matters as opening hours of shops, provision of car parking, and the closure of Queens Square to cars. The need for the consumers' group waned as a Citizen's Advice Bureau developed from the community association, and the local authority created a Weights and Measures Department. Eventually the community association became the Crawley Council of Social Services (C.C.S.S.), which continues today as the Crawley Council of Voluntary Services (C.C.V.S.).

Mention of cars leads to the fact that the planners in the 1950s did not, and possibly could not, anticipate the growth of car ownership. When houses were being built in Northgate, for example, the first site to be developed had 133 houses and 27 garages in special blocks. That was considered to be more than enough. Indeed, at first there were insufficient car owners to rent out all the garages and some people rented them who did not own cars. Then, as car ownership grew, the C.D.C. areas became overrun by on-street car parking. The only possible solution was to expand the width of the roads by taking away some of the grass verges, so allowing cars to be parked without blocking the roads.

By the 1960s, the community had developed. After 15 years, most of the original planned expansion had taken place and its population target was reached. The former active members of the community mellowed; at any rate their aims had been mostly achieved or their fights resolved. Crawley has always been a prosperous town, with one of the lowest unemployment rates in Britain. The local borough council assumed the response to community needs. A swimming pool was opened in 1964. Poverty and race relations do not seem to be large

75. Queens Square, Crawley. When first opened, motor traffic was light and a road with parking spaces was feasible in the shopping centre. Eventually the Square was fully pedestrianised.

problems in the area; there have been greater problems with drug abuse, especially when Crawley was accused of being the distribution centre for the south of England. It seems that its position will continue to be focal for a variety of networks.

The mature New Town: ***quo vadis*****?**

When looking at recent history, it is difficult to stand back from events in which most of the population of the New Town, or readers of this book, have taken part. We can only really see events from our own involved perspective. Because of this, it is possible to examine some of the events of the last 20 years, and surmise that these may be of relevance to the future — pointers perhaps of the path of development which the town is at present treading.

Take the issue of the size of Crawley. The original master plan, and town design, was based upon a target population of fifty thousand. In 1961 W.S.C.C. produced a draft development plan for the whole county. Crawley by then had a population of 54,000 in the U.D.C. area and it was planned to raise that to seventy thousand. By 1964 there were 59,000 people in Crawley and the C.D.C. was dissolved. Housing passed to the borough, but the management of commercial estates passed to a New Town Commission, based in London and with a local office. Crawley council asked the county to permit the town to grow to 100,000 to deal with a severe local labour shortage. This had been made worse particularly by the continued expansion of Gatwick Airport, whose unskilled workers could earn considerably more than the skilled tradesmen in Crawley.

By 1970 there was little room left in the designated area. Furnace Green and Southgate West were the last two neighbourhoods to be built within the original one. Broadfield, when started, progressed beyond the New Town area onto Horsham R.D.C. land, as did

Ifield West and Bewbush. Similarly, the east of Pound Hill, up to the line of the new motorway (the M23), was at first in Cuckfield R.D.C. area and subsequently in the Mid-Sussex Council area. In that part of Worth which lies outside Crawley, a good deal of development has also taken place in Copthorne and Crawley Down. Towns always spread beyond their civic boundaries, which nowadays can cause planning problems. A Pound Hill pensioner who paid rates to Crawley could get a free bus pass: her elderly neighbour who paid rates to Mid-Sussex could not. It is not surprising that residents are confused by such inconsistent treatment.

By 1977 the population of Crawley was about seventy-five thousand. Broadfield neighbourhood was already planned to contain a population of 14,000, the largest in Crawley and much larger than anything thought of when the town was first planned. To deal with this a second major shopping area developed at Broadfield in place of the usual small neighbourhood shopping area. Work on Broadfield started in 1971. In reality, it was planned so differently from the rest of the town as to present itself as a separate town, cut off from the rest by the by-pass and the Horsham Road. Bewbush was tagged on, from 1975 onwards, and it will eventually have a population of ten thousand. With these two neighbourhoods, the original concept of the New Town seems finally to have been destroyed.

The population of Crawley was 81,255 at the 1981 census. The largest neighbourhood was Pound Hill with over 11,000 people, 3,000 more than the second largest, Broadfield. Southgate, Ifield, Langley Green and Tilgate each had some seven thousand. Bewbush had reached almost 5,000 and was rapidly expanding. The oldest neighbourhoods, Northgate and West Green which each contained about four thousand people, were the smallest. The disparity in sizes of the neighbourhoods was marked.

The other interesting revelation from that census was that there was a large number of people in the age-group 55 years to 59 years, over 5,000, and these were all approaching retirement. They were the first migrants to the area, many of whom were holding valued supervisory posts. This presents a new challenge to the town. At the moment, having such a comparatively young population, the death rate in Crawley is about eight per thousand. The national average is about twelve per thousand; the local figure will inevitably rise now.

Despite financial constraints the local council built a golf course on the edge of Tilgate Forest in 1967. A sports centre was opened in 1974, adjacent to the swimming pool, and when Bewbush was being developed a second sports centre was built there, for the western edge of the town. The Crawley Sports Centre was subsequently renamed the Leisure Centre, and a mixture of sporting and general entertainment was presented. Eventually, an arts centre was opened on The Hawth, originally planned in 1974 but delayed. Now Crawley is well-provided with entertainment areas, parks and sports pitches, even though they took thirty years to complete. This is a legacy of the way in which the New Town plan was carried out. Cultural activities had a very low priority; there are some local amateur theatrical activities which are well supported, but culture is not something with which Crawley is associated.

The Crawley Borough Council area has changed its boundaries several times. When local government reorganisation took place in 1974, it was intended to transfer both Gatwick and Horley to Crawley. This caused an outcry in Horley, and many of the local inhabitants protested vigorously. Their wishes were heeded, and so Horley was placed instead under Reigate and Banstead council. There it remains, somewhat isolated, having little in common with Banstead and not much more with Reigate. Nowadays, many of the Horley residents regret this decision: it is not really sensible to separate Gatwick and Horley into different local government units. Interestingly, had Horley become part of Crawley borough then the political complexion of the town may have changed in the 1980s!

It is no longer relevant to talk of the target population for the town. The borough still tries to erect houses where it can, given the local government constraints of the time, and in 1976 it was finally given the housing stock of the original corporation. This meant that about fourteen thousand homes were in local ownership. Government policy, however, is for many of them to be sold off to the sitting tenants (or their children) at a price well below market valuation.

Coupled with the fact that most of the new houses in the town are for private ownership, the complexion of the town is changing. The term 'balanced community' was used at the inception of the New Town. Attempts by planners to mix social classes in small areas, however, are not welcomed by any of them. There are informally well-defined areas in the town. The 'balance' was always more of an attitude: a determination to make the community successful which was shared by all new migrants. Given the prominence of a property-owning population, it will be interesting to see whether the Labour Party can still remain in control of the town.

Commercial sites are now being sold off, and many of the shops in the town centre are owned by pension funds or insurance companies. These are not interested in a 'balanced' shopping centre; they want to maximise rents. Despite attempts by the council to stem the tide we are now witnessing a town centre dominated by branches of multiple stores, operating a self-service system with minimum staff — and minimum service. The High Street is in danger of becoming a long money market, interspersed with fast-food shops. At the same time, inflated rents in Manor Royal, caused by the sale of freeholds, are changing its nature. Central government policy takes easy precedence over local wishes or needs.

It is more accurate nowadays to speak of the commercial estate rather than the industrial estate, since much of the original industry is moving out. This trend has been going on for some years. Gatwick needs warehousing, hence the demise of the village of Lowfield Heath, rather in the same way as villages were destroyed for sheep farming five centuries ago. Factories constructed in the 1950s and 1960s are demolished and rebuilt to suit the needs of modern business, and Manor Royal is becoming an estate dominated by warehouses and hi-tech units. If nothing else, this type of employment reduces the workforce needed. In 1987, Youngmans, the original Manor Royal factory, announced that it intended to leave Crawley to move into cheaper premises elsewhere to the south-west. Traditional industry needs more space than modern undertakings do. As rents rise, then the older firms will move out and new skills will be required from the workforce.

Gatwick's new North Terminal opened in 1988, as the airport still continues to grow. The safety record has been good; two notable accidents involved a Turkish and an Afghan aircraft. Fears of overcrowded airspace appear in the press from time to time, and the residents of Charlwood know quite well that some aircraft fly very low after take-off. British Caledonian Airways, the successor to B.U.A., was the dominant airline at Gatwick for about 15 years, though it eventually became overshadowed by the British Airways/British Airtours/Poundstretcher organisation. In retrospect it should not have been too much of a shock when British Airways took over the ailing British Caledonian company; frequent denials of the merger should have been the clue!

There has been an eruption of large hotels in the area over the last 15 years. It has not always been easy to keep up with some of the changes of names or ownership. These — and a mushrooming of guesthouses and a grossly disfigured countryside due to the spread of airport carparking — are continuing trends.

Conclusion

One visible feature of the town is the spread of offices in the centre as well as on the periphery. In 1987 the local branch of Friends of the Earth surveyed the area and found that there was one and a half million square feet of unoccupied office accommodation in the town, and that another half million was planned. In time this will all be filled and yet more required. Complaints are made, however, that there are just not enough small units available. Those who build and lease out large office blocks are only really interested in big companies which would want to lease the whole of the premises. The countryside is also being invaded by commerce and there are a number of hi-tech estates: the large site in Tilgate Forest on Pease Pottage Hill is an example, and permission for another is sought on the site of Forge Farm in Tinsley Green. Since the M25 and M23 network has been completed, there is an impetus to develop sites within easy reach of the major roads.

In April 1989 was published a report commissioned by Crawley and District Industrial Association and the Institute of Personnel Management. It was concerned with how to survive full employment! This document pointed out forcibly what many were already aware of, namely that with less than two per cent unemployment in the town, an ageing population, a falling number of school-leavers and over 10,000 new jobs to be provided in the town by the mid-1990s, there was a chronic labour shortage in Crawley. This was made worse by a severe housing shortage. The report made it clear that the solution for many employers would be to move away from the town.

Schools in Crawley were given large playing fields when first built. At one time Thomas Bennett School had the largest roll of any comprehensive school in the country. Now, since school rolls are smaller, it has been decided that the playing fields are too big and, as an example of the effect this will have, a part of the Hazelwick School site was sold off to allow a large food supermarket to be built. This shop has plenty of car-parking space and is within a few minutes drive of the motorway, which points to another trend, the provision of hypermarkets with vast areas of car-parking surrounding them. In Manor Royal, alongside the A23, there is a huge site for the sale of furniture, carpets, D.I.Y. materials and car spares. Others are planned. Smaller shops in the area fear the loss of trade.

It is ironic that at a time when the town is at last experiencing an ageing population, with growing numbers of those who will not be so mobile and have to rely on local shops, the trend is antagonistic towards the smaller, local shops. There are several housing schemes for the elderly, at least for those who can afford to purchase homes designed for the elderly. These are attractive to site developers. Such a clientele does not need large plots with gardens, and the local authority does not demand so much car-parking space. Thus more housing units can be crowded on available sites. The provision of private housing for the elderly is already well under way in the town.

There is now a growing awareness of the importance of the environment, and more people are looking at what the historic past of Crawley can still offer them. It has been a long-standing source of irritation that the corporation and its successors appeared to have little interest in the old buildings which were in the district when the New Town was planned. There are a few examples of the imaginative use to which old buildings can be put, such as Jordans Farm Barn, which provides a factory social club, the Ifield Barn Theatre, in a medieval barn adjacent to Ifield church, and two of the timber-framed buildings in the High Street, which have been lovingly restored and rebuilt to provide modern premises yet still retain their original features.

The planned High Street relief road could lead to a revitalised town centre; on the other hand it could just lead to faster traffic flows. The planners have to reappraise their policies. Local government is now more market-orientated. Does this mean using all land to bring in the biggest income, or can non-economic interests also have a place? Surely social amenities are still valued. There are potential benefits to Crawley from visitors and tourists, provided that there are places to visit. It is a fact of life that historic buildings can offer more attractions than modern houses. Crawley Museum Society organised a public meeting in March 1989 to protest at the way the High Street was being developed. It was well

76. Good Friday at Tinsley Green. Playing marbles on Good Friday had been a tradition in Sussex for centuries. It was revived at the *Greyhound* in Tinsley Green and still continues. The player is 'Pop' Maynard, a well-known folk singer from Copthorne.

attended and the local papers recorded much support from their readers. The main point in their defence made by the local borough councillors was that they considered themselves virtually powerless in planning the business redevelopment of the town centre.

The latest change to affect Crawley is the building of what may prove to be the last neighbourhood in the town. This is Maidenbower, on the site of Frogshole Farm (which itself is likely to become a public house). When this is finished, Worth church will at last be in an urban setting and the sole remaining rural retreat in the borough will have gone. When all the land between Gatwick and the motorway is built upon, perhaps then the story of the growth of Crawley from a collection of isolated farms to an identifiable but rambling urban unit will be complete.

We have not yet experienced urban decay — that will be for another generation. In the meantime we are left with a town with its own identity, a strong economy and, on the whole, a contented population. There is one ominous trend. Inflated prices drive the young out of town. Something will have to be done to keep young married couples in Crawley. And the financial implications of a rapidly increasing proportion of elderly in the local population have still not yet been grasped.

Crawley is a pleasant place to live in; it has many trees and open spaces, and is still a town in the country. Yet it is dynamic, not static. The feeling of change remains. There is a need, therefore, to answer the question 'Where is Crawley heading?'. It is virtually certain that Crawley originally was a medieval planned development. Then, in the 1940s, it was once again the subject of a marvellously planned expanded development. What is planned next . . . or is planning no longer the word to use?

Further Reading

Armstrong, J. R., *A History of Sussex* (Phillimore, 1974).
Bastable, R., *Crawley: A Pictorial History* (Phillimore, 1983).
Bastable, R., *Crawley: The Making of a New Town* (Phillimore, 1986).
Bracher, P., *Ifield Mill, its Owners and Occupiers* (Crawley Museum Society, 1986).
Brandon, P., *The Sussex Landscape* (Hodder and Stoughton, 1974).
Bridge, Rev. A., *Worth Church* (Fred. Sherlock Ltd., 1911).
Cleere, H., and Crossley, D., *The Iron Industry of the Weald* (Leicester University Press, 1985).
Fisher, E. A., *The Saxon Churches of Sussex* (David and Charles, 1970).
Gibson-Hill, J., *Rescue Archaeology in Sussex* (University of London, 1974).
Gibson-Hill, J., and Henbery, E. W., *Ifield Mill: a Survey* (Crawley Museum Society, 1980).
Goepal, J., *How I Chose Crawley Street Names* (Crawley Museum Society, 1980).
Goepal, J., *The Development of Crawley* (Crawley Museum Society, 1980).
Goldsmith, M., *Crawley and District in Old Picture Postcards* (European Library, 1987).
Gray, F. (ed.), *Crawley, Old Town, New Town* (University of Sussex, 1983).
Hanson, E., and Warner, R., *Quakers in Ifield, 1676-1976* (Ifield Meeting, 1976).
Harper, C. G., *The Brighton Road* (Chatto and Windus, 1892).
Henbery, E. W., *Ifield Mill Restoration* (Crawley Museum Society).
Hooper, T. R., *A Surrey and Sussex Border Church* (Morgan and Scott, 1925).
King, J., and Tait, G., *Golden Gatwick: 50 years of Aviation* (B.A.A./R.Ae.S., 1980).
Leon, H., and McLachan, H. G., *Two Sussex Parishes, Ifield and Crawley* (La Société Inter'l de Philologie, 1917).
Longleys of Crawley (James Longley & Co. Ltd., 1983).
Lucas, E. V., *Highways and Byways in Sussex* (Macmillan, 1904).
Mawer, A., and Stanton, F. M., *The Place Names of Sussex*, vols. I and II (Cambridge University Press, 1929 and 1930).
Morris J.,(ed.), *Domesday Book, Sussex* (Phillimore, 1976).
Reports of the Commission for the New Towns (H.M.S.O., 1963 et seq.).
Reports of Development Corporations (H.M.S.O., 1948 et seq.).
Sewill, R., and Lane, E., *The Free Men of Charlwood* (Published by the authors, 1967).
Straker, E., *Wealden Iron* (David and Charles reprints, 1969).
Sussex Archaeological Collections (Sussex Archaeological Society, 1848 et seq.).
Sussex County Magazine (S.C.M., 1926-56).
Sussex Industrial History, Nos. 7 and 8 (Sussex Industrial Archaeological Society, 1978 and 1979).
Sussex Notes and Queries (S.A.S., 1926-71).
Sussex Record Society (S.R.S., 1902 et seq.).
Tait, G., *The Gatwick Express* (G. Tait and Associates, 1984).
Victoria County History of Surrey, vol. 3, edited by H. E. Malden (University of London/Dawsons, 1967).
Victoria County History of Sussex, esp. vol. 6 (part III), edited by T. P. Hudson, and vol. 7, edited by L. F. Salzman (University of London/O.U.P., 1987; O.U.P./Dawsons, 1940/1973).
The War in East Sussex (Sussex Express and County Herald, 1985).
West Sussex County Times, formerly *Horsham Advertiser* (1871 to date).
Worssam, B. C., *Iron Workings in the Weald Clay* (Proceedings of the Geological Association, 1964).

Index